RING OF
LIBERATION

RING OF

Deceptive Discourse

in Brazilian

Capoeira

With a Foreword by
Robert Farris Thompson

J. Lowell Lewis

LIBERATION

The University of Chicago Press

Chicago and London

J. LOWELL LEWIS is a lecturer in the Department of Anthropology and Centre for Performance Studies at the University of Sydney and an amateur *capoeirista*.

THE UNIVERSITY OF CHICAGO PRESS, CHICAGO 60637
THE UNIVERSITY OF CHICAGO PRESS, LTD., LONDON
© 1992 by The University of Chicago
All rights reserved. Published 1992
Printed in the United States of America
00 99 98 97 96 95 94 93 92   5 4 3 2 1
ISBN (cloth): 0–226–47682–0
ISBN (paper): 0–226–47683–9

Library of Congress Cataloging-in-Publication Data

Lewis, John Lowell.
   Ring of liberation: Deceptive discourse in Brazilian capoeira / J. Lowell Lewis.
      p.   cm.
   Includes discography.
   Includes bibliographical references and index.
   1. Capoeira (Dance)   2. Capoeira (Dance)—History.   I. Title.
GV1796.C145L48   1992
793.3′1—dc20   92–3749
                                                       CIP

To my parents, Felice and Fran,
and to all capoeira masters, past and present,
Axé

Contents

Maps, Tables, and Figures

Foreword

Once the African-Brazilian martial art called capoeira was distant. Now it's right next door. North American women and men play this blend of dance and combat in Oakland, San Francisco, Los Angeles, Denver, Santa Fe, Boston, New Haven, Washington, D.C., Atlanta, and New York City.

In the last-named town lives Jelon Vieira, originally from Bahia, a famous capoeira master who brought the art to our shores in 1975. He is now joined, at this writing, by historic *Angola*-style capoeira masters in New York, João Grande and, from time to time, Moraes.

Under demographic pressure, America is becoming perhaps the world's "first universal nation": Native American, Asian, African-American, Latino, East and West European. The rise of capoeira in North America is appropriate to this trend, for it draws on many sources. Songs in Portuguese accompany the playing of the game, but African words from Kongo and the ancient cities of the Yoruba are also sometimes embedded in these songs. Capoeira women and men move to the resonating beat of one of the oldest instruments on the planet, the musical bow. They call it *berimbau*. Judging from details of morphology and play, the *berimbau* is an elegant creole fusion of impulses coming into colonial Brazil from Kongo and Angola.

Oblique, wheeling, down, and up, the motions of capoeira are preeminently sub-Saharan in their bearing, though there are exceptions, notably in recent (*atual*) or *Regional* styles of capoeira. But even here things get ground down by percussive emphasis in the Afro-Atlantic manner. Take the cartwheel, which capoeiristas call *aú*. Nothing could be more universal. I saw children cartwheel near Vila Real in Portugal in the summer of

1988. But *Angola*-style capoeiristas nuance this universal sign of self-mastery and high spirits in their own, highly specialized, Africanizing way. They pretzel their legs, and bring them in close, when they cartwheel, as opposed to the open "V-form" of the legs in the Western phrasing of the maneuver. Plus, they consciously name their nuance *aú fechado* [closed cartwheel], as Lewis discusses in chapter 4.

During fieldwork in north Kongo in the summer of 1990, I met Samba Jean, a Mu-Kongo expert in the martial arts of Africa. He told me Bakongo name cartwheels with an idiophone "of wheeling motion," *na wú*. This may well be the origin of the term, *aú*, in the parlance of capoeira athletes. In any event, *aú* in the *Angoleiro* manner seems vaguely cognate with the pretzeled legs of young men "breakin'" in contemporary hip-hop. And both manifestations compare to the pretzeled "closed" legs of a black cartwheeler portrayed by Debret in the streets of Rio in the early nineteenth century. The latter person was part of the celebration of the funeral of the son of an African leader who had died on this side of the water.

Lowell Lewis brought the last-mentioned reference to my attention in 1985. Over the past years, in fact, when I needed clarification on this or that point in capoeira lore, I called him. I struck my efforts against the whetstone of his expertise. Now, with this volume, all African-Americanists have his insights and information at hand.

Lewis trained with *Angoleiros* in Bahia. This means his text is backed with sweat as well as erudition. His book connects. He does not, for instance, loftily call *rasteiras* "disequiliberating blows." He calls them what they are: sweeps, takedowns, trip-'em-ups. We are given clarity. We are given history. We are given nuance. All of which inspired this writer to strike out and discover in what ways capoeira links up with *candomblé Nagó* and Kongo in addition to *umbanda*. Exú, for instance. He is the grandmaster trickster of them all, ubiquitous in the *terreiros* from Acre to the Atlantic, from Belem to Rio Grande. And capoeira is part of his domain because, as João Bosco made patent in a song, Exú is lord of trip-'em-ups, boss of all *rasteiras*.

In February 1991, I followed a research lead to Venezuela.

Sule Wilson, of the Schomberg library in Harlem, showed Daniel Dawson, of the Caribbean Culture Center on West 58th in New York, who, in turn, showed me, a drawing. The drawing was dated August 15, 1874. The scene was an Afro-Venezuelan village square where two well-built young black men were having at it, smashing into each other with what African-Brazilians would call *cabeçadas* [head-butts].

I had seen putative antecedents of this move in Kongo in the summer of 1990. There, south of Kinkala in the village of Boko, I witnessed several head-butt styles of combat and Samba Jean glossed them for me in Ki-Kongo. *Ngwindulu mu-tu* [hitting a person with your head] has many variants, including *ku matu,* striking your head against your opponent's temples, *mu ndeko,* hitting his head with the sides of *your* head, *mu dúmuka* [literally, "by jumping"], where you butt him under the chin with your head.

And so, to test the continuity of such moves, I went to Venezuela. In Curiepe, the Harlem of the Barlovento coast, east of Caracas, in the state of Miranda, I met the locally famous drummaker, Bernardo Saenz. Saenz stood before a complement of *kulo e puya* drums, which he himself had carved and strung. They were long, narrow, and tuned with an exterior cord harness—similar, in many respects (excepting the fact they had been carved from local laurel), to the *tuutila* harness drums of northern Kongo documented by Laman at the turn of the century at Sundi in Nganda. Jesus García reports in his excellent study, *Africa En Venezuela,* that in the course of fieldwork in the Republic of Congo he found "three drums, identical, in their manner of construction, to the drums *culo e'puya* of Curiepe." He found these drums in the Lekoumou Region where the Beembe and Kamba Kongo peoples live. Lewis notes a similar tuning style on capoeira drums in Bahia (chapter 5).

Saenz talked about drums, talked about dance, and finally shifted to the subject of the martial arts. "We blacks in Venezuela," he told me, "have a kind of self-defense [*defensa personal*] which we call *broma. Broma* means, literally, "just joking." This sounds, to me at least, like a feint, a stratagem in itself, comparable to the *malícia* mind-set in the *Angola* style of capoeira in

Brazil. Saenz added that blacks playing *broma* in Curiepe "use whatever you've got"—karate observed on television, a little wrestling—in addition to the older moves of the ancestors, the *sweeps, head-butts,* and *kicks*. The latter three moves formed the ancestral core, apparently the same situation defining "knocking and kicking" combat among the blacks of the Sea Islands off Georgia and South Carolina, though much more work has to be done there before we know for sure.

Saenz said, *"Tenemos coces, mas virando, parado no"* [we have kicks, but (they are executed with the body) turning, not standing still]. Saenz demonstrated. It was a rough-and-ready, nonacademy, street equivalent to what in capoeira could be called *armada de frente*. That same spin-kick came to Martinique. There a local *ladjá* [the capoeira of Martinique] master, the late Eugène Mona, showed me in August 1990 a tree-altar to his Kongo ancestors, who brought the moves across the water.

Of all the martial arts of the Black Atlantic world, capoeira is supreme. Open this book and *dúmuka*. Jump into a world of black creative motion. The *roda* (ring) awaits you, the song has started:

> *Ô lemba* é lemba*
> *Ô lemba é, ô é lemba*
> *Ô lemba é lemba*
> *Ô lemba tu barro vermelho.*

Robert Farris Thompson
Yale University

---

*'Lemba' is known in North Kongo as an ancient trading society.

Map of Bahia prepared by Joanna Yardley.

Preface

PROLOGUE

The two men squatted facing each other in the hot sun, sweat pouring off their faces, their clothes wet and clinging to their bodies. Behind them colleagues played musical bows and tambourines as the crowd pressed in on the cleared area in the plaza which was the arena for their contest. The festival had already been going on for two days and the capoeira players—for that was the name of the sport the men were playing—had kept the action going continuously for most of that time. The games had moved from time to time, from the market plaza to the main plaza and back, once even onto the portico of the church, but breaks in the action had been brief, and the players had achieved a state of exhaustion that bordered on trance. Yet it was precisely this bone weariness which the men sought, as a kind of liberation, freeing them from social obligations and personal worries, relaxing bodies to an elastic flexibility and focusing their attention on the game and the game alone.

Most of these men and boys had known each other before the festival, with varying degrees of intimacy. Some were brothers, cousins, fathers and sons; others good friends or casual acquaintances, and a few had just met for the first time, or had heard of each other by reputation. But now they were beginning to understand each other deeply, in a way that had nothing to do with kinship, occupation, wealth, status, or previous history. These men had no use for such extraneous information now, they were immersed in a fundamental communication of bodies and wills, of slashing feet and twisting torsos: they were seeing into each other, trying to discern physical habits, emotional weaknesses, and rational resources which could be brought to bear in the ring. As the two men hunkered, trying to slow their breathing, they each stared into the other's eyes, as if to take the measure of his soul.

Finally one of the musicians, himself a fellow player, grew impatient and started to sing:

s: dá, dá, dá no nêgo   give, give, give it to him
    no nêgo você não dá   you're not giving him a thing

The other players, and some of the spectators, came in on the chorus:

c: dá, dá, dá no nêgo   give, give, give it to him [1]

Goaded by the singers, the two men slowly leaned in toward the empty space as the chant continued, extending their hands toward the middle of the ring as if to say "after you." Never taking his eyes off his opponent, one man turned and stretched into a back bridge, leading into a slow-motion back handspring, while the other slid into a head stand on the side of his head, one elbow bent into his ribs for support. Instead of completing his backflip, the first man stopped in midair, his body held in a curved position which seemed to defy gravity. Using superb strength, the second player extended his bent arm and straightened his neck into a normal headstand, then pushed himself up into a handstand. Meanwhile the first man reversed back onto his feet and lunged into his adversary's torso with a head butt. Seeing the attack coming, the second player turned his handstand into a cartwheel, freeing one arm which he bent at the elbow to threaten the face of the head butter. The latter aborted his head attack and turned his back, kicking with the following leg so that it flowed smoothly through the space just vacated by his cartwheeling opponent. The game was on.

We were in the town of Santo Amaro da Purificação in the heart of the sugar-growing region around Salvador, hometown of many famous capoeira players both past and present. The occasion was the thirteenth of May celebration, anniversary of the lib-

---

1. Here and henceforth, S: stands for 'solo' (the call) and C: stands for 'chorus' (the response).

eration of the slaves by Princess Isabel at the close of the Brazilian Empire in 1888. In addition to capoeira games, the other main activity of this festival was *candomblé,* the African-Catholic religion characteristic of Bahia, versions of which are now practiced throughout Brazil. I had seen several capoeira players also take turns playing drums for the *candomblé* circle, to promote the descent of spirits into the heads of the dancing initiates.

The two contestants now striving in the capoeira ring were well known to me and even better known to each other, since one had taught the other how to play. One was a well-known *mestre* ('master') from Salvador, capital of the state of Bahia (northeastern Brazil), and the other had been his student (*aluno*) for many years and was now a master himself, recently returned from teaching in São Paulo. In spite of the closeness of their relationship, however, neither was giving anything away to the other in this contest. The fact that each knew the other's tricks, and that they were both excellent players, made for an exceptionally exciting and beautiful game and the audience was enthralled, shouting comments and encouragement. The older master was small and wiry, a veteran of many battles, which made him a wily tactician. The younger master was big and powerful, with amazing endurance and speed, and was known to be feisty, not averse to giving an unwary opponent a good thrashing.

The bout had been going on a very long time now, perhaps twelve minutes. Even though the masters had paused several times to find their wind, they were demonstrating extreme endurance given the intensity of their struggle and the difficulty of their moves. It was a mark of respect for their efforts that no other players had cut in to change the pairing of contestants. Experts and casual observers alike were fascinated with the variety of attacks and defenses, the beautiful yet deadly moves these two could improvise, and everyone wanted to see the resolution. As another sign of the importance of this contest, the audience had thrown quite a bit of paper money into the ring. If the players chose to, they could begin a variation of the game by competing to pick up the money, thereby claiming it for themselves. So far they had been so intent with the direct interaction, however, that they had been ignoring the money, letting it collect in the center of the ring, where it was occasionally arranged into a pile by a fellow player from the sidelines.

All the musicians, and quite a few of the spectators, were themselves players waiting their turn in the ring or on the instruments. I myself was a fledgling player, a student of the older master for some months, and I had struggled in the arena and taken part in the music at various times during the festival. Since this was an outdoor, public game, there were only two types of instruments being played to accompany the action in the ring: tambourines (*pandeiros*) and musical bows (*berimbaus*). *Berimbaus* are the lead instruments, without which there can be no capoeira contest, and the lead bow was currently being played by Vavá, a local master whose father had popularized another Bahian martial dance, the stick fight called *maculêlê*. Vavá had begun the chant which had gotten the masters moving again, but had stopped singing as soon as the action became intense.

Moving effortlessly from feet to hands and back again, the men were now extremely close together, yet they did not pull their blows, striking with full force but finding only air. The interplay was building to another climax, the two bodies windmilling in a blur of sweeps, kicks, escapes, leaps, almost too fast for the eye to follow. Suddenly Braulio, the younger master, broke off the action and began walking around the cleared space in a conventional interlude, itself a kind of game called "take a turn around the world" (*dá volta ao mundo*). *Mestre* Nô, the older master, followed him around, both of them breathing heavily. Without warning, Braulio did a cartwheel into the center, bending his elbows in order to lower his head toward the ground, and picked up the pile of money with his mouth. He ended up on his feet at the far side of the ring, took the money in his hand, and started laughing. The crowd exploded with laughter and approval as Nô looked disgusted with his former student. The older man had forgotten the money in his concentration on the contest, and his student had taken advantage by suddenly "remembering" it.

After some negotiations, with the intercession of several players on the sidelines, Braulio was convinced to return the money to the center of the ring and the game was restarted, both players squatting once again "at the foot" (*ao pé*) of Vavá's lead *berimbau*.

As they crouched there, *Mestre* Nô suddenly leaped backwards into a double backflip, lowering himself on the second revolution to pick up the money in *his* mouth. He came to rest on his haunches, mouth stuffed with bills, looking like the cat who ate the canary. This time it was Braulio's turn to look sheepish as the crowd laughed approvingly. Excited and moved by this inspired trickery, without stopping to consider the consequences, I burst into song:

s:	ô me dá o meu dinheiro,	oh give me my money,
	ô me dá o meu dinheiro,	oh give me my money,
	valentão	tough guy
	ô me dá o meu dinheiro,	oh give me my money,
	valentão	tough guy
	porque no meu dinheiro	because on my money
	ninguém ponhe a mão	nobody puts a hand

As I started singing, many of the players looked up to see who it was, especially since I obviously had a foreign accent. Although it is accepted for anyone to join in on a chorus in capoeira singing, even audience members who are not participating in the physical contest, usually only masters or respected senior players initiate songs, since the soloist must carry the song, giving a clear indication of pitch and rhythm, and must know the verses of the calls for each song. Therefore as I was ending the verse I became quite nervous as I realized what I had done. Would anyone respond to my call, or would they all keep silent, a snub to the presumptuous foreign novice who dared to interfere in the creation of this exceptional game?

It was with relief and thankfulness, then, that I heard a full chorus come in on the refrain:

c:	ô me dá o meu dinheiro,	oh give me my money,
	ô me dá o meu dinheiro,	oh give me my money,
	valentão	tough guy

I didn't try to continue the song for more than a few repetitions, since I realized that I only knew that one solo verse, but as I sang I understood that the reason the chorus had responded enthusiastically was that I had done the most important thing right. I had chosen an appropriate song to capture that moment in the game, to highlight the action and allow the audience and players a chance to express their delight in the quality of play.

The exhilaration I felt was increased because I had (unconsciously) tested and confirmed my understanding of the conventions of the game and, therefore, of a small, specialized aspect of Bahian culture. Indeed, I was actively participating in the recreation of that culture through the practice of one of its central pastimes. Soon after this song, the bout between Braulio and Nô ended as a new partnership moved into the ring. As frequently happened, there was no real resolution to the contest between them. (The money was donated to a local academy.) Some thought that Braulio had gotten the upper hand, others argued for Nô. In this context, winning or losing, though a subject for debate, did not seem to be the central concern of the audience or the players.

This story, drawn from my period of fieldwork in Brazil, introduces several of the themes that will be developed in the course of the following work. Although I am writing in the ethnographic tradition, and thus with a theoretical interest (signs of which emerge toward the end of the story), I also hope to include in my audience fellow capoeira players, martial arts fans, students of African-American culture, and others whose interests are more descriptive. Trying to write for diverse readers is similar to the problem, currently under intense scrutiny, of how to write any account which purports to capture (or free) other voices. It should be obvious from the narrative above that I do not propose to break any new ground in this regard. Most of the account, as above, is in my own voice, but one that has been transformed by experiences in the ring, and by conversations outside it, in various countries. Where I do report the words of others, as in the songs above, I will try to do justice to issues of context, informed by an interest in the emerging field of discourse analysis.

The problems of fidelity to the understandings of cultural others are given a peculiar twist in this study, since, in addition to giving 'voice' to my fellow capoeira players, I also need to try to give them 'body.' That is, a crucial part of this narrative is the description of nonverbal interaction in the ring, for which any linguistic representation is especially problematic. Indeed, one of

the theoretical foci of this study is to examine the relations between communicative channels in cultural expression, to continue
an exploration of the widely employed metaphor of social action
as a kind of 'text.' In what ways are physical play and musical play
like or unlike language play in this particular unified field?

I first discovered capoeira in classic ethnographic fashion by
going to Brazil, all in ignorance, and stumbling on a game in front
of the Mercado Modelo (tourist market) on a bright Saturday in
Salvador. Years later the story began again, in a 'properly' postmodern fashion, as initial dissertation research at the University
of Washington led me out of the library and onto the damp grass
of Volunteer Park in Seattle. Hoping to discover exotic capoeira,
I was bemused to find that it was being played next door all along.
In yet another unexpected move, I soon saw that it would not do
to simply 'understand' capoeira as an intellectual exercise, but that
I would need to exercise my flabby body trying to 'stand under'
the whirling, dangerous feet of limber players. This was no job
for an armchair anthropologist.

BASIC TERMS

Before I can begin to discuss the origins and contemporary
practice of capoeira, it will be helpful for the reader to know certain basic facts about it, including some of the key terms which
will be used repeatedly. The word 'capoeira' refers to a game or
sport played throughout Brazil (and elsewhere in the world) today, which was originally part of the Afro-Brazilian folk tradition.
It is a martial art, involving a complete system of self-defense, but
it also has a dancelike, acrobatic movement style which, combined
with the presence of music and song, makes the games into a kind
of performance that attracts many kinds of spectators, both tourists and locals.

Space to play capoeira is always defined in terms of a ring,
roughly or precisely circular in shape, and of varying dimensions,
depending on the setting. In street games the ring is formed by
spectators and players crowding in to watch the action, while in
tournaments the ring is drawn on the floor and the diameter is
fixed. Note that the same word which defines the shape of the
play space, *roda* ('ring' or 'wheel'), also is used to refer to the

performance event itself, a game of capoeira. Players will say, "Let's have a *roda* tomorrow," or "I saw him at the *roda* on Sunday." I will always use *roda* in this latter (metonymic) sense henceforth, or refer to an 'event,' 'game,' or 'performance,' while calling the physical space the 'ring,' or 'arena,' in order to avoid confusion.

The word 'capoeira' itself is of uncertain origin (see chapter 3). In the nineteenth century the players were referred to as *capoeiras,* participants in *capoeiragem,* the activity. In contemporary usage, which I will adhere to below, the game is referred to as 'capoeira,' and those who play it are called *capoeiristas.* A senior instructor of capoeira is known as a *mestre* ('master') and is frequently referred to by a 'war name' (*nome da guerra*), which is received during the course of training. In the text, I will give the capoeira war name, Mestre Quick, followed by the original family name in parentheses (John Smith) the first time they are mentioned. Thereafter, I will dispense with family names, but Appendix C provides a list of all the masters cited, including both of their names.

In order to simplify extensive descriptions of physical interplay, I will resort to the generic pronoun 'he' rather than the nonsexist 's/he' or 'he or she' alternatives. I justify this partially by noting that capoeira is still largely, and traditionally was exclusively, a male activity, though this character is changing at present. I am in favor of this change and aware of the sexual politics involved in the use of language, but was able to find no acceptable alternative to the conservative usage which would not hopelessly muddy the already difficult descriptions of nonverbal interactions.

Capoeira is always done to music, so some players 'play' musical instruments and sing around the perimeter, while others 'play' the game, the physical part of the sport, inside the ring. In most cases, everyone who plays a musical instrument is also expected to enter the ring from time to time, in order to participate fully in the game, so there are (usually) no musicians who are not also players in this sense. This semantic confusion between the two senses of 'play' does not occur in Portuguese, where 'to play (instruments)' is *tocar,* while 'to play (a game)' is *jogar.* To avoid confusion in English, I will refer to action in the arena as 'physical play' or 'movement dialogue,' in order to distinguish it from music-making. This is also necessary because I wish to avoid easy alternatives like 'fight' or 'spar' on the one hand, which are too martial, versus 'dance' on the other, which is too neutral. A central feature of capoeira play, and a recurring theme of the book, is the necessary tension between what Huizinga called 'agonistic' versus 'ludic' tendencies in the interaction: between conflict and playful cooperation.[2]

As mentioned above, the lead instrument in the capoeira ensemble is the *berimbau*, which is a single-stringed musical bow. I will accordingly refer to it as a 'bow' or as a *berimbau* indiscriminately. The *berimbau* is today virtually an index[3] of capoeira, since it is used in very few other contexts, and the state of Bahia is the acknowledged heartland of capoeira and of Afro-Brazilian culture in general. Confusion sometimes arises because Salvador, the capital of the state, is also called Bahia; named after the 'Bay of All Saints' (*Bahia de Tôdos os Santos*) by which it stands. In colloquial speech, then, it can become Bahia, Bahia, similar to New York, New York. To avoid this confusion, I will refer to the city as 'Salvador' and to the state as 'Bahia,' except in cases where the distinction is unimportant, that is, where both are intended at once. Denizens of either the state or the city are called *Baianos* ('Bahians').

THE FIELDWORK

The bulk of the analysis and synthesis in this work is the result of eighteen months of fieldwork, primarily in the city of Salvador, between 1981 and 1983.[4] As the story above indicates, that material is supplemented by frequent trips to the Recôncavo region

2. Actually Huizinga saw agonistic contests, including war, as one kind of play, and did not oppose the terms in quite the way I have here (cf. Huizinga 1955, esp. chaps. 2–4). The point I want to make is that in some play there may be no contest (ludic but not agonistic) and in other forms the contest may be 'playful,' subordinated to more important considerations than merely winning. This second sense is what I usually intend by the word 'ludic.' What I characterize as 'agonistic' play is that in which the contest is dominant and winning is everything, or nearly so.

3. 'Index' is used here in the Peircean sense, as something understood to be connected in space and/or time to something else (see chapter 1).

4. In addition, I spent five months in Brazil, two months of it in Bahia, in 1973–74, before I was officially doing research.

which borders the Bay of All Saints, especially the towns of Santo
Amaro da Purificação, Cachoeira, and Muritiba. I visited the latter two only twice, but had frequent contact with capoeira players
from Muritiba while in Salvador, and I went to Santo Amaro
about a dozen times. In addition to this experience in Bahia, I
made two trips to Recife (state of Pernambuco), two to Rio de
Janeiro, and one to São Paulo. On all of these trips outside Salvador I met capoeira players and masters, attended *rodas* and capoeira tournaments, and generally collected as much information
about local capoeira as I could in a limited time. Also, I have made
a point of visiting (and training with) most of the capoeira teachers in the United States, especially in New York and San Francisco, and I had the opportunity to see some of them play capoeira
in Brazil as well. All of these experiences are brought to bear on
the interpretations which follow, but the focus will be on capoeira
in the city of Salvador and environs.

Within Salvador, I visited twenty-five official capoeira academies, some of which also functioned as dance studios and schools,
several of which I frequented regularly. Due to the instability of
the rental situation, and the economic difficulty of maintaining
classes for students who are often poor, there isn't much point in
cataloging their names and locations because such information
goes out of date quickly. For example, in 1968 Rego listed ten
capoeira academies in the city, only two of which still exist on the
same site, and one of those had closed and recently reopened
under new management (1968: 390–92). The fact that I visited
twenty-five active locations, and heard about at least ten others,
compared to Rego's much shorter list, suggests that formal instruction has increased since the 1960s, although many young
men in Salvador still receive informal 'instruction' in the streets
and on the beaches. D'Aquino notes that in 1980 only five academies were officially registered with the Federação Bahiano de
Pugilismo ('Bahian Boxing Federation'), which is an indication of
the failure of that organization to represent capoeira adequately
(1983: 62).

One response to the current interest in creating 'dialogic' or
'polyphonic' ethnography (Clifford 1988: 21–54) is to rely on
transcriptions of other voices and various techniques for assuring

the fidelity of recorded conversations to the relevant contexts. In this case, as I have indicated, one would need videotape at least and, of course, problems of distorted representation in that mode are not qualitatively different from those in written language. There are some videotapes and audio recordings available of capoeira, for the interested reader, and I provide a partial list appended to the bibliography. Unfortunately, I was unable to provide a tape to accompany this book, but I hope to undertake one as a separate project in the near future.

What *is* of special theoretical interest in the narrative which follows is that I attempt an in-depth analysis of all three major communicative channels in capoeira expression: movement, music, and text. These general areas of academic interest have usually been addressed separately by respective specialists, or, especially in the case of dance, ignored altogether. The goal of this work is to provide a plausible account of how these media work together, and sometimes against each other, in the creation of the complex expression that is capoeira play. If I come anywhere near achieving this goal, perhaps the result will encourage others to continue the trend toward a more holistic approach to the play of signs in the recreation of cultural meaning.

ACKNOWLEDGMENTS

Many people have my gratitude for their help in the completion of this work, only some of whom it is possible to mention here. Of course, my greatest debt is to the masters and the students of capoeira who put up with my questions, treated my bumbling efforts to learn the sport with tolerance, and were my hosts and friends both in Brazil and in the United States. First of all, I want to thank the masters who were my main teachers: Mestre Nô, Mestre Moraes, Mestre Acordeon, Mestre Waldemar, and Mestre Canjiquinha. To Nô, a bond of friendship that will never be broken, based on countless *rodas,* in and out of the ring; to Moraes, a bond of understanding that goes beyond rationality, and a comradeship that crosses boundaries; to Bira (Acordeon) thanks for opening the door, being my first teacher and resource, and special thanks to your parents Maria and José Goisia Almeida for their many kindnesses in Salvador; to the late Mestre Waldemar, voice of the angels (then as now), gratitude and respect for the master who gave so much even in the midst of adversity; to Mestre Canjiquinha, for his unfailing humor and sly sense of *malícia;* and a special word of gratitude to the late Mestre Cobrinha Verde (Rafael Alves França). Though they may pass on, their presence lingers with us: *Axé!*

Many other masters and students aided me substantially in Salvador, as well. Thanks to: Mestre Itapoan for his classes and the use of his legendary library; and to Mestres Marcelino (Mau), João Pequeno, Virgílio, Paulo dos Anjos, João Grande, Curió, Braulio (de Nô), Cobrinha Mansa, Um por Um, Vermelho (all three of them), Caiçara, Gato (Velho), Gatinho, Ezekiel, Lua, and the many others who told me and showed me what capoeira was all about. Special thanks go to Olavo (Galo Cego) Paixão dos Santos, champion *berimbau* maker, player, and friend, and to the gang from Muritiba. I also owe a great debt to Jair Moura for his generosity with materials and his impressive knowledge of capoeira history.

In Salvador I was aided by the resources of the Centro dos Estudos Afro-Orientais and its director Dona Yeda Pessoa de Castro. Also active with archival and moral support were the personnel of the Museu Afro-Brasileiro and its curator Dona Graziela Ferreira Amorim. I'm sure the readers will share my gratitude to the legendary Carybé, whose wonderful line drawings illuminate so much of this book. Among the many who aided me both intellectually and personally in Salvador, special thanks are due to: Ralph Waddey, Nelson Araújo, Thales de Azevedo, Antonietta de Aguiar Nunes, James C. Riordan, Gilberto Sena, Ziza, Maria Mutti, and Lucio Mendes.

Among the many who hosted and instructed me in Santo Amaro, my greatest debt is to Mestre Vavá, his brother Viví, and the members and supporters of their group, Os Netos do Popó.

In Rio de Janeiro I owe special thanks to Mestre Camisa and the Grupo Senzala, including Mestres Garrincha, Peixinho, and Gato. I also want to thank Armando Puga and his family, and Ele and Nazaré Semog for their kind hospitality.

While in São Paulo I was kindly hosted by my friend Gladson

de Oliveira Silva and his family, and special thanks are also due to Mestre Suassuna, Mestre Brasilia, and to the members of the Federação Paulista de Capoeira.

In Recife I owe a special debt to Luiz Augusto de Carvalho Carmo and his family, as well as to master João Mulatinho and the close-knit group of fellow players there.

Of those who aided in the production of this manuscript, primary thanks go to the members of my dissertation committee: Jean-Paul Dumont, E. Valentine Daniel, John R. Atkins, and Simon Ottenberg. All of these friends provided many sorts of help, emotional and practical, as well as intellectual, and without their faith and vision this book would certainly never have been produced. The following colleagues also read and provided valuable suggestions on aspects of the work: Robert F. Thompson, Christopher Waterman, James B. Watson, Roberto da Matta, John MacAloon, Sally Allen-Ness, and C. Daniel Dawson. Special thanks are due to Catharine Howard, who attended to the accuracy of the Portuguese transcriptions and translations, and who provided valuable insights on several points. For preparing and checking the Laban notation (Appendix A), I am grateful to Director Ilene Fox and the staff and resources of the Dance Notation Bureau in New York City. Among the other friends and colleagues who have given me support and encouragement in the United States, I would like to single out for thanks Kenneth Dossar, Jelon Viera, Gary Harding, Ken Harris, Marcelo Pereira, Elisio Pitta, Almiro Aquilino, Catharine Evleshin, Zonnie Bauer, Jeron Freightman, Michael Williams, Samia Panni, Pamela McClusky, Karen Morell, Themba Mashama, Henry Young, and Michael Z. Goldstein.

Major funds for the fieldwork research were provided by the Fulbright Foundation's Institute for International Education and by the Graduate School and Department of Anthropology, University of Washington, to whom I am extremely grateful. Additional support in the manuscript preparation was provided through a fellowship for recent recipients of the Ph.D. by the American Council of Learned Societies.

I would also like to thank my editors at the University of

Chicago Press, T. David Brent and Kathryn Kraynik, for their unflagging support and patience. Finally, there are my parents, whose many gifts can never be repaid, and my wife Suzanne and son Galen, who continually help me to keep it all in perspective.

Introduction

Capoeira is a cultural genre widely known in Brazil, although there are wide differences of opinion as to exactly what it is. Even among adepts of the sport there are frequent disagreements over fundamental issues. For me to describe capoeira to an outside audience (as a semi-insider), it would be possible to highlight any of several different characteristics (for example: martial arts, dance, ritual, musical performance, or theatre), each of which comes to the fore at various moments during a typical event. From this perspective, capoeira is a blurred genre, in a sense slightly different from (but related to) that outlined by Geertz (1983, chap. 1). I refer to him here primarily because all three of the metaphors he suggests as basic to current understandings of culture—game, text, and drama—are central to the interpretations of capoeira interaction which follow. Of these, the fundamental one, since it is the one most firmly grounded in the players' own conceptions of what they are doing, is game or sport.

Following Huizinga, many scholars of play have attempted to make a systematic distinction between these two terms, without a clear consensus emerging (Huizinga 1955: 195–96; Blanchard and Cheska 1985: 52–53). Among capoeira players, there is a tendency to use 'game' (*jôgo*) as the basic, unmarked term, especially relevant to informal occasions and more traditional styles of play; whereas 'sport' (*esporte*) is marked as the term of preference for more formal occasions, like tournaments, and for more institutionalized kinds of play. So when referring to capoeira in addressing an outside audience, especially for the news media or any government agency, players will frequently use the term *esporte*, while among themselves and informally the term *jôgo* is far more common. I will follow this lead without attempting a careful consistency, since both terms are in active use in the description of most kinds of capoeira activity.

Another common way to refer to capoeira events, especially among older players, is as *brincadeira* ('a child's game'), a noun derived from the verb *brincar*, 'to play (as a child).'[1] The lexical domain of 'play' in Brazilian Portuguese thus distinguishes musical play and adult play, already mentioned in the Preface, from this sense of childish playfulness.[2] The titles of the three central chapters of the book are chosen to reflect this division in the Brazilian language of play. Chapter 4, "Jogar," is devoted to the physical interactions; chapter 5, "Tocar," focuses on the musical patterns; and chapter 6, "Brincar," concentrates on verbal artistry. Note that, except for *tocar*, there is only a loose correspondence between these titles and the meanings of the terms, but the fact that all of these kinds of play are essential to the players' definitions of capoeira activity indicates clearly that here is where one should begin to look for an understanding of the game.

In his most famous article, Geertz proposes that Balinese cockfight is a kind of "deep play," and this is a phrase I (and others) find extremely fortunate for thinking about many forms of cultural expression, including capoeira. Like the Balinese cockfight, capoeira also takes the form of combat, but the outcome is (usually) only a metaphorical death, and the real end is more akin to liberation: a liberation from slavery, from class domination, from the poverty of ordinary life, and ultimately even from the constraints of the human body. A question Geertz does not address, however, is precisely *why* play should be so revealing of deep cultural patterns. Why does it seem to be, like ritual, such a direct doorway into the rich field of meanings at the heart of daily life? Perhaps part of the answer has to do with how play serves as a framework for contextualizing social encounters. This was Bateson's central insight regarding play (e.g., 1972: 177–93), and one which Goffman has extended into a general approach to understanding human interaction.[3]

CULTURE PLAY

If this study is of a certain kind of play in Brazilian culture, it is grounded on a theory which in turn derives culture, at least in part, from the activity of human play. In one of the most penetrating discussions of the importance of play, Gadamer describes it as "the to-and-fro movement which is not tied to any goal which would bring it to an end" (1975: 93). By omitting agency from this construction, he stresses the autonomy of play, not dependent on any particular subject or subjectivity, while at the same time emphasizing the fact that it can constitute, in its essential form, pure "self-representation" (1975: 95). That is, as many scholars of play agree, in its most general form it has no aim or purpose except play itself. For Gadamer, the combined force of these two qualities draws the players in, overshadows them in the activity process, and encourages them to "play themselves out" in it. These ideas resonate immediately with themes from capoeira discourse, as when adepts experience the voice of the *berimbau* as 'calling' (*chamando*) them to come and play. But as play develops from childlike self-absorption to organized cultural expression, it opens itself out to an audience; it moves from mere self-representation to "representation for someone." In Gadamer's scheme, capoeira lies somewhere between a mere game, in which players are primarily caught up in their contest world, and art forms which find their perfection in the experiences of an audience. Exploring this hazy boundary should be valuable for an understanding of how play worlds create contexts for 'serious' cultural meaning and will be the main business of chapter 7.

The paradox of losing oneself and simultaneously finding one's self in the experience of play is prominent in Gadamer's analysis and is echoed by many other students of the subject, who frequently associate it with the idea of 'freedom.'[4] As Sebeok put it, "The only ordinance that applies to Pure Play is the law of liberty" (1981: 3). In these views, play is seen as 'free' in two senses at least: (1) it must be entered into voluntarily, as part of one's free will; (2) one experiences a sense of freedom in the activity itself. Patterson has argued persuasively, in his seminal work on slavery (1982), that the idea of 'freedom' was not a spontaneous invention, but arose in reaction to the institution of slavery. That is, the concept of 'freedom,' as commonly used in the Euro-American tradition, is not primarily grounded in an infinite possibility field, the *freedom to*, but rather originates in the idea of the loosening of bonds or restraints, the *freedom from*.

A review of the two freedoms in play noted above seems to substantiate his view. In the first place, play must be voluntary, because one cannot be coerced into it. Coercion destroys playfulness, because if one cannot choose to play one does not feel playful. Anyone who has been forced to take music lessons, for instance, has experienced this. Second, the sense of freedom in play comes from a loosening of social restraints, a suspension of the rules of 'normal' behavior, which is experienced as a sense of personal release, therefore pleasure. Children naturally are in play until adults set social limits for them, and one of the themes of children's play is to repeatedly test those limits. Of course, play can also test physical limits as well, and absorption in play can make one 'forget about' one's body and even 'lose track of' time, both ways of transcending limits temporarily.[5]

If Patterson's analysis is correct, it follows that capoeira is able to express the ideal of freedom in play so well because it was an outgrowth of slavery. It has this in common with similar art forms throughout the Americas, many of which have flourished because they seem to embody this joyous sense of the potential for liberation, which is especially intense when it comes from an intimate experience of oppression. For example, the physical interplay in capoeira is improvised, which not only allows for but demands maximum creativity on the part of the players. The same is true of jazz in the United States, another art stemming from the institution of African slavery, and one which has already achieved the status of an international art form. In both cases there are also constraints or structures within which creativity should operate, and it is precisely this interplay between constraint and freedom which drives and renews the continuous improvisations.

Thinking about capoeira in all its freedom, it might be seen as an exuberant dance, but a major constraint on this creativity is the imperative of self-defense, since the sport is also a martial art. The movements are frequently acrobatic, involving total body involvement in all dimensions, but while executing these improbable contortions, one always has an eye on one's partner, who is also one's adversary. This is a major difference between capoeira and break dancing, for instance, although many of the moves look superficially similar in the two activities. Some students of black performance arts believe that capoeira, which was being played in New York's Central Park by the mid 1970s, had an influence on the development of breaking, while others disagree (see Dossar 1988; Thompson 1986). In any case, it seems that breaking was a fad that has now largely passed away, whereas capoeira, already an old art dating at least from the late eighteenth century, is still growing and shows signs of becoming an international sport. I believe that part of the reason for this difference may be that breaking was 'too free,' being primarily (merely) an expression of individual creativity in movement. Since capoeira is a delicate balance between domination and liberation, between fight and dance, those creative tensions generate an endlessly fascinating interplay.

In thinking about cultural patterns generally, social scientists have mostly been concerned to describe typical or habitual interactions and concepts. Such customary usages must be rule-governed, which therefore means that actors have stereotyped roles to play and typical concepts of those roles. Durkheim, for example, took great pains to emphasize the lack of freedom in social systems, the extremely constraining nature of social reality. Accordingly, many scholars have come to see play as a subset of social action in which typical patterns are temporarily suspended, thus providing a sense of freedom but usually within carefully predetermined limits of space and time. It follows that play comes to be seen as a diversion from normal life, a 'break' in quotidian patterns which, in functional theories, often serves to reinforce the sociocultural order. It is from this perspective that common distinctions like 'play' versus 'work,' or 'recreational' versus 'instrumental' behavior have arisen.[6]

Once ordinary conventions are (temporarily) suspended, there are several possibilities as to what can occur. Some kinds of play represent anarchic alternatives to normal interaction, like Brazilian Carnaval. Here a common theme is status reversal (Turner 1977: 166–203), in which normal roles are simply inverted—for example, the poor dominate the rich.[7] Although participants in such celebrations may interpret status reversals as the total suspension of all social rules, this is usually only a convenient fiction. In most cases 'anarchic' festivals are in fact carefully controlled by the elites, for whom true chaos is a persistent fear, since it would be extremely threatening to the status quo. A more common alternative to the quotidian is the world of games, in which the playful freedom comes precisely from a secure knowledge of the rules in force. Games are not set up to be chaotic alternatives to order, rather they constitute alternative rule systems which, unlike social life, are relatively simple and consistent. It follows that games can be revealing of general cultural patterns partly because they can be seen as microcosms of society, or at least of some aspects of social interaction. As microcosms they can be comforting, since people reason by analogy that a finite, consistent set of rules must regulate social life as well. This helps explain the paradoxical process of games being perceived both as 'escapes' from normal life, while also serving as models for reflection on deep cultural patterns in the outside world.

Sometimes even such controlled reflections are dangerous, however, since they can reveal things that are potentially destructive to the frameworks of meaning and interaction that societies depend on. Play domains accordingly contain a built-in safeguard, namely, their supposedly 'nonserious' nature: games are, after all, *only* games and are not to be taken as 'the real thing.' Usually this mask is enough to prevent U.S. citizens from being too appalled by the implications of football or Spaniards by the bullfight, but the line between the two worlds is fragile and always in danger of dissolving.

The fact that games can expand to encompass human life (as with gambling addicts) or can threaten to tear the social fabric (as with soccer riots) indicates the persistent difficulty of keeping play within controlled bounds. Huizinga was one of the first to formulate this problematic, dwelling both on the boundedness of the play space itself, similar in this respect to many kinds of sacred spaces, while also constantly insisting on the fundamental, or precultural, nature of the play experience.[8] Recent work has followed this lead, but more has been written about play as microcosm in organized games and sports than about the varieties of noninstitutionalized play behavior in society, the constant 'interplay' between freedom and constraint in the generation of all meaning systems. One of the most careful analyses of the second type is that of Grathoff (1970), who demonstrates that even in very well-regulated societies, what he calls "social inconsistencies" frequently arise. These are situations of interaction in which social types and "typificatory" schemes fail to give meaning to an emergent context. In such cases, participants are reduced to "playing at a theme" in an attempt to reconstitute coherence in the social field (Grathoff 1970: 53f.). Coherence is achieved when an existing typificatory scheme is reestablished or when new social types are actively invented, as a result of this play, and thus a new framework of meaning arises. Although Grathoff does not mention them, anthropological encounters are fertile fields for the generation of social inconsistencies and might be taken as prototypes for, or limiting cases of, the problem of context creation in society.

This was the view proposed by Wagner in *The Invention of Culture* (1981), in which he has the encounter between anthropologist and hosts forcing both to rediscover themselves while they create a new discourse to bridge the gulf of strangeness. This discourse becomes known as 'culture' when it is reformulated for public consumption by the anthropologist upon his return, but the hosts may well call it something else. Within any group, encounters between 'self' and 'others' constantly require the renovation and reinvention of common understandings. This was the case of Grathoff's concern, in which the freedom of play is often called upon to reestablish coherence. The arrival of an exotic anthropologist can be seen as an extension of the everyday cultural mediation that allows people to overcome problems in communication. The difference between the normal maintenance of cultural usages and the special case of the anthropological encounter is merely quantitative, in this view, having to do with the size of the gulf between 'self' and 'other.' The larger the gulf, the greater the shock of the encounter and the greater the creative play needed to bridge the gap with a new mediating discourse.

Given what has been said so far about play in culture, it is easy to see why a form of deep play like capoeira might have developed. Chapter 3 discusses the origins of the game in a situation of cultural encounter and conflict between European, native Amerindian, and African traditions in the Brazilian setting. Such an encounter inevitably creates many social incongruities, necessitating a very free play in the creation of cultural types in order to bridge gaps in understanding. These inconsistencies were further exacerbated by the institution of slavery, which necessarily causes "distorted" communication due to the power inequalities of master-slave relations.[9] These two major factors, along with a host of smaller ones, created an extremely fertile field for the generation of play forms in Brazil, of which capoeira is only one. Since a person often learns to play capoeira as a child, at least in Bahia, perfecting one's technique and understanding well into adulthood, the game combines both youthful and mature approaches to playfulness. Perhaps this too has added to its development as an extremely elaborate and enduring art form whose creative potential has yet to be fully realized.

If something like this theoretical approach to play is accepted, then it becomes fairly clear why study of ludic forms is a good avenue into the heart of matters social and cultural. When play is organized into games, it becomes a concentrated field for the generation of, and reflection on, signs which reverberate throughout the society at large. These overtones are especially pervasive precisely because play, being a creature of freedom, resists the boundedness of arenas and enters into every sphere of social life, sometimes in disguise, to lend vitality and coherence to human encounters. Play exists as an organizing activity, as a meaningful orientation, established since childhood and most useful precisely where other frameworks break down. All play has the potential for depth, but some play is clearly deeper than others. Capoeira is especially rich because it combines human physical interaction, instrumental music, singing, and oral poetry into complex expressive events.

These semiotic domains are mutually embedded, interactive channels which influence each other in complex ways, and their mutual influence will be the main theme of this work. In addition, these domains, which make up the microstructure, are themselves embedded in a hierarchy of signification that extends into the macrostructures of Bahian and Brazilian social interactions and cultural beliefs. The game functions as a sign *of* history, preserving cultural patterns from former times, and as a sign *in* history, evolving along with changes in the social order.[10] I will consider the undertaking successful if I can demonstrate some of the main relations within the microstructure of capoeira and relate them to broad cultural themes in Brazilian society at large.

THE METAPHOR OF DISCOURSE

Of the three main semiotic channels active in capoeira play—movement, music, and song—only the last one is, strictly speaking, a kind of discourse, since the song lyrics count as texts. Because a principal theoretical goal of this work is to contribute to the semiotic project, a general understanding of signs in culture, a fruitful first step is to examine the limits to an analogy between language and other codes. Of course, linguistic models of culture are not new in anthropology (one thinks immediately of cognitive and structural approaches), but these have proved less than satisfying for several reasons. Typically one or two ideas have been taken from one subfield of linguistics (such as phonology or semantics) and applied generally to systems of cultural knowledge. Since language is itself a subsystem of culture, that is, embedded in a matrix of nonlinguistic signs, such an approach seems to put the cart before the horse. This does not mean that conceptual tools from linguistics cannot be applied to other expressive domains, but such attempts should be part of a clear strategy for elucidating a general semiotic theory within which culture and, in turn, language are seen as special subtypes.

In order to make the development of such a theory possible, semioticians are turning increasingly to the work of C. S. Peirce, whose approach, unlike that of Saussure, is not grounded in the linguistic sign, but is based on a comprehensive phenomenology.[11] This is not the place for a detailed explication of the system, except to say that it provides the theoretical underpinning for this work, as well as many of the analytical tools. Elsewhere, I have explored in detail the implications of several of Peirce's fundamental triads, especially the key notion of 'interpretant' in the 'atomic' triad of the sign (Lewis 1986; see also note 18 below). The semiotic terms used most frequently in this discussion will be those of his most famous triad, types of relations between sign and object: iconic, indexical, and symbolic.[12] Glosses for these and other terms will be provided in the text or in notes, as necessary.

Another problem with earlier attempts to see cultural systems in linguistic terms might be called the question of coherence or integration. In other words, how well do the parts of any given sign system work together to produce an orderly whole? While it is clear that language, for instance, has definite rules and regularities, recent studies of linguistic universals have demonstrated that there are also many anomalies and idiosyncracies and that universals are perhaps better seen as tendencies or probability vectors (for example, Comrie 1989: 19–23). This kind of discovery has been a key factor in the critique of Chomsky's early view of language as the competence of an "ideal speaker/hearer." If some degree of indeterminacy is true for language, what might one expect of systems such as painting, carving, music, or expressive movement? Can they be seen as 'systems' at all, and, if so, are they more or less integrated than language and verbal thought? This is, of course, an empirical question and it seems clear that there will be considerable variation between societies for any given (nonlinguistic) mode of expression.

Nonetheless, the Peircean framework provides a working hypothesis here which seems intuitively appealing. Language is the privileged domain of symbols for Peirce: signs taken to have an arbitrary relation to their objects as a matter of habit or convention. This is especially true at the levels of phonology and syntax, where rule operation seems to be the most consistent. In contrast, extralinguistic signs are often primarily iconic and/or indexical, with the symbolic relation latent or even 'degenerate.' It follows that such domains are more loosely integrated; because icons and indexes are less fixed by habit, they have the tendency to intermingle and propagate into complex branches and trees of relatedness. If this is true, then it is perhaps the very fertility of the sign fields we call art, dance, or music that has greatly complicated attempts to organize them into consistent systems, even within one social setting. This helps to explain why language has failed as a model for nonverbal expressive systems: it is overdetermined for such a purpose.

A third reason for the danger of seeing cultural systems as 'texts' is related to the two above, but perhaps it can also provide, paradoxically, a new way of understanding sign systems in general: this is the problem of context. A major weakness of both cognitive and structural models of culture has been that methods were focused on the construction of paradigmatic frameworks which abstracted words and ideas from their contexts in use. The results were hypostatized schemata which have repeatedly been shown to be overly intellectual, overly self-consistent, and overly global. Also these analytical models, in their guise as 'science,' purported to be context-free (that is, universal), which only served to mask the fact that they were simply new anthropological contexts, with very tenuous connections to the worlds of indigenous interpretation.

The formidable problem of context has also been the focus of recent critiques of theoretical linguistics and philosophy of language, which have resulted in several new approaches to language and meaning. Fields such as speech act theory, discourse analysis, conversation analysis, and the ethnography of speaking have in common an interest in the context-sensitive aspects of language: a view that meaning arises out of the culturally mediated discourse event, which is crucially dependent on physical setting, kinesic and proxemic cues, and shared presuppositions about what constitutes appropriate communication, among other things. Analyses of situated speech have shown that contexts for the interpretation of meaning are not only given in advance (by setting, social roles, shared knowledge, etc.) but are also constantly being changed and renegotiated in the process of communication.[13] Note that many of the 'contextualization cues' (Cook-Gumperz and Gumperz 1976; Gumperz 1982) that are crucial to the interpretation of talk are not symbolic but indexical signs, metacommunicative signals that refer back to aspects of the ongoing discourse. These can be and frequently are nonverbal signs—eye contact, facial expression, gesture and posture—which 'comment on' the talk underway.

In capoeira, the main channel of communication is not talk, it is action—the interplay of two bodies in the ring. In the course of this activity, songs are sung which can be seen as 'comments on' that encounter and which also serve thereby to alter the context of play. This is an interesting inversion of the usual hierarchy of verbal/nonverbal relations. That is, capoeira songs and shouted comments can and do serve as contextualization cues for action in the ring, similar to the way raised eyebrows or curled lips can affect the meaning of linguistic utterances. This is the main justification for referring to capoeira as 'discourse,' in what seems to be an extension of the textual metaphor into nonverbal domains. In fact, the study of language as discourse really does the reverse: it represents a step toward the semiotic, embedding linguistic signs (symbols) in a larger context of indexical and iconic relations. By making this move explicit, through the fortunate coincidence of capoeira play, this study can perhaps strengthen the position of those who view language as discourse, while simultaneously situating verbal discourse in the more fluid play of signs in general.[14]

Seeing capoeira play as discourse has proven fruitful as a way of thinking about physical interactions and musical patterns in the game. For example, for reasons I will elucidate in chapter 4, there is a sense in which basic interaction patterns resemble conversational 'turn taking,' where partners alternate initiatives ('attacks') and responses ('escapes'). This is the justification for my continual use of the metaphor 'physical dialogue' to refer to movement interactions. In addition, there are complex 'opening and closing' conventions which govern entrances to and exits from the ring and similar norms which influence initiatives in singing and taking up instruments. The concept of interpretive frame, a central tool in the analysis of situated speech and mediated communication, has greatly aided my understanding of what I call 'games within the game': these include subroutines such as *chamadas* ('calls') and the 'turn around the world' mentioned in the Preface. Using the term 'discourse' also enables me to exploit the very general sense in which the word has come to stand for large-scale social and cultural patterns of understanding, as in the work of Gramsci and Foucault. This common academic usage aids my attempts to relate capoeira interactions to Brazilian cultural 'discourse' outside the ring.

PERFORMANCE

This introduction has been loosely following the form of Geertz's argument in "Blurred Genres" (1983), while suggesting certain emendations which add to the theoretical force of metaphors he cites. Instead of 'game' theory, I have argued, what is needed is a better understanding of the more general, unbounded category of 'play' (of which games are a subtype).[15] Likewise, the literary metaphor of 'text' is hampered by an association with written language, whereas something like 'discourse' situates investigation in the logically and historically prior domain of spoken language (in turn embedded in general sign systems). Finally, the metaphor of 'theater' might be usefully expanded to include a view of social life as a field for performance.

From Weber, Parsons, and the "social action" theorists, to Turner's view of ritual as a kind of "social drama," many different schools of thought have found the theatrical metaphor a useful tool. I would add to this tendency a convergence from the field of linguistics as well. Part of the force behind the move toward viewing language as situated discourse comes from a renewed interest in what Chomsky called "performance," which for him were precisely those aspects of language without regular patterns, hence without theoretical interest. Since the early work of Labov, at least, many linguists have felt the need to return to 'natural' speech events for data and have been finding interesting regularities in varieties of performance. To be sure, linguistic performance is clearly distinct from theatrical or musical performance in the strict sense, but I would suggest that both meanings can be seen as part of the same trend toward viewing culture as process: toward seeing patterns and rules as emergent in interactive contexts, rather than as static and predetermined structural frameworks.[16]

Therefore I see no contradiction in portraying capoeira both as 'deceptive discourse' and as a kind of social (and personal) drama, a *theater of liberation*. By doing both, I hope to take advantage of this convergence onto the idea of performance and to use the power of both linguistic and dramatic metaphors in the analysis. This kind of conceptual convergence is something of a two-

edged sword, however, since an uncritical conflation of events
with categories can obscure more than it reveals. An example of
this problem that has direct bearing on capoeira is the category of
ritual.

Turner's work has led many to apply terms from ritual process, like 'liminality' and 'communitas,' to phenomena in the secular social world. This move is appropriate, I would argue, only as
long as the analogic distinction is carefully maintained. Turner
takes pains to separate truly liminal states, like those found in rites
of passage, from the 'liminoid' states common in the social processes of large-scale, industrial societies (1982: 20–60). Following MacAloon, it seems to me that ritual frames differ from
other kinds of ceremony and festival settings in two ways (1984:
250–54). They make reference to the ultimate, usually spiritual,
foundation that provides a grounding framework within which
the particular (by implication all possible) events are embedded;
and they assert the possibility of an unmediated contact with that
ground, a contact that can fundamentally transform human life.
To this I would add that, in most cases, the spiritual domain also
contains a moral component, which provides the means for a criti-
cal judgment of behaviors which are ritually framed. It seems to
me that one should resist the temptation to label all habitual or
traditional group action 'ritual,' but rather should carefully examine given ceremonial frames with an eye for what interpretive
possibilities they suggest to participants.

Most adepts agree that capoeira as it is practiced today is a
secular event and that its connection with spiritual practices, such
as *candomblé* or Catholicism, are indirect at most.[17] Nonetheless,
rodas often begin with an invocation which explicitly gives praise
to God (*Deus*), and many songs refer to saints and deities, both
Christian and African. In spite of this, I believe it is inaccurate to
refer to capoeira games as rituals and a distortion to call the sport
a 'ritual combat' when one simply means a 'mock combat.' The
existence of the *ladainha/chula* invocation (see chapter 6) does
provide a ritual framework within which the game can be situated, and it is possible that in the past this frame was taken as
determinative of events (or that in the future it will be). The current effect of such invocations (optional in many games), for most

players, is merely to endow the proceedings with an air of moral seriousness and thereby to encourage mutual respect among players. To be sure, a person is free to seek spiritual help before or during the contest, but this is seen as an individual choice and not part of the group concern. For some, the game can be a spiritual practice, while for others it is simply an invigorating pastime, and the vast majority seem to view the ring as a spiritually neutral arena.

Careful attention to the negotiation and interpretation of context requires that categories like 'ritual' not be applied to interactions casually or metaphorically. Since contexts are not predetermined but emergent, sacred and secular moments may coexist or alternate repeatedly within the same ongoing interaction. Sacred language may be used to comment on secular activities (and vice versa), such that an event or stretch of talk is impossible to categorize neatly and unambiguously. The same kind of interpretive complexity can apply to other kinds of competing context frames, not just sacred and secular, and to interactions between past and present meanings, or between naive and expert understandings. Once again Peirce tells us, through his category of the interpretant,[18] to expect polysemy in sign systems, rather than shared meanings. Consensus is not the norm, but is a difficult and fragile condition, always breaking down and forever in need of renegotiation. Shared activities like games, rituals, and speech genres provide familiar frameworks for consensus building, and therefore cultural creation, but each time one is enacted the result is at least partly new. This is why change rather than continuity is the rule in cultures, even though the former is often masked by, or subsumed into, the latter by the force of habit.[19]

OTHER FRAMEWORKS

In spite of the many criticisms of Lévi-Strauss and structuralism, some of which I have alluded to above, I believe there is still a wealth of insight contained in his work, and it would be less than honest to deny his influence on some of the analysis to follow. Binary thinking is an important, even fundamental, mode of human cognition, though it is certainly not the only such mode. Gadamer's "to and fro" motion will be seen to reverberate throughout much of what follows, revealing complementarities players use to organize the game into several kinds of order. These oppositions are always mediated in interesting ways, and it is the process of mediation between extremes which seems to me most productive, in the last analysis, to an understanding of capoeira in Brazilian society. This is a neglected aspect of structuralism which has been used productively by some authors to account for fundamental patterns within a carefully contextualized ethnographic belief system.[20]

In an attempt to deal with the movement aspects of capoeira more adequately, I exposed myself to the fundamentals of Laban Movement Analysis (henceforth LMA), one of several analytical systems competing for supremacy in the field of movement description.[21] There is some precedent for the use of LMA in anthropology, the most well-known being the choreometrics project begun by Lomax, Bartenieff, and Paulay (1968). LMA is a complex theoretical approach, still in the process of development, including a complete notational system. Although I am far from being an expert in its use, the system did provide me with a detailed framework for observing physical interplay and suggested to me some analogies between the physical and social orders. Some LMA terms will be used in the text, but the object is not a comprehensive movement description of capoeira, which in any case I am not qualified to attempt. Instead, I try to dig deep enough into movement patterns to reveal some key features of this repertoire as it relates to other semiotic channels and to the total expression of meaning in the game. To supplement the verbal description of the basic capoeira movement, the *ginga*, I provide it in Laban notation in Appendix A, which is solely for the interest of experts in the system. Otherwise, technical LMA terms will be glossed as they occur in the discussion.

Many of the points just made could be reiterated with regard to analysis of the musical performance system, mostly in chapter 5. Although not an ethnomusicologist, I have had some training in that approach, as well as independent musical training. I have become a competent capoeira musician (much better than my physical play) with extensive experience in games throughout Brazil and the United States, although I still have a lot to learn. In any case, I believe I have captured the musical performance structure more completely than previous attempts, but again make no pretense to having the final word. I only hope to have revealed enough about the musical patterns to demonstrate how they function with song texts and movement in the total event process. Like most eclectic efforts, this work perhaps lacks the depth of the specialist in any one of the subsystems of capoeira expression, but the point is precisely not to ignore any one aspect in favor of another: to achieve a balanced approach with sufficient insight overall to reveal essential patterns. Since capoeira is very deep play, it is a long way to the bottom, which may indeed be boundless. Although this is not the first work on the subject, the project still seems very near the beginning stages. Therefore I eagerly await more work on this wonderfully complex phenomenon and only hope that this book aids somewhat in the explorations to come.

The Origins of Capoeira

The only weapon of self-defense I could use successfully was
that of deception.
                    —Henry Bibb, a slave in the United States

Did capoeira originate in Brazil or in Africa? This frequently
posed question is the cause of controversy, both among contemporary players of the game and between scholars of Afro-Brazilian
traditions. The question itself reveals much, both in its presuppositions, and in the context from which the controversy arises.
Notice that there are only two sites suggested, Africa and Brazil;
a significant third choice is implicitly excluded, namely Portugal.
Since the songs of capoeira are sung mostly in Portuguese, and
since Catholic saints, along with other Christian elements, are repeatedly mentioned, it would be impossible to deny that Lusitan-
ian culture has strongly influenced capoeira, yet no one would
argue that capoeira originated in Portugal.

The main reason for this is that capoeira has an undeniably
African esthetic. In movement style, musical structure, and many
other areas, the sport is fundamentally non-European. If the African component is primary, the question then becomes, how integral is the Brazilian influence? Is this a Brazilianized African
sport or a Brazilian sport with African roots? Put in this way, the
question seems harmless enough, and an outside observer might
wonder why it should be so hotly debated. The answer is that the
question is relatively innocuous from a historical perspective, but
crucial from an ontological one. That is, this question of origins
is central to the self-understandings of many players: it is a fundamental question about identity.

In his review of the conditions for the possibility of violence in Sri Lanka, Daniel (1990) has argued for a new perspective on the question of central concern here, which he formulates as a rereading of the traditional conflict between myth and history. The contradiction, as he frames it, is only tangentially related to issues of falsehood and truth, rather he sees the mythic as primarily 'ontic,' as a way of *being* in the world, as opposed to the 'epistemic,' which is a way of *seeing* the world (1990: 227).[1] This distinction is even more subtle than it might appear at first, since history is always partly mythic, in this view, and myths or legends can be, and frequently are, epistemic. In the case of capoeira, it is clear that many players have such an ontic interest in the game's origins, since for them the game is primarily a way of being in the world. Thus issues of historical origin, which to most scholars are 'empirical' issues involving epistemic debate, are frequently seen by participants in the sport as issues of ethnic identity.

In the United States, for instance, blacks who practice capoeira tend to argue strongly for an African origin to the sport, since they can then claim it as their own more directly, without having to think of it as an exotic, Brazilian import.[2] Likewise, some of those in Brazil who identify themselves as an exploited and marginal subgroup, typically the darkest and sometimes the poorest, tend to argue the same way. They think of themselves as blacks first and Brazilians second, identifying strongly with the homeland and seeing racism as the chief impediment to their social mobility in Brazil.[3] Many others think of capoeira as a Brazilian invention, especially those of higher socioeconomic status, which on the average corresponds to lighter colored skin. This is by no means a strict dichotomy, and racial politics are not nearly so polarized in Brazil as they are in the United States, but it is still clear that the struggle over origins involves a politics of power, of dominant and counterhegemonic discourses, of racism and cultural imperialism.

In such a debate there is no neutrality, and I cannot hide behind a cloak of academic authority or objectivity to argue that I am immune to these power struggles. Nonetheless, I must admit that I have not found an alternative to the traditional academic interest in an epistemic view of the past, with all its verificationistic tendencies (Daniel 1990: 228). That is, as I think about oral traditions and stories of the origins of capoeira, I cannot stifle urges to consult historical and anthropological sources, to evaluate and compare such stories against what is 'known' from these other sources (not necessarily less mythic). As a result of these academic habits, I will be casting doubt on some oral traditions and legends of capoeira origins from an epistemic perspective. I do this not because I wish to disempower the proponents of alternative discourses, but simply because my interests differ from theirs and it seems dishonest to hide my opinions simply because I am in solidarity with the political agendas of those who think otherwise. Wherever possible, I will suggest alternative interpretations of the past without arguing for the 'truth' of any one view, and at times I will have something to say about the effects of capoeira legends on the beliefs and practices of those who adhere to them.

One example of how the debate works itself out in practice can be seen in alternative views of a group of martial arts similar to capoeira, found in other parts of the New World. In Martinique, there is a sport called *l'agya,* and in Cuba one called *mani* (the latter perhaps extinct), both of which involve acrobatic, mock combat set to music.[4] Also, there is a stick fight from Trinidad called *kalinda,* which is similar to the Brazilian *maculêlê,* mentioned in the Preface.[5] There are also oral accounts of a black martial art called "knocking and kicking" in the southern United States.[6] Some students of black culture argue that these various arts come from a common source (usually in Bantu central Africa), which explains their similarity. This is currently a popular view for many, but less is heard of an equally plausible explanation: that slavery created a host of similar institutions in the Americas, from which elements of many African cultures were combined in similar ways. Either scenario could account for the differences between the various arts, but it is interesting that the first interpretation tends to dwell on their similarities, wanting to see them all as essentially 'the same.' This has the political effect of increasing the potential for solidarity among black people from different countries by recreating their common origins in Africa. Since adequate descriptions do not exist of any of these other martial arts,[7] the question of their origins, or even their commonalities, seems undecidable (for now) from an epistemic perspective, although this does not sway those for whom the ontological priorities are clear.

In any case, all students of capoeira history would agree that if there had not been an African slave trade to Brazil, the game could not exist as it is played today. Accordingly, it is to that trade, and the slave society that resulted from it, that I will now turn to examine what may be known about the origins of the sport.

AFRICAN SLAVERY

When Pedro Alvares Cabral made the first official landing in Brazil in 1500, Portugal already had a tradition of African slavery extending back to medieval times and had been engaged in commercial slave trade for almost sixty years. Under the aegis of 'Henry the Navigator' (who never went to sea in his life), Portugal had been pushing down the coast of Africa, pursuing a systematic exploration venture the object of which was lucrative new trading ports, and one of the earliest commodities was the human kind. When the native population of Brazil proved inadequate for the labor needs of the new colony, the Portuguese did not hesitate to begin transporting Africans there as well.[8] So 'successful' was the venture that it quickly grew into one of the largest enforced migrations in human history, carrying a total of approximately three and one-half million people to Brazil alone in the course of 350 years (Curtin 1969: 49). If one adds the mortality rate on slave ships, which probably averaged ten to thirty percent,[9] then the enormity of the disruption caused to African societies by this trade can be imagined (cf. Vansina 1966; Birmingham 1966). The fact that Africa underwent the depredations of the slave trade and later colonialism is a major problem in the reconstruction of cultural continuities, since it makes it more difficult to discover what traditions were carried to Brazil by the slaves. Modern Africa can be 'translated' into precontact Africa only with great care and little certainty.

Africans were brought to Brazil from the western, southern, and southeastern coasts of the continent, from Mauritania all the way to Mozambique. Trying to trace cultural influences from such a diverse collection of tribal and linguistic groups, given the lack of understanding and interest Europeans usually showed toward those 'cargoes' at the time, is a daunting task. Brazilian authors always mention the fact that, upon the declaration of the Republic in 1891, Ruy Barbosa burned all colonial records relating to slavery in an alleged attempt to rid Brazil of all memory of that shameful institution (Verger 1964: 2). Since Barbosa was the Minister of Finance, however, others have suggested that his act was meant to avoid suits against the new government by ex-slaveholders desiring compensation for their lost property. In any case, Verger brings some order to the problem by suggesting four main cycles of slave imports into Bahia, the capital of colonial Brazil:

1. The Guinea cycle during the second half of the sixteenth century.
2. The Angola cycle in the seventeenth century.
3. The Mina Coast cycle during the first three quarters of the eighteenth century.
4. The Bight of Benin cycle between 1770 and 1851, to be precise. (Verger 1964: 3)

In the sixteenth century, 'Guinea' was the Portuguese name for the entire west coast of Africa above the equator. The traffic during this period was relatively light, probably less than a thousand slaves per year on average, and many were drawn from the Senegambia area (Schwartz 1985: 339). By the beginning of the seventeenth century, African slaves were beginning to outnumber Indians on plantations, and the pace of slave trading accelerated considerably, with averages in the five to ten thousand per year range. The majority of slaves during this 'Angola' cycle were taken from ports such as Cabinda (north of the Kongo River), Luanda, Benguela (both in present-day Angola), and Mossamedes (modern Namibia), mostly drawn from groups speaking Bantu languages. The 'Mina Coast' is in present-day Ghana while the 'Bight of Benin' is east of that in modern Nigeria. All these cycles represent central tendencies only, especially the last two, and they vary somewhat for other ports in Brazil. For instance, it is generally agreed that more slaves from Bantu groups were brought through Rio de Janeiro during the last two cycles, while Bahia was receiving primarily groups from West Africa north of the equator. Many authors have argued (for example, Plaut 1980; Kubik 1979) that African culture, insofar as it was preserved in Brazil (especially in Bahia, the area of chief concern), has two main 'layers': a deep core of Bantu traditions established since the seventeenth century, and a newer layer of West African traditions firmly established in the eighteenth century and renewed throughout the nineteenth.

Herskovits was among the first in this country to begin finding "survivals" of specific African cultural elements in the life of U.S. blacks (1958 [1941]). In Brazil, however, the tradition is significantly older, partly because the African heritage is so much more apparent, dating back to the pioneering work of Nina Rodrigues, who distinguished Nagô (Yoruba), JeJe (Ewe), Minas (Fanti/Ashanti), Haussá (Hausa), Tapa (Nupe), Gurúnci, Fulá (Fulani), Mandinga (Mandé), and Bantu groups (1977 [1906]). It should be kept in mind that by the time of the slave trade many groups in the West African area had already experienced conversion to Islam. This was noted early on in Brazil, where Islamized blacks were commonly known as *Malês*. These people tended to be inimical to Christianity, so they were forced to hide their religious practices, and they were usually unwilling to consider even the token conversion to Catholicism practiced by other Africans. As a result, the *Malês* led several rebellions in Salvador in the early nineteenth century (cf. C. Moura 1981) and were virtually extinguished as an independent group. Since they were unwilling to syncretize their beliefs with the dominant religion, there are few traces of their cultural influence on modern Brazil, but one or two can still be found in the capoeira world. For example, one type of shirt often used by players is called *abadá*, a word which derives from the Arabic name for a prayer shirt used by the *Malês* (Cascudo 1970: 1).

INFLUENCES ON CAPOEIRA

The idea of 'survivals' has long been out of favor in anthropology, since it tended to reinforce a piecemeal, pseudo-evolutionary view of culture change. As societies came to be viewed as systems, more or less internally integrated, the interests of anthropologists shifted away from trait lists and cultural diffusion. Nonetheless, integration is never perfect nor total, diffusion does occur, and there are genetic relations between cultural systems, not unlike those between languages. In discussing possible origins for and influences on aspects of capoeira practice, therefore, I intend to adduce evidence for the ongoing discussion about the past of the sport and perhaps shed some light on theories of change and continuity in expressive culture. This section should not be read as a refusal to focus on the current performance of capoeira nor as a failure to see it as a system in its own right.

Influences on capoeira from the indigenous Amerindian population are the hardest to find and the most difficult to document, since the original coastal groups were never well studied and were absorbed so quickly, for the most part, into Bahian and Brazilian mainstream culture. It is often in the latter form, secondhand as it were, that native culture influenced capoeira, since it formed an essential part of the cultural matrix called Brazilian folklore, of which capoeira is a part. African blacks and Indian slaves labored side by side on the sugar plantations for decades in the earliest period of Brazil's history and had ample opportunities for exchanging ideas and practices. When blacks escaped to the bush, they sometimes took refuge with native groups (Bastide 1978: 93–94), and when they formed their own fugitive communities, natives often joined.

The stereotype of the *caboclo* is testimony to this fertile fusion of African and Brazilian tribal traditions, which contributed creolized religious cults, myths, and folk art forms of many styles to Brazilian culture. The term *caboclo* has a range of different meanings in the various regions of Brazil, most of which refer to some degree of indigenous descent, but almost always a mixed one. One exception to this is in Afro-Brazilian religion, especially *candomblé* and *umbanda,* where *caboclos* form a class of spirit beings associated with dead or mythical indians (see Wafer 1991; Brown 1986). In the Amazon Basin, the term often refers to relatively acculturated Indians, living like ordinary Brazilians, as opposed to '*indios*' or '*silvícolas*' who maintain more of their traditional practices. In capoeira, *caboclo* is used in a sense common throughout Bahia, for anyone from the interior ('rural regions') similar to our antique terms 'hick' or 'hillbilly.' Calling someone a *caboclo* in capoeira discourse is a form of mild teasing which may foreground a person's unsophisticated or uneducated side, but it can also allude to the spiritual power thought to emanate from the indigenous or untamed realms.

Several terms used in capoeira songs seem to be of Tupian origin, such as *paraná* ('a body of water,' cf. the Paraná river), and perhaps even the word 'capoeira' itself (see below). Whether these are direct influences from indigenous culture, or the secondhand legacies of Amerindian/Brazilian mainstream culture, is difficult to determine.

Influences from Africa itself can be specified somewhat more exactly than indigenous elements, but the difficulties are still formidable. For example, de Oliveira (1971) and J. Moura (1980) quote a letter from an Angolan named Albano de Neves e Souza, noting the similarities between capoeira and a dance called *ngolo* practiced by the Mucope people near Luanda. *Ngolo* was reputedly a zebra dance done by young men on the occasion of a female puberty rite called *efundula*. The best zebra dancer was awarded the choice of a wife from among the newly initiated women without having to pay a bride price (de Oliveira 1971: 68). Some students of Mestre Pastinha, a famous Bahian capoeira master, now deceased, corroborate this story. They say that Pastinha's own master, an African, told him that capoeira came from a "dance of the zebra" in Angola. Thus far I have found no reference to the Mucope in the anthropological literature, but Loeb (1948: 14–17) discusses an *efundula* ritual, also a female initiation, among the Kuanyama Ambo in an area (now Namibia) considerably south of the Angolan port of Luanda. In the fourth stage of this Ambo *efundula*, the girls are called *oihanangolo* or 'ash girls' (since they are covered with ashes) and imitate men, being then free of all taboos and restraints. The only overt similarity to capoeira in Loeb's account comes from his description of a different dance practiced by the Ambo: "The boys have a kicking dance in which they jump out from their group and kick as high into the air as possible, to the admiration of the girls" (1948: 12).

Given this conflicting and sparse evidence, it is difficult (from an epistemic perspective) to support claims, prominent among the students of Mestre Pastinha, for a unitary Angolan origin of capoeira, even though an early name for the game was "Capoeira Angola." Acrobatic dances are reported as part of male initiation ceremonies in many parts of the African coastal area where slaves were taken and, if capoeira is seen as having had multiple African influences, it is quite likely that puberty rites were important to its development. Among the Maconde people of Mozambique, for example, there is an acrobatic initiation ritual which involves religious specialists bending over backwards to pick up coins with their lips, a practice extremely reminiscent of the capoeira money game.[10] Throughout this region of Africa, including groups like the Shona of Zimbabwe, musical bows almost identical to Brazilian *berimbaus* are also found (Maraire 1982). In the film "Bitter Melons" (1974), San bushmen of the Kalahari can be seen in an "ostrich mating dance," doing a combination kick-and-duck very similar to a key interchange in capoeira. Sometimes capoeira can look very much like wrestling, though this is not its usual form, and wrestling is certainly a widespread tradition throughout West Africa. Wrestling is also practiced by native Amerindian groups in Brazil, so once again it is difficult to distinguish direction of influence or to rule out the possibility of convergence or independent invention.

Clearly Bantu elements in capoeira include many of the African terms in the songs, such as *Aruandé* (referring to the slave port of Luanda), *mangangá* ('medicine man,' see below and chapter 5), and *moleque* ('street urchin'). Kubik, Thompson, and others argue that the basic rhythmic structure is Bantu (see extended discussion in Wa Mukuna 1982), and it is probable that the *berimbau* itself is a legacy from southern Africa. West African elements include the two-tone gong *agogô* (Yoruba), names of *orixás* (or saints known to represent them) in the songs, and direct and indirect references to *candomblé*. Since mainstream Bahian culture also includes many of these same words and elements, the capoeira world can be thought of as a somewhat specialized version of that system, with variations increasing in other parts of Brazil.

THE CULTURE OF SLAVERY IN BRAZIL

From its very beginnings, Brazil was seen by Europeans as a source of export products, and to a large extent its history could be written as an economic history of the cycles of demand for its resources. Brazil's fortunes rose and fell as a direct result of the European demand for its cash crops and minerals, in a pattern common among colonial enterprises. Among the various items that have determined Brazil's fortunes, none has been more important than sugar, which dominated the economy from the end of the sixteenth to the middle of the nineteenth century. The organization of the sugar industry, then, has been a major factor in the development of Brazilian society and culture in general, influencing economic and interpersonal relations throughout the country, even in areas where sugar was never the main crop. The center of the sugar industry until relatively recently was the northeast region of Brazil, especially the states of Bahia and Pernambuco. It is here that the pattern of large cane plantations developed, complete with local mill and refinery (*engenho*), owned by a Euro-Brazilian *senhor* (gentleman planter) and worked primarily by African and Creole slaves.

Even when sugar lost its dominant economic position in the mid-nineteenth century, it remained an important crop, and this pattern of large plantations reproduced itself in other sectors, especially in the northeast where paternalism and oligarchical control of resources are still endemic. On huge cattle ranches in the interior of Brazil, or on later plantations of cacao, coffee, and other export crops, slave labor was gradually replaced by a more modern form of debt peonage or institutionalized poverty, but the broad outlines remain the same, and certain aspects of the culture of sugar plantation life still mark interactions between the classes and races, even in the modern urban setting.

As in the United States, the children of plantation slaves were often allowed to play freely with the master's children from infancy until they were large enough to begin work. This fostered an initial closeness, perhaps a virtual sibling relationshp, between dark and light children, followed by a painful estrangement. Slaves in Brazil coined new words to refer to the sons and daughters of the master: *ioiô* and *iaiá*. These Africanizations of the Portuguese *senhor* and *senhora* often contain an emotional force expressive of the betrayed trust of a former playmate. A slave newly arrived from Africa might hate and fear the white master, but a second-generation slave, a *crioulo,* raised with a white child who later becomes the master, must have had a far more complex set of emotions with regard to him or her. The relationship will have been central to that slave's own character formation (unlike the newly arrived African) and will inevitably have affected his or her own self-image. As if this were not complex enough, add the fact that the little slave child was not infrequently engendered by the master also, who used his power for sexual access to the slave women. In these cases, the mulatto child was the half-brother or sister of the *iaiá* or *ioiô,* making their social distance seem all the more unjust. The classic work on the psychological effects of slavery on the formation of Brazilian culture remains that of Freyre (1956 [1933]; 1963 [1936]), even though it is highly speculative and anecdotal. Although the approach is outdated, and many scholars object to his tendency for sweeping generalization, Freyre's work remains valuable as one of few attempts to reconstruct the relation between social and psychological patterns during this era.

The words *iaiá* and *ioiô* occur frequently in capoeira songs, carrying all the baggage of slave-era injustice into the modern world. Many scholars of slavery have emphasized that, although slaves were powerless in most senses of the term, by virtue of this inequality masters also became dependent on their slaves in certain ways.[11] For instance, by manipulating their labor, the main source of their value to the master, slaves could influence conditions on plantations, perhaps even gain a measure of control over their daily lives. Through such tactics as malingering, slowdowns, inefficiency, intentional misunderstanding, and sabotage, slaves could communicate to the master displeasure with the way things were being run. By working well, on the other hand, they could demonstrate approval. This situation is captured in many capoeira songs, such as:

c: vâ dizer ao meu Sinhó   go tell my master
    que a manteiga derramou   that the butter spilled

s: a manteiga não é minha   the butter isn't mine
    a manteiga é do ioiô   the butter is the *ioiô's*

This song clearly evokes a scenario of slave resistance. The slave does not own the butter, so the implication is that he doesn't care that it spilled; he may have allowed it to spill, or even spilled it on purpose. Since the master could not know whether the accident was deliberate sabotage or mere negligence, it would be difficult for him to punish anyone, and such uncertainty itself was surely a powerful slave weapon. The manipulation of the system of production is one of the ways slaves gained some leverage over their masters indirectly, without resorting to outright rebellion or escape. Scott (1985) has argued that these types of dissimulation are a common pattern among subordinate groups worldwide, peasants as well as slaves, becoming formidable "weapons of the weak" whenever the cost of direct confrontation is too dear. In the capoeira world, such trickery became transformed into a positive value called *malícia,* and the understanding of that key term will be a major theme of this work, since it manifests itself in many aspects of the game, from deceptive tactics to deceptive discourse.

CATHOLICISM AND SLAVERY

The main justification for the participation of the Roman Catholic Church in the practice of slavery was that the 'pagan' Indians and Africans should have their souls saved, even if this meant the imprisonment of their bodies. Thus the church fathers insisted that all slaves be baptized and taught the rudiments of the catechism. This training was the responsibility of the individual masters and their chaplains, so it was often extremely perfunctory or nonexistent since there was no economic advantage to be gained by Christian instruction. In some cases, the blacks were not even allowed into the chapel to hear mass, but had to stand outside and participate as well as they could. Although the plantation owners were supposed to give the slaves Sundays and holidays off, they sometimes failed to do so, especially when the sugar was being harvested and the mills were in operation.

As a result, Catholicism among the slaves was frequently quite superficial, consisting of stock phrases and practices which appeased the consciences of the masters, but were often merely masks for underlying African beliefs. For example, the gesture of crossing oneself was undoubtedly one of the first signs of Christianity learned by African slaves. By making the sign of the cross, the slave could easily demonstrate his good Catholic faith without language, and perhaps without even the knowledge of what it signified to Christians. Thompson, among others, has noted that in Africa the image of the cross predated Christianity; that among Kongo groups, for instance, it was used to signify the divisions between heaven and earth, living and dead (1981: 43–44). While the gesture itself was easily learned by a new African slave, it is doubtful that the Christian meaning would be absorbed quite so rapidly, especially given linguistic and sociocultural barriers. Many slaves probably crossed themselves initially without understanding what they were supposed to be doing, perhaps interpreting the gesture as they would have in Africa, especially those for whom the cross was already an important icon.

Over time, with increasing exposure to Brazilian Catholicism, slaves learned the 'accepted' meanings (interpretants) for the gesture (see chap. 1, n. 18), but this did not by any means require them to forget the African interpretations. It might very well be a source of satisfaction for slaves to 'put one over' on their masters by deceiving them in thought while pleasing them in deed, as they did in so many other areas of slave life. Nor did such an act have to be strict duplicity, since among many African groups there is nothing contradictory about a both/and view of religion in which gods from various traditions can be included in the same pantheon. For instance, it is well known that African kings or chiefs who became Christian or Moslem did not always feel compelled to abandon their former deities and rituals, in spite of pressure to the contrary from missionaries.

The act of crossing oneself is ubiquitous in a Catholic society like Brazil, now as in the past. For instance, in the city of Salvador today, when a bus passes a church most of the riders will cross themselves. In the game of capoeira, the gesture can be used in a great many different ways, ironically as well as seriously (see chapter 3), and the variety of these contexts suggests that multivocality was part of its past as well.

Another religious practice common to plantation life was the 'giving of the blessing,' which usually included crossing oneself as an integral part. This might occur as a regular ritual in the evening, as the slaves paraded by the big house (Bastide 1978: 72; Pierson 1967: 81), or whenever a slave happened to meet the master in the course of a day: "Symbolically, both children and slaves were supposed to ask for a blessing (*bênção*) on seeing the senhor, and he was expected to give it" (Schwartz 1985: 288). The slaves were all too aware that the very master who was blessing them today could flog them tomorrow. This duplicity is captured in capoeira by naming one of the most common kicks "the blessing." *Bênção* is a fundamental capoeira attack, having many variations, but consisting basically of a front kick striking the opponent with the heel or the flat of the foot (see fig. 2.1).

There is a common joke, or scenario, acted out using this kick, which captures an essential aspect of the principle of *malícia*.

Figure 2.1 *Bênção:* The Blessing

On his first day of class, the instructor offers his hand to a new student for a handshake in a gesture of welcome. When the student reaches out to take the hand, the master unleashes his 'blessing,' knocking the student to the ground or against a wall. The lesson to be learned, amid gales of laughter, is something like, "Never let down your guard," or "Never trust anyone too far." The harshness of the lesson is compatible with the harshness of the system, both past and present, in which behind each blessing is a potential kick in the gut. In this concise, nonverbal scenario, capoeira players express the hypocrisy of the social system, both past and present, by unmasking the friendly handshake. I believe it is probable that the kick got its name from the blessing practices of slave society and that the scenario got its force from a wealth of similar interactions, highlighting the hypocrisy of a church that sanctioned systematic dehumanization.

Although the scenario of the blessing probably had its origins in the slave era, the blessing of the master eventually became a part of general Bahian culture. In recent times, many children have been taught to ask the blessing of their parents or other elders as a gesture of respect. This generalization of the earlier practice adds a new dimension of potential complexity to the scenario and to the force of the blessing kick as a named attack. One form this more current set of meanings may take is as a vehicle for the resentment or ambivalence young people (and most *capoeiristas* are young) feel toward their elders. As I will argue in chapter 3, such emotional ambivalence is often common between students and their capoeira masters. Note finally that asking the blessing is also integral to the ritual practice of some *candomblé* houses (see Wafer 1991: 149), so it is likely that religious connotations from that domain may also influence understandings of capoeira blessings in some cases.

The word *malícia* comes from the same Latin root as the English 'malice' or 'malicious' and has a set of related, but generally more benign, meanings. In the course of this work I will attempt to lay bare the full pragmatic scope of the term, since it seems to be at the heart of the practice of traditional capoeira. The first component of *malícia* is this notion of double-dealing or cunning, a lesson learned in slavery but still valuable in the modern world.

Capoeira masters who befriended me in Brazil frequently admonished me to be careful and not to trust anyone too far. Mestre Nô used to tell me, "You are not sufficiently malicious" (*malicioso*, the adjectival form), by which he meant that I was too trusting. This was a lesson that should be learned in the capoeira ring, but applied to life outside as well. The notion of extending principles of the capoeira game to life in general is common to the teachings of all masters. As Bira Almeida has expressed it, capoeira is not just a sport, it is a "way of life" (1981: 17).

HOLIDAY FESTIVALS

Perhaps because the burden of work fell so heavily on the slaves, opportunities for celebration and recreation were seized with a wild intensity. Early in the plantation era it was discovered that slaves tended to work better if they were allowed time off once in a while to sing and dance in their own way. This was a pragmatic tactic on the part of slaveowners, dictated by economic self-interest on the part of those who practiced it (by no means all), but it resulted in the preservation of many African cultural forms, syncretized to create new Afro-Brazilian arts. Since Sunday was the Christian day of rest, slaves were sometimes allowed to do as they wished at least part of the day. Even if Sundays were not granted in a given case, there were saints' days and religious holidays which were frequently celebrated even in the midst of cane harvests (Schwart 1985: 102–4). One reason to give slaves time off was to allow them to grow their own food in garden plots, but the highlight of many such days was a musical 'jam session' known as a *batuque*. According to Mendonça (1973: 117) this word derives from the Bantu *batchuque*, "a type of drum and its accompanying dance." The music and dances which developed out of these *batuques* are arguably the most important and characteristic of the Afro-Brazilian performance art forms.

Descriptions of slave *batuques* from the colonial era frequently emphasized their erotic nature, since this was shocking and titillating to the European travelers who witnessed them, but certain other features were sometimes noted as well. The music was 'repetitious' or 'monotonous' to European ears and was always accompanied by dancing. There was enthusiastic interplay between the dancers and the musicians, involving the whole 'audience' in clapping hands and singing responses. The sessions were usually held in a circle, with one or two dancers at a time in the center (see, for example, Koster 1966: 121–22). Many of these same elements are found in modern capoeira, in many types of traditional *samba* (especially rural and informal varieties), and even in some types of religious cult activities.

Slaveowners and religious authorities frowned upon the practice of African rituals, prohibiting such things as animal sacrifice, but they were not always able to tell the sacred from the profane when it came to music and dance. A royal letter to Brazil in 1780 stated that, "His majesty ordered that no superstitious or idolatrous dances be permitted; while the dances of the blacks, though hardly innocent, could be tolerated; hoping, through this lesser evil, to avoid other greater evils" (Tinhorão 1975: 130, *in* Plaut 1980: 26). In most traditional African societies, music is a spiritual matter, varying from the mere indication of the participant's spiritual state to actual messages exchanged with spiritual powers (cf. Chernoff 1979; Nketia 1974). A clear distinction between sacred and profane, as Durkheim proposed, may be appropriate to Western religious thought, but it turns slippery when translated into an African medium. For instance, dances which seemed erotic to most colonial-era Europeans, and therefore profane, might have been experienced by some Africans as sacred evocations of fertility, the sexual union of opposing cosmological forces (Jahn 1961: 82–90). Taking advantage of European predispositions, the slave was sometimes able to 'hide in the open' with musical celebrations that had traditional African significance, but were inaccessible to the uninitiated. For Africans, there were messages in the song lyrics, messages in the dance interactions, and even in the musical forms themselves, which were often completely hidden from Euro-Brazilians.

During the *batuques* there were probably both erotic and spiritual moments, and in some cases perhaps both combined, but there was also a time for the men to take over the circle in competitions of strength and dexterity (physical and verbal). Here is a description from more modern times by an old *sambista* (*samba* player and composer) from Rio de Janeiro:

[T]he days of the *bambas*, who would compete at *samba* leg-blows inside a circle of drummers until all hours of the dawn, between one improvisation and another, after the thing was for men only. When someone shouted "All skirts get out of here!" the leg-blow competitions would begin among the best, with attacks from the front, back and sides. Only those with strong reputations would stay on their feet, and even so, anyone could lose his big name in the blink of an eye . . . Stuff for real men only. Of course it was nothing but a game, an interesting show, a kind of duel or competition among *batuqueiros*. During this spectacle in the dirt patio, the percussion instruments would never stop playing, and the improvised verses would come out beautiful and spontaneous, sometimes satirical, criticizing any old thing. (Alves 1976: 108–9, *in* Plaut 1980: 44)

Although this account is from the turn of the twentieth century, fragmentary descriptions from colonial travelers and contemporary oral traditions suggest that this kind of activity has been part of *batuque* circles for a long time. Further evidence comes from the widespread variety of similar genres found today, and in the recent past, in Bahia and other parts of Brazil. Notice that the word *batuqueiro*, someone who plays in a *batuque*, has essentially the same meaning here that it had in slave times. The term *bamba* refers to an adept at these 'manly' pastimes, which included improvised versifying as well as physical dexterity. This same title has been used for capoeira adepts as well, as in the case of Mestre Bimba, whose story will be central to later developments in the sport (Moura 1979: 22).

There was a game practiced until recently in Bahia called *Batuque* (I capitalize it here to distinguish it from the generic forms) which seems to have been virtually identical to what Alves describes above. Moura has suggested that this Bahian *Batuque*, which he filmed, may have been the precursor to capoeira (1979: 25–29 and personal communication). Whether or not this is true, it is interesting that there are many similar genres in various regions of Brazil, all involving male competitions of strength (especially tripping contests) often combined with verbal dueling.

For instance, in Rio there was a practice called *roda de pernada* ('round of leg-blows'), which is probably one name for what Alves was describing, and there is a notorious kind of tripping *samba* known as *samba duro* ('hard samba,'), which I have seen in Bahia and elsewhere. Since trips and foot sweeps are central tactics in capoeira as well (see chapter 3), and since competition in the singing is also present (though not as common now as it seems to have been in the recent past), it seems safe to say that capoeira is related to these other genres. Though it is difficult or impossible to reconstruct exact derivations between folk arts over time, it seems possible that capoeira, in its physical interaction, was once a simpler game, similar to the several tripping contests mentioned here, which gradually evolved its present rich and complex movement repertoire over the course of many generations. It is also possible that there is a relation between the elaboration of the physical contest and a decline in the importance of verbal competition, which seems to be a trend in the capoeira of recent times.

SLAVE RESISTANCE

In the previous sections I have argued that slaves resisted the system that oppressed them in a number of indirect ways. On the plantations they were sometimes able to use their labor as a weapon against the masters in order to improve their conditions or simply as a psychological release. They were able to take advantage of their cultural and linguistic differences in order to preserve elements of their music, dance, and religion, and these differences also aided in labor protests. They could pretend to misunderstand orders, but they could also dissimulate by following directions to the letter while ignoring the spirit of the law. One of the anecdotes I heard in Bahia will serve to illustrate this 'overliteral' type of resistance:

> A new African slave arrives on a plantation and is being shown the ropes by the overseer. While weeding a field the lunch bell rings, but the slave ignores it, since he doesn't know what it means. The overseer explains, "When you hear that bell stop what you are doing at

once and go eat, since you are only allowed fifteen minutes for meals." Sometime later the slave is out walking
the fields with the master of the plantation. They come
to a muddy spot and the master asks the slave to carry
him across. When they are halfway across the mud, the
lunch bell rings and the slave drops the master and hur-
ries off to eat.

In addition to indirect tactics of resistance available within
the system, of course, slaves could and did resist directly either by
outright rebellion, or by trying to escape and flee into the bush.
Unlike the United States with its free northern states, there was
no legal refuge for Brazilian slaves, but there was a vast, largely
untamed hinterland that was either uninhabited or populated by
indigenous groups not yet under Portuguese domination.

Rebellion was the most dangerous option, since the penalties
were the harshest and the chances of success so slim. Nonetheless,
there were isolated uprisings from the very beginning, which
gradually increased in frequency by the late eighteenth and early
nineteenth centuries. Fueled by the success of the slave revolt in
Haiti, by the American and French revolutions, and by an increase in slave imports due to a resurgence in the demand for
sugar, these rebellions eventually led to a series of reforms, but
slavery itself was not abolished until 1888 in Brazil. The consequences of rebellion can be illustrated by the case of the Islamic
Africans, mentioned above. They were the leaders of many of the
rebellions of the early nineteenth century, including the largest in
1835. The fact that they left almost no cultural marks on the
highly creolized culture of Bahia is evidence for the ineffectiveness
of their all-or-nothing strategy.

A far more popular tactic of resistance to slavery was escape to
the bush, which was commonly practiced from the beginning to
the end of the slave regime. Groups of fugitive slaves formed villages called *mocambos* or *quilombos* (both words of Bantu origin)
which varied in size from a dozen members to tens of thousands.
The largest community was the famous 'kingdom' of Palmares in
the region of Pernambuco, which lasted most of the seventeenth
century, approximately eighty years. During its height, Palmares

was composed of perhaps a dozen villages, with an estimated population of eleven thousand in 1645, fifty years before its demise (Bastide 1978: 84).

There is a persistent oral tradition connecting capoeira with the *quilombo* of Palmares. One version of the story has it that Zumbi, the last 'king' of Palmares, was himself a capoeira master. In these accounts, it is the excellence of capoeira as a fighting technique which helps explain how the community resisted conquest so successfully.[12] This legend, although culturally (ontically) meaningful, seems historically doubtful for a number of reasons. First of all, none of the firsthand accounts of the conflicts mention capoeira by name, nor any specific battle tactics or dances that are reminiscent of the sport (cf. Freitas 1982; Kent 1965; Carneiro 1958). Although the fugitives did use their knowledge of the bush and guerrilla ambush tactics to good effect, they also used guns whenever they could get them, and even made their own. One account mentions that Gana Zona, the brother of King Ganga Zumba (who preceded Zumbi as leader of the community), was the official armorer, in charge of the furnaces where weapons were forged (Carneiro 1958: 203–4). Given the type of warfare necessary to the defense of these villages, it would have made sense to concentrate on weapons training rather than hand-to-hand techniques like capoeira, especially since the fugitives were frequently outnumbered by the invading troops. These arguments cannot be taken as conclusive, but they support the contention, developed below, that capoeira was likely to have been, at best, in an embryonic form during the seventeenth century. There is evidence from within capoeira discourse, and it is theoretically plausible, that the pastime required the existence of a well-knit, synthetic Afro-Brazilian culture (and therefore an urban setting) before it could emerge, probably not until the late eighteenth century, as something like the sophisticated game known to practitioners today.

Schwartz has pointed out (1970: 202–26) that even though the fame of Palmares has led many to think of it as the prototypical *quilombo*, it should in fact be considered atypical in most respects. The overwhelming majority of *mocambos* in Brazil were rather small in size and, rather than being isolated in the inaccessible interior, were often located close to plantations and towns. In Bahia, a large number of such small fugitive enclaves existed on the periphery of Salvador, and Schwartz notes that this proximity to other settlements made it easier for them to survive, simply by stealing what goods they needed. In this way *quilombos* were not required to set up their own infrastructures of cropping and manufacturing, as Palmares did, but could simply exist parasitically on the existing system. Perhaps part of the reason that Palmares lasted as long as it did, aside from its remote location, was that its relative self-sufficiency placed no real economic burden on the planters, except insofar as it was an inducement for other slaves to run away. In Bahia, however, none of the small, parasitic *mocambos* were allowed to flourish, precisely because the landowners felt the constant economic drain of their robberies and were always complaining to the authorities. Kent also notes that after Palmares was finally wiped out, Brazilians learned their lesson and made a point of not letting *quilombos* become well established (1965: 187).

The existence of so many fugitive communities in the history of Brazilian slavery is evidence for the fact that flight from captivity was a major strategy Africans adopted in response to their plight. It was a dangerous strategy, since the penalties were severe upon recapture, but not as dangerous as outright rebellion. Both rebellion and flight involve total noncooperation with the system of slavery and thus are regarded by modern Brazilians as the most noble responses to it. I suggest that this is one reason for the persistent association of capoeira with Palmares, since capoeira today represents the spirit of rebellion, of noncooperation with oppression, of liberation. Modern players wish to identify themselves with what they consider to be the purest and strongest form of resistance to oppression, and Palmares has become a symbol of such total and successful resistance against great odds.

While it is true that flight and aggression are lessons taught by capoeira play, they frequently are transmuted to become *indirect* aggression and *mock* flight. I believe that most, if not all, possible responses to domination are encoded in the capoeira interactions and that a great number of them, the vast majority, involve accommodations with and adaptations to that domination. These compromises still involve resistance, since I take it as a given that most slaves are resistant to their captivity, but of a more subtle and therefore less glamorous kind. Just as in the case of flight, the most common strategy was to run 'close by,' to pretend to run, only to return to plague the master; so the most general response to slavery was not to rebel directly, but to pretend to cooperate.

In this way, through the give and take of plantation life, a culture of slavery was created, a complex system with the constant threat of violence, but with recourse to that violence only when other channels broke down. It is the value of deception, of apparent accommodation, which I hope to show is at the heart of the play in capoeira, and which remains an integral part of modern Bahian culture at large. The complex drama of adaptation to domination through *malícia* keeps vitality in the game of capoeira one hundred years after the abolition of that terrible institution from which it was born.

The association of capoeira with slavery in the 'ethnographic present' can be seen immediately in the names of the academies and clubs teaching the sport in Brazil today. One of the biggest independent capoeira associations, based in Rio de Janeiro, is called Grupo Senzala. On the old colonial plantations, the slave quarters were called the *senzala*, usually a row of huts with doors all facing the 'big house.' Other capoeira clubs have such names as Quilombo, Palmares (fugitive slave communities mentioned above), Pelourinho (location of the slave auction block and whipping post in Salvador), and even Kunta Kinté (Alex Haley's African ancestor in *Roots*), under the influence of North American television. The most commonly used uniform among capoeira clubs is white pants with no shoes (shirt optional), an imitation of slave costume, which usually consisted of homespun cotton and bare feet. Of course this was only the costume of field hands; household slaves and others were more elaborately dressed.

Contemporary oral traditions connect capoeira with slavery as well, as has already been mentioned. One common story has it that capoeira was a martial art developed by slaves to aid in rebellions and escapes, but that it had to be disguised as a dance to fool the masters, who had forbidden all martial training to slaves. Since most blows are struck with the feet in capoeira, some say that this practice developed when slaves were manacled and couldn't use their hands. Another common attack in the game is the head butt (*cabeçada*), which can be done with both hands and feet chained together. I will discuss these and other oral traditions in detail in later chapters.

Although slaves were generally denied access to weapons, for fear of rebellion, such things as knives and machetes were essential to their work (for example, cutting sugar cane), and to this day knives and machetes (and razors, a later, urban addition) are sometimes used in exhibitions of capoeira. Freyre has suggested that capoeira developed its unique, acrobatic style as a means for unarmed men to attack others armed with guns (1963: 322). Capoeira players agree that, even after abolition, a *capoeirista* would never carry a gun, or even use one captured in a fight. It was a matter of pride that one didn't need a firearm to emerge victorious. This tradition casts further epistemic doubt on the belief that capoeira was important in the foundation and maintenance of such *quilombos* as Palmares, where guns aided greatly in defense.

One major way that the slave regime in Brazil differed from those in other colonies in the Americas was in the relative success that Brazilian slaves had in gaining freedom. Policies regarding manumission and the purchase of freedom by slaves were more liberal in Brazil than in the U.S. South, for instance, and many slaves availed themselves of these opportunities. Brotherhoods of freedmen were formed under the protection of the church in order to pool funds for the purchase of freedom for relatives and friends. In addition, attitudes toward miscegenation were somewhat more relaxed among the Portuguese than was the case with other Europeans, resulting in a large proportion of mixed bloods, many of whom were granted freedom preferentially. These *pardos* were also able to buy their freedom more easily, since they often had superior access to paying jobs as artisans and sugar specialists. The result was the creation of a large class of mulatto freedmen, which by the late eighteenth century represented at least forty percent of the population of Bahia. The size of this group was unprecedented in the Americas; in the American South freed slaves were never more than six percent of the free population, while in Jamaica that figure was closer to three percent in 1800 (Schwartz 1985: 462).

Although there were substantial urban centers very early in Brazilian history, it was not until the eighteenth century that a large percentage of the total population began concentrating in cities. This trend accelerated after the declaration of the republic in 1889, and a significant number of these new urbanites were ex-slaves leaving the plantations to look for opportunities in the cities. It was the creation of large neighborhoods of poor people of African and mixed descent, especially in Salvador, Rio de Janeiro, and Recife, that, I believe, facilitated the next step in the evolution of capoeira into a fully mature art form. One major piece of evidence for this view is that the earliest mentions of capoeira as a martial activity come from novels and police archives in Rio de Janeiro. Accordingly, it is to the urban context that the discussion of the recorded history of capoeira will have to turn.

The History of Capoeira

The reader will wonder why, amid so many other definitions of terms, I have not yet tried to define the word 'capoeira' and discuss its derivation, which would surely throw some light on the question of origins. Unfortunately, in spite of the fact that much ink has been spilled on the subject, it seems unlikely (as with most other debates about origins) that a definitive etymology will ever be reached. In his recent review of the arguments, Holloway notes that "the resulting debate resembles a linguistic version of antiquarian disputes over empirical details in history" (1989: 643), and I could say something similar about 'speculative history' in anthropology. I refer the interested reader to Rego, from whose excellent summary of the arguments I take the two most likely sources (1968: 17–29).

The overwhelming favorite in the oral traditions of living *capoeiristas*, including the oldest masters in Salvador, derives 'capoeira,' the game, from '*capoeira*,' a secondary growth (usually grasses and shrubs) that appears after virgin forest has been cut down. The story connecting the two phenomena has slaves (1) escaping into this second-growth bush in their flight from captivity, and/or (2) practicing the sport in these grasslands, near the plantations, but hidden from the masters and overseers. The first alternative would make sense if the most successful escapees were those who also practiced capoeira, thus the place they escaped to (or the place they practiced) became associated (indexically—see chap. 1, n. 12) with the thing being practiced. 'Capoeira' as secondary growth derives, according to several etymologists, from the Tupian *caá* ('forest', 'woods') *puêra* ('extinct') (Rego 1968: 21). Both of these senses of capoeira, secondary growth and martial activity, seem to have entered the language at about the same time, in the early nineteenth century.

The word 'capoeira,' however, had been around at least since the seventeenth century in its Latinate, Portuguese derivation from *capão* ('capon,' a castrated cock), meaning 'a cage for capons,' and by extension a cage for chickens in general. It remained for Gerson to make the link to the game, by noting that at the location of an old poultry market in Rio de Janeiro, male slaves used to play capoeira in their spare time (Rego 1968: 24). Since the game of capoeira also resembles a cockfight, the capon cages could have been associated with its practice in two ways. This scenario is appealing because, aside from the fact that cocks and other birds are mentioned prominently in capoeira songs, it places the early evolution of the game in an urban context, rather than a rural plantation setting. Some scholars, like Kubik, have even suggested a Bantu derivation for the word capoeira (Kubik 1979: 29).

The earliest reference to capoeira as a sport or fight, uncovered so far, dates from approximately 1770 and consists of a series of newspaper columns written by a journalist from Rio, Joaquim Manuel de Macedo, which were later made into a book.[13] He portrays the antics of a Portuguese lieutenant known as Amotinado ('the unruly') whose job it was to guard the viceroy, the Marquis de Lavradio, during his amorous nocturnal escapades. De Macedo describes this lieutenant as a fierce fighter, hence the nickname, and identifies him with capoeira, but it is not clear how he came to practice the art, nor are any details given of any other players. Since little official attention was paid to the activities of slaves and ex-slaves during this period, it is possible that Amotinado was one of the earliest Luso-Brazilians to learn something of capoeira, thus giving it a hint of respectability for the first time.

Nothing more is heard about capoeira until the early 1800s, when various accounts begin to appear in the police archives of Rio de Janeiro. In 1809, the Guarda Real de Polícia (Royal Guard Police) was created under the auspices of the Emperor Dom João VI, in exile from Portugal. The director of the guard was a Major Miguel Nunes Vidigal, described as "a competent capoeira, with cool composure and an agility worthy of any test, respected by the most feared toughs of his time. He excelled at stick, knife, fist, and razor play, absolutely unbeatable with blows of the head and feet" (Barreto Filho and Lima 1939, in Rego 1968: 295). Although reputedly an adept of the game himself, due to this appointment Vidigal became a formidable enemy of street capoeira. He persecuted his fellow players until his death in 1853. About a year after he died, a novel based on his career, *Memoirs of a Militia Sargeant*, was written by Manuel Antonio de Almeida.

Vidigal, like Amotinado, was a military man, and both were described in very similar terms as expert fighters. As representatives of the elite social order, though perhaps not members themselves, they incorporated and legitimated aspects of the Afro-Brazilian subculture, but they were in no sense typical of it. Only with Vidigal does one begin to get some image of the milieu within which capoeira was being routinely practiced, and then only from his opposition to it. Although no federal statute was officially enacted against the practice of capoeira until 1890 (Rego 1968: 292), this didn't stop the authorities from attacking what they perceived as a threat to public order.[14] During the period of slavery, any activity connected with African culture could be viewed as subversive at the whim of the authorities. Indeed, Holloway has demonstrated that one of the most frequent police charges against slaves and others jailed in Rio de Janeiro during much of the nineteenth century was the offense of 'capoeira' (1989: 654–64).[15]

Rugendas, an Austrian artist who toured Brazil in the 1820s, painted two interesting pictures of early capoeira activity in Bahia. One entitled "Jogo de Capoeira" ('game of capoeira,' see fig. 2.2) shows what could be a boxing match, except for the drum accompaniment and the distance of the combatants from each other. From where they are standing, they could not hit each other with

Figure 2.2   *Jogo de Capoeira*

fists, but they would be in range of a number of the whirling or
lunging kicks so typical of modern capoeira. Even more revealing
is a watercolor entitled "São Salvador" (fig. 2.3), which seems to
be set in the part of the city known as the peninsula of Itapagipe,
a famous site of capoeira contests and the location of the slave
church O Senhor do Bomfim ('The Lord of the Good End'). In
this depiction, one of the contestants is clearly going into a low
move known as *negativa* (same root as our 'negative'), characteristic of the distinctive capoeira tactic of staying close to the
ground.

     During the period of the Brazilian Empire (1808–89), there
were running battles between police and *capoeiras*[16] on the streets
of Rio de Janeiro, Salvador, and Recife. Carnaval groups would
use them as bouncers or guards to protect the musicians and dancers from the crowds. When two groups met on the street during
parades, fights often ensued over right of way (de Oliveira 1971:
82–86). In one famous case, however, the *capoeiras* were called
upon to aid the city of Rio de Janeiro against foreign mercenaries.
On July 9, 1828, the second battalion of German grenadiers and
an Irish battalion rioted in protest against the punishment of one

Figure 2.3   São Salvador

of their number. According to Marinho, Major Vidigal contacted the *capoeiras* of Rio and told them to take care of the situation, whereupon the latter harried the mercenaries back to their barracks in a hail of "head butts, blows, kicks, 'tails of the stingray' [a capoeira kick], and razor cuts" (1945: 21).

This story shows that, even though the practice of capoeira was generally looked down upon by members of the Brazilian elite in the nineteenth century, there was also a certain ambivalence toward the players, based on their undeniable prowess at fighting. A native Brazilian couldn't help but feel proud of the skill with which these men were able to overcome adversaries much better armed than themselves, and this was probably the motivation for such men as Vidigal and Amotinado studying the game in the first place. This is the first recorded case in which *capoeiristas* were called on to aid the powers that be, but it was by no means the last. During the War with Paraguay (1865–70), many conscripts were needed and slaves who volunteered were promised their freedom. Burns reports that approximately six thousand slaves gained their freedom in this way (1970: 183). Among the slaves and freedmen who fought in Paraguay, many were said to be adepts of capoeira who made reputations at the front as effective fighters.

The development of capoeira in the urban setting was associated with criminality, in the minds of the police and the upper classes. This involved the creation of lower-class stereotypes, referred to by various terms, like 'capoeira' itself, and the more general category of *malandro*. This social type corresponds roughly to our 'street tough' or 'hoodlum,' with a fairly wide range of possible variations from slick pimps and con-men to scruffy muggers, drunks, and pickpockets (cf. da Matta 1980). Therefore calling someone a 'capoeira' was the same as calling him a *malandro*, though not all *malandros* knew capoeira.[17] The aggregation of a substantial group of, mostly dark, habitually impoverished people in the inner cities of Brazil greatly increased after the abolition of slavery, when many ex-slaves fled the plantations looking for better work. The creation of these neighborhoods, still very much a part of urban life today, has led to a rich 'street culture' with local variation from city to city, but with a number of common features. This inner-city society is intimately associated with Afro-Brazilian music, dance, costume, diet, and religion, especially in Salvador, and it has been a rich source for novels and poetry.[18]

A *malandro* is someone who engages in *malandragem*, which can signify almost any kind of shady activity, and which in some contexts can also be a synonym for the practice of capoeira. Both words connote the making of one's living in a less than honorable fashion, but not necessarily illegally: one can be a gambler, a beggar, a gigolo, or simply a person with no visible means of support. Often such a person will be perceived as someone with time on their hands, as a vagrant, a vagabond. Accordingly, another potential synonym for the practice of capoeira is *vadiação*, from *vadiar*, 'to be idle, to loaf, to bum around.'[19]

Chronically unemployed blacks living in cities had to evolve new strategies for survival, strategies much like those known as 'hustling' in the United States. The fact that higher strata of Brazilian society looked down on these activities, stigmatizing them with pejorative names, was a legacy of the slave regime which the poor did not have the luxury of worrying about. In this setting, capoeira became a survival strategy as well, in some cases provid-

ing money to participants directly. Sometimes *capoeiristas* would
play the sport in plazas and on streets, hoping to get passersby to
throw their money into the ring. In order to entice them to do
this, an entire subroutine developed within capoeira, the money
game, complete with special rules and appropriate songs. I described something of how this works in the Preface, and I will
return to it in chapter 4. Regular money games are still found in
Salvador in front of the Mercado Modelo and at the Terreiro de
Jesus, though the rules have been simplified somewhat, or even
forgotten, in recent times.

Another well-known strategy is to play a game of capoeira in
front of a small bar, hoping to get free drinks from the owner or
his customers. I witnessed this several times, especially in the interior of Bahia, and songs are sometimes used directly to help
lubricate the proceedings:

c:	ô i ô i	oh ee oh ee
s:	você tem cachaça aí	you've got rum over there
c:	ô i ô i	oh ee oh ee
s:	você tem mas não quer dar	you've got but don't want to give

In addition to these direct means of gaining money or free
food and drink, there were indirect means of survival connected
to the role of capoeira player and *malandro*. One could sometimes
create a public persona so fearful that people would be intimi-
dated into giving one what one wanted. Small shopkeepers and
landlords might be inclined to give one free meals, or to let one
'borrow' things without having to return them, especially if one
were part of a gang of similar toughs (which was common during
the nineteenth and early twentieth centuries).[20] There might even
be reciprocity in these relations if one in turn protected business-
men from robbery or attack by other gangs. Finally, the practice
of capoeira was valuable as a martial skill, in this urban context,
to allow one to survive fights with rival gangs and with the police.

After the declaration of the Brazilian Republic in 1889, capoeira players were used in some cases as ward heelers or political
bullies to force people to vote for certain candidates or parties. In
this case, the authorities were taking advantage of the fearsome
reputation of capoeira toughs, but the players themselves also

benefited both monetarily and in terms of political patronage, no doubt. The practice was especially widespread in Rio, but soon fell into disfavor because of the unruly scuffles that tended to break out around polling places.

Although the lifestyle of a *malandro* was reviled by higher-class, Europeanized Brazilians, this did not necessarily mean that the rascals had a negative image of themselves. For the disciple of capoeira, the practice of *malandragem* (roughly, 'hooliganism') could be a positive cultural value representing one's ability to survive in adverse circumstances by using one's wits and physical skills. Thus a similar type called the *picaro* in Spain became idealized to form the foundation for 'picaresque' literature;[21] and a 'rascal' in the English tradition is frequently portrayed as someone who is also clever, crafty, slippery, and cunning. Thus, when used in general parlance, the quality of *malícia* is usually applied by speakers to others with this basic ambiguity: variations on playful censure and/or grudging admiration. In this form it can be a focal trait in the conception of cultural stereotypes like *malandro,* which can have a similar range of ambiguity, often crucially dependent on the contrast between insider (us) and outsider (them). So when *capoeiristas* refer to their games as *'malandragem,'* they are playing on this double sense by contrasting a general social stigma toward their activities (especially in the past) with their own pride of participation in the sport.

Another synonym for a *capoeirista* is *mandingueiro,* which originates from a name for the African group(s) generally called the Mandé or Mandinka people. In Brazil these people had a reputation for knowledge of herbal healing and related magic, as they also did in Africa, since such specialists were widely traveled. Eventually the term *mandingueiro* became synonymous with anyone of African origin who had esoteric knowledge related to healing, especially the making of protective fetishes to ward off evil influences, regardless of ethnic identification. Capoeira adepts were frequently known for this kind of knowledge, since they employed fetishes, known as *patuá,* to protect them in the dangerous games, and in street fighting in general. Some of these *patuá* were said to be able to defend the wearer against bullets, so they were greatly valued in battles with the police. Since Zumbi, of Palmares

fame, was said to be impervious to bullets because of a similar
medicine, this contributed to the speculation that he also knew
capoeira. Another legendary *capoeirista* who had knowledge of
fetish-making was Besouro ('Beetle') of Santo Amaro, whose
story will be retold in chapters 3 and 6.

In 1890 a law was passed specifically prohibiting the practice
of capoeira and, as a result, police repression became even more
extensive and more effective. Adepts of the game, when caught *in
flagrante,* were sometimes exiled to the prison island of Fernando
de Noronha, as happened in the celebrated case of Juca Reis
(Marinho 1945: 24–28). It is likely that this internment garnered
so much attention precisely because the victim was a member of
the ruling elite, otherwise it would probably not have raised a
single eyebrow. As a result of constant harrassment, capoeira was
all but extinct in Rio de Janeiro and Recife by the first decades of
the twentieth century. In Bahia, however, it managed to survive,
perhaps because the police were not as effective in enforcement
there, perhaps because it had a stronger base in the interior, outside the capital city of Salvador. Accordingly, I will now turn to
the main field site for this research and discuss the recent history
and current practice of capoeira in Salvador and the surrounding
region of Bahia.

3

Capoeira in Salvador

The sketchy records available from the early history of capoeira suggest that its development, at least by the nineteenth
century, was intimately associated with city life. Of course, there
were large towns and cities in Brazil fairly early in its history, and
many rural plantation masters also maintained homes in ports like
Salvador to facilitate the export of sugar and other goods. But
even though the rural-urban interface has been complex all along,
the bulk of the population of Brazil was rural throughout most of
the colonial and imperial period, and it was not until after the
republic that urbanism accelerated to include a majority of Brazilians, especially those of color. Therefore the struggles between
police and *capoeiras* in imperial Rio de Janeiro were symptomatic
of a new Brazilian urbanism, forecasting new types of class and
racial strife. It seems likely that the gradual movement of ex-slaves
into the free labor market, coinciding largely with the gradual
movement of Brazilians from country to city (a process which is
still continuing), also provided stimuli for new developments in
capoeira. These changes included new settings for capoeira play,
at the very least, and perhaps a profound reorganization of its
practice, corresponding to the emerging Afro-Brazilian cultural
matrix that was intensified by city life.

I have been arguing that, whatever its origins, capoeira (like
Afro-Brazilian culture in general) has changed and evolved gradually over the course of many generations. It seems undeniable that
part of this process, and perhaps the formative part, is intimately
linked with urbanization. Certainly the fact that the earliest historical records of capoeira as a martial practice come from the
streets of Rio supports this view. In the previous chapter, I mentioned the vagabond stereotype and capoeira as *vadiação*. This

kind of 'leisure' time, the fruit of chronic underemployment, was certainly not found on the plantations. In addition, I noted that capoeira as self-defense involves the practice of hand-to-hand (and foot-to-foot) techniques suitable for street fighting in close quarters, but less effective in open terrain where guns are the weapons of choice. These indications, and several others mentioned below, suggest that, if capoeira did not originate in an urban setting, it was certainly perfected there.

If the record of capoeira activity in Rio de Janeiro is sketchy and indirect, and even more so for Recife, there is almost no historical data for capoeira in Salvador before the twentieth century. Yet oral traditions indicate that Bahia was definitely an early center of the sport and after it was officially outlawed in 1890, capoeira seems to have been all but eradicated everywhere but there. Reasons for the persistence of capoeira play in Bahia are highly speculative, as with so much else in this account, but one important factor may have been the unique cultural geography of the region around Salvador.

The word 'Bahia' means bay, as mentioned in the Preface, and it was at the mouth of this large 'Bay of all Saints' that Salvador was founded as the first capital city of the crown colony in 1549. The area surrounding this bay, called the *Recôncavo* (see map 3.1), was already a main center of the sugar plantation culture, owing to its fertile soil and the ease of transportation by boat to the port city of Salvador. The intercourse between capital city and the Recôncavo was an important aspect of the economic and cultural development of the region, creating a rich mix of urban and rural traditions that constantly fed one another. There are several indications that this unique cultural geography was important to the early development and later preservation of capoeira. For example, perhaps the most famous capoeira master of all, Besouro, now often referred to with the title *Cordão d'Oro* ('sash of gold'), was from the Santo Amaro region, the setting for the Preface. Many other famous Bahian masters were born in the Recôncavo region as well, including the recently deceased masters Cobrinha Verde, who claimed to have trained with Besouro, and Waldemar, who was born on an island in the bay. Another legendary master, who died in the 1950s, was Samuel Querido de

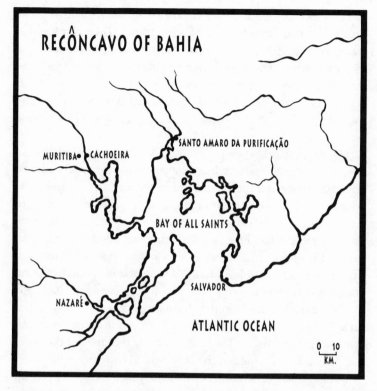

Map 3.1 Prepared by Joanna Yardley.

Deus ('Beloved of God'), said to be able to defeat young opponents when in his seventies. When anthropologist Ruth Landes visited Salvador in 1938–39, she was taken by Edison Carneiro to witness a contest with Querido de Deus and her description of that bout provided an early inspiration for this work (1947: 100–107).

Samuel was the owner of a kind of small sailboat called a *saveiro*, which he used primarily for fishing. For hundreds of years these *saveiros* have plied the inland waters of the Bay of All Saints, transporting food, people, and other cargo from the Recôncavo to Salvador and back. This economic connection also fostered cultural interchange between rural and urban worlds, with boat owners acting as intermediaries and brokers in both senses. The Salvador waterfront was, and still is, a traditional site for capoeira games, especially around the markets located there. This is partly because so many *capoeiristas* are known to have been employed in waterfront activities: as fishermen, boat owners, stevedores, and merchant sailors. Songs of the bay and the sea are among the most popular themes in capoeira lyrics. Even the basic move in capoeira, the *ginga*, has as one of its meanings 'to row (a boat)' and the motion of the body when doing the *ginga* resembles rowing (see chapter 4).

During the fieldwork period, I made several trips to towns in the Recôncavo and saw styles of capoeira, and other related arts, quite different from those practiced in the city. Several masters I interviewed had come from the interior to Salvador in order to perfect their capoeira, then returned to the Recôncavo to teach and lead more relaxed lives. A few maintained homes in the interior and commuted back and forth for the economic benefits of city commerce. When Jair Moura, a student and researcher of capoeira history, set off to find and film Bahian *Batuque*,[1] he finally found some old players in the Recôncavo, near the town of Nazaré. To further illustrate the kind of interaction common to this central region of Bahia, I will relate briefly the story of the other major Brazilian martial art, the stick fight known as *maculêlê*.

This game (as *maculêlê* is also called) had been practiced for many years, no one knows exactly how long, in the region around Santo Amaro da Purificação. Toward the end of World War II, an old player of the game called Popó (Paulino Aloisio Andrade) decided to get together a group, including his own children, to teach them the sport, since its practice was on the wane.[2] When the group was ready, Popó had them parade through the streets of Santo Amaro during a festival, and that day has now become a traditional time for the presentation of *maculêlê* in its home town. The current leader of the group is Vavá (Valfrido Viera de Jesus), one of Popó's sons, who appeared as a capoeira player in the Preface.

Another son of Popó, Zezinho, went to live in Salvador and started a group which presented 'folklore' shows, as they are called. Such shows are now common tourist attractions in the cities of Brazil (and the world), but at the time this type of performance tradition was just beginning. In Salvador many people were attracted to learn *maculêlê*, and its performance soon became a standard part of folklore shows in the region. As with most tourist art, elements of the original transmission are frequently changed for the new contexts. One example of this in *maculêlê* is the addition of machete play in addition to stick fighting. Machete fights (*facão*) are especially dramatic in these shows, as the lights are turned off and sparks fly at the clash of steel blades. This is the kind of flashy attraction which goes well in spectacles, including the element of added danger, but machetes were clearly not part of the original practice (Mutti 1978: 10, 21–22).

Today *maculêlê* is practiced in many capoeira clubs and academies throughout Brazil, sometimes as part of a typical workout, sometimes only on special occasions. The sport, for better or worse, has become part of general Brazilian culture. The original group from Santo Amaro, with some new members, continues to practice and perform *maculêlê* at present, and recently (1983) they traveled to Europe and Africa on a tour. Vavá is also a master of capoeira, which he perfected by traveling to Salvador to study with teachers there. Stories such as these demonstrate clearly that relations between the interior and the capital have been central to the development of Bahian folk arts of many kinds, including capoeira and *maculêlê*. In some cases, rare arts are 'preserved' in the Recôncavo until rediscovered by urbanites and turned to their own purposes. This apparent preservation is an illusion, of course, fostered by the fact that rural life often seems more culturally conservative, since rates of change tend to be slower than in cities under normal circumstances. In other cases, the city provides a stimulating cultural diversity and forum for specialization, which can then serve to reinvigorate rural practice.

It is probable that both of these processes have been important to the evolution of capoeira play at different times in the past. During the peak of the persecution of capoeira, after 1890 through the early decades of this century, it seems likely that organized repression was more effective and better organized in the cities than in the countryside. If this was the case in Bahia, the Recôncavo may have provided a refuge for capoeira practice within easy reach of city players wishing to avoid detection. The intimate rural-urban connection characteristic of Bahia is not present to the same degree in either Rio de Janeiro or Recife, which may partially explain why the sport survived primarily in Bahia, and it was from there that it was to have its renaissance, to become a national and international sport.

ORAL TRADITIONS

Since there is little historical data on capoeira in Salvador before the 1920s, I will attempt to provide a picture of what players have told me about traditional patterns from earlier times. Most of the accounts I heard referred to periods within the memory of living informants or their teachers: that is, from approximately the turn of the century up to the present. The exceptions to this have been discussed in the previous chapter and concern tales of capoeira origins in Africa or on the plantations.

For many decades, long enough to establish it as a tradition, regular capoeira games (*rodas*) were held on the streets and in the plazas of Salvador. Young men and women growing up in the city were exposed to these events as a matter of course. They watched their elders play and participated as audience from a young age. The games were a pleasant and exciting pastime (*folguedo*) for spectators in many of the poorest neighborhoods of the city, and young boys would spontaneously imitate the moves of the men, as they still do on the beaches of Bahia today. As a young man got older, if he was especially interested in capoeira, he would hang around the games until he was noticed by an adult player who agreed to apprentice him, or he would seek out a local player to be his *mestre*. A student who had been accepted was called *discípulo* or *aluno* ('disciple' or 'student'). The *discípulo*/*mestre* relationship was an informal one, involving an older player showing moves and explaining tactics to a younger player. When the *mestre* decided a young player was ready, he would take him along to a *roda* and let him play, serving as his protector if things got too rough. In general, though, a player learned by playing and his main training was in the school of 'hard knocks.'

There were essentially three venues for capoeira games during this early period: regular local *rodas*, pickup games, and festival competitions. Many neighborhoods had regular *rodas* once a week, usually on Sundays. These games were always under the supervision of a given master, or sometimes a group of masters, whose job it was to oversee all aspects of the events. In the case of disputes, the hosting master was responsible for settling things down, and in his absence another senior master was delegated to assume that role. If money was thrown in the ring by spectators, the senior master was in charge of dividing it up. Players had to have the permission of this master in order to participate, and strangers were usually not allowed in the ring unless one of the regulars vouched for them. In general, these were low-key, relaxed events, more like training sessions than serious competition, unless a guest or guests from other neighborhoods were in attendance. One such *roda* was hosted by Mestre Waldemar for many years in the district of Liberdade/Pero Vaz. After a hiatus, the tradition was resumed at Fazenda Grande by one of his students, Mestre Virgílio (Virgílio Ferreira), except that the games were moved inside, in accordance with modern practice.

What I am calling pickup games were spontaneous events that could be held virtually anywhere at any time. Again these were most common on holidays or Sundays when people were in a festive mood, but they could also happen at other times when players were together and had time on their hands. One motive for this type of event was to raise money or to promote drinks at a local bar. Some players who were chronically unemployed relied on this kind of activity to supplement their incomes, and it is this type of game especially which fits the stereotype of *vadiação*. Many teachers, then as now, urged their students to avoid the players (*malandros*) who might start *rodas* in the central city during business hours, or late at night, since these games were usually not supervised by a reputable master and anything could (and did) happen. Similar games are still found in Salvador today and some of them have become regular events, such as the Saturday morning game in front of the Mercado Modelo. Players who try to earn money in the street still have shady reputations, so many *capoeiristas* now tend to avoid all street games, except on special festival days.

During periods of intense police persecution, which seem to have been intermittent in Bahia, the regular *rodas* sometimes became regular 'floating' games: that is, the site would change from week to week. In these cases, masters would take turns hosting, according to whose neighborhood was chosen, and the location was passed by word of mouth. These were not pickup games, however, since they were still planned and a given master was still in charge. On his record, Mestre Pastinha describes being called in to assume this role, to 'organize' or 'mount' (*montar*) the *roda*, in various places. If the police should find out about one of these games and stage a raid, there was a special beat of the *berimbau*, called *cavalaria*, which was used as a warning (see chapter 5). When players heard that beat, they would immediately disperse in all directions to avoid arrest.

In the past, the most important games of the year for the capoeira adept in Salvador were held on the festival days which precede Carnaval. Starting in December with the festival of *Conceição da Praia*, there are a series of neighborhood celebrations in local plazas throughout the city, the well-known *Festas do Largo*. This festival cycle has become an institution in Salvador, which many people anticipate eagerly each year as a gradual warm-up to the madness of *Carnaval* in February or March. Each district hosts a celebration for several days (and nights) with booths for eating and drinking, bands for dancing, and amusements of all kinds. These *festas* traditionally included capoeira play as well, and games can still be seen at the most important ones, like Bomfim and Rio Vermelho. Several older players told me that the most important *roda* in this series was the first one, *Conceição da Praia*, which was considered in the past to be the championship arena. Whoever dominated that event was usually acknowledged to be the best *capoeirista* of the year. The name of this *festa* refers to a church that is right on the waterfront of the lower city, across from the central market,[3] further evidence for the importance of the harbor setting in the capoeira world.

Although there are still *rodas* to be seen at the *festas* today, these games no longer have the prestige that they did in the past. Over the years, the *Festas do Largo* have gotten more and more crowded, and the crowds have gotten rowdier with alcohol and other intoxicants. As a result, festival games are hard to watch, due to the throngs of people, and they are frequently anarchic. These games were never in the control of a single master, but in the past all the masters present would cooperate to see that play was under control. Since most masters avoid these games today, due to the chaotic atmosphere of the festivals, often only the toughest street players will be in attendance. Under these conditions, a dispute can quickly lead to violence. Capoeira at the best of times flirts with violence and aggression, so at the worst of times, which these occasions can be, blood may flow. Generally, the quality of play at these events is not the best, since many of the players are amateurs inspired by drink and the moment, and often the music is drowned out by the crowd noise. Even so, tradition dies hard in Bahia, and, occasionally, when the conditions are right, one can still see excellent capoeira at one of these *festas*.

A new development is the case of Mestre Caiçara (Antonio da Conceição Morais), who is paid by the city to appear with his group of students to present demonstrations of capoeira at various *festas*. In this case, anyone wishing to play in the *roda* must get Caiçara's permission to enter, and he serves as arbiter of conduct in control of the events. Since his demonstrations are usually treated as a show by the audience, however, spectators rarely try to join in. Therefore the action doesn't usually have the spontaneity and inventiveness of a truly open game, resembling instead the capoeira presented in folklore shows for tourists.

This brief background, sketchy as it is, should be enough to provide a context for the more recent history of capoeira in Bahia. As noted, these traditional practices were frequently called by the name "*Capoeira Angola*," a reference to the presumed African origin of the sport. Although games varied from place to place according to personnel and setting, the style of play was basically the same (except for individual variation), and all players knew more or less what to expect when they faced each other in the ring. During the next period of capoeira history this situation would change, and the impetus for that change came from a single master who decided to take capoeira off the streets and to teach it in 'academies.'

RECENT CAPOEIRA HISTORY

In 1927, Mestre Bimba (Manoel dos Reis Machado) founded the first formal academy for the teaching of capoeira as a martial art, called Centro de Cultura Física e Capoeira Regional. Though it wasn't officially licensed by the government until 1937, this marked the beginning of the institutionalization of capoeira as a sport (de Almeida 1982: 15–16). Bimba's example was quickly followed by Mestre Pastinha and capoeira began moving into studios and schools, although it remained on the streets as a folk art as well. In 1953, after witnessing a demonstration by Mestre Bimba's academy, the president of Brazil, Getulio Vargas, declared that capoeira was "the only truly national sport" (de Almeida 1982: 18). Predictably enough, the move into institutions, though it helped to revive capoeira, also caused it to change in many ways. Mestre Bimba developed a method for teaching capoeira, and an approach to its play, that was significantly different from those in the traditional settings. Bimba's capoeira began to be called *Regional* ('regional,' the 'region' referred to was presumably the state of Bahia) after the name of his academy, and in time the name was extended to signify the style of capoeira played by his students. In contrast, Mestre Pastinha attempted to preserve a more traditional approach to the teaching and playing of the game, retaining the old name, *Capoeira Angola.*

Perhaps the most significant thing about Bimba's academy was his special interest in attracting students from the middle and upper socioeconomic sectors of Bahian society. He was concerned with creating a respectable image for his sport capoeira, to counteract the old *malandro* stereotype, so he began teaching an intensive capoeira 'course' (*curso*), complete with a diploma, for a sizeable fee. The course succeeded in attracting many upwardly mobile, lighter-skinned young men, university students and future professionals. This change in the social background of the participants influenced corresponding changes in the style of play, and over time these two distinct types of capoeira emerged: the newer, innovative *Regional* style, and the older, more conservative *Angola* style.

Mestre Bimba had been trained in the traditional way, and for many years was considered to be a champion in regular capoeira circles. His father was an adept of *Batuque,* and one story often told is that Bimba combined *Batuque* moves with Asian martial arts, such as Judo or Jiu Jitsu, in order to create his new capoeira style. Mestre Itapoan has pointed out that this scenario is highly improbable, since Bimba never studied any of the Asian systems, although he does argue that *Batuque* was an influence on *Regional* capoeira (de Almeida 1984: 14, 28). The idea for teaching capoeira as a martial art in an academy setting might well have been suggested by the success of the Asian approach in Brazil, however, especially since Bimba later adopted the use of colored belts, presumably from that source.

Spurred on by a vision of a modern, sport capoeira, Bimba's students began leaving Salvador to open academies throughout Brazil by the 1950s. Rio de Janeiro, and then São Paulo, became centers for the growth of this new, old sport. In 1972, capoeira was officially proclaimed a Brazilian national sport, under the jurisdiction of the Federação Brasileiro de Pugilismo (Brazilian Boxing Federation), and at the same time local and national tournaments were organized. By the mid-seventies there were capoeira academies throughout Brazil, and the first masters had begun teaching classes in the United States and Europe.

Although frequently associated with the academy of Mestre Pastinha, *Capoeira Angola* was never restricted to that arena, but was always a folk art, with an emphasis on freedom of expression and individuality. Unlike Bimba's approach, which included a standardized method and diplomas for 'graduation,' the classes in Pastinha's academy were more informal and varied in content depending on who was leading them on any given day. Many *Angoleiros* (traditional capoeira players) learned elsewhere, from other masters or simply on the streets in casual games. The influence of Bimba's method on modern capoeira has been great, especially outside of Bahia, since it was mostly his students who carried the sport to other cities in Brazil, establishing academies and promoting tournaments. Even within Bahia, contemporary play has been influenced by *Regional* practices, although it could be argued that other modernizing factors have been just as significant.

This division between the more modern *Regional* style and the conservative *Angola* style of play was most marked in the early years of the institutionalization of the game, from the 1940s to the late 1970s. More recently, there has been a trend to reunite these two schools of play under the motto *"Capoeira é uma só"*

('There is just one capoeira'). This trend seems to have been partly in reaction to the failure of the Brazilian Boxing Federation to unify the sport, exacerbated by discontent with the conduct of tournament play. In the early years, much time was spent in discussion, trying to agree on competition rules, scoring, names of moves, and the like. Acrimonious debates on these subjects caused much frustration and hard feeling, and the resulting rifts are still evident in relations between masters at present.

Mestre Camisa (José Tadeu Carneiro Cardoso) in Rio de Janeiro, himself a former *Regional* instructor and student of Mestre Bimba, has for some time been reincorporating *Angola* techniques into his instruction and seeking out old *Angoleiros* to honor and learn from. He and the other masters of the association Grupo Senzala have refused to participate in organized tournaments in recent years, on the grounds that they are not the traditional way for a player to demonstrate his expertise. Such tournaments, either independent or sponsored by the Brazilian Boxing Federation, were formerly the hallmark of the new sport capoeira in the *Regional* approach.

From the other direction, there are players trained in the traditional *Angola* manner, such as Mestre Nô in Salvador, who encourage the modernization of capoeira so that it will not die out. Nô calls his capoeira *atual* ('current' or 'up-to-date'), and this is the term I have chosen to denote the emerging unified style, which tends to be a combination of some of the *Regional* innovations with aspects of traditional *Angola* play. Any capoeira which falls between the extremes of the other two styles will be called *atual* (an increasingly large proportion of all play), though it is not a term used in this way by the players themselves (except for Nô). Mestre Nô maintains that changes in style of play are simply evolutions in the game, reflecting how people want to play it, and are playing it, today. Students of Nô who are instructors (and he has produced more teachers than any other master of his generation) are generally following this lead, and other independent Bahian masters, such as Mestre Paulo dos Anjos ('Paul of the Angels'), take a similar approach.

Some masters in Bahia are still consciously following the *Regional* approach, such as Mestre Itapoan (Raimundo Cesar Alves de Almeida) and Mestre Ezequiel (Ezequiel Martins Marinho), and there are some who are trying to resist the tide of innovation and retain a 'pure' *Angola* style, like Mestre Moraes and Mestre João Pequeno. Moraes is becoming increasingly influential at the present time, and his Grupo de Capoeira Angola-Pelourinho has been growing rapidly as an organization both in Brazil and the United States.

With the formation of capoeira academies in Bahia and, later, in other states, under the influence primarily of Bimba's *Regional* institute, training methods changed dramatically. Even in Pastinha's traditional *Angola* academy, there were some innovations; relationships became routinized and new roles were created. The role of senior *mestre,* formerly in charge of local outdoor games, changed somewhat when he became the head of an academy. He not only had to oversee the games, but was also chief administrator who decided what was to be done and by whom. He had to organize the financial and operational aspects of the school, which meant taking on more responsibility and learning how to delegate his authority. As a result, the senior *mestre* did not always lead classes himself, but frequently delegated this task to a *contra-mestre,* a new role created by the needs of the academy.[4] Before the advent of academies, a man trained with his chosen *mestre* until the latter told him he was on his own, that he had become an adult player, at which time he could call himself a *mestre* and take on disciples. With the growth of academies, this process became more structured, and in Bimba's academy the process of training was broken into a series of stages the player must pass through. These stages were initially marked by the awarding of colored scarves, in imitation of the silk neck scarves worn by some traditional players to prevent razor cuts. Over time, the colored scarves were replaced by a series of colored belts, probably under the influence of the belt rankings in Asian martial systems.

It is not easy to isolate causal factors behind the development of the new, *Regional* style of capoeira, but an initial attempt would probably include the complex interaction of at least three major forces. One set of factors is generated by the imperatives of the institutionalization process itself, perhaps the main impetus behind the emergent status of *contramestre.* Another set of determining factors clusters around the issues of social class and ethnic identity. I have demonstrated that capoeira has its Brazilian roots in slavery and was therefore originally the plaything of the lowest economic strata of Brazilian society, primarily those of Afro-Brazilian ethnic identity. Although the *Regional* form of capoeira was the creation of a poor black player, Mestre Bimba, it was developed to appeal to middle- and upper-class players. Its continuing evolution was influenced by their active participation and manipulation in Bimba's later years and after his death. Finally, there may be a set of causal factors having to do with the 'modernization' process itself, insofar as these can be analytically separated from class and institutional influences. By this I not only mean to imply fidelity to a given historical period, but rather something like the convergence of genre-internal imperatives with local and world cultural processes. Accordingly, the emergence of the *Regional* style could be seen as parallel to other types of modernization in Brazil and the world, and the latest *atual* synthesis might be called a 'postmodern' trend. Whether or not one accepts the existence of the third kind of process, it is not enough to argue simply, as many have, that expressive forms like capoeira simply respond to determining changes in social, economic, and/or political structures. Instead, I want to ally myself with those who have demonstrated that expressive performances co-create contexts for the social and cultural world as it is changing around them and try to demonstrate how that happens in this case. For example, this kind of approach helps to explain why debates about the origins of the game, or even about rules for play, should be so crucial for those whose emerging identity is tied to the sport.

The trend toward the reunification of capoeira styles has at least been reinforced, and perhaps was originally inspired, by the influence of foreign capoeira players. For fifteen years, Brazilian masters have been training students in the United States, to name just one country, and some of these students have gone to Brazil for intensive exposure to the sport. Initially, instruction in the United States was mostly in the *Regional* style, which was the primary method in all the capoeira exported from Bahia. As U.S. players became more sophisticated, and with their travels to Brazil, they discovered the different approach characteristic of the *Angola* tradition and began to moderate their play in response to it. This was especially true of black players, who saw in the *Angola* style a continuity with their own African heritage. This process coincided with a general movement in Brazil for experienced players to research the roots of their sport. It is hard to document the extent of foreign influence in the turn back to the older style, which seems to be leading to a reunification of capoeira, but it is clear that any analysis restricting itself to indigenous class or ideological factors is missing something.

Learning Capoeira Today

In the Preface, I alluded to the fact that I had already begun to learn capoeira in the United States before going to Brazil for formal fieldwork. When I began researching the sport, I discovered that a group had been practicing irregularly in Seattle for some time, under the informal leadership of Jeron Freightman, who had studied with several different Brazilian teachers. Soon after I made contact with this group, we hosted a workshop with Bira Almeida, one of the pioneer masters on the West Coast. This was my first exposure to capoeira in the flesh, and I knew my body was in for an ordeal. Inspired by Bira, our group began meeting on a regular basis and several of us made trips to the Bay Area for workshops with him and his students. One of those trips was on the occasion of the first U.S. capoeira tournament (1982), in which Bira's group hosted the students of Jelon Viera from New York. Jelon was the first master to begin giving regular lessons in the United States, starting in 1975.

These contacts prepared me somewhat for what I was to encounter in Brazil, and when I arrived I already had a list of masters and classes to visit. Since I knew Portuguese, thanks to a previous trip to Brazil, there was none of the usual early fieldwork disorientation. I landed at the airport in Rio de Janeiro in the morning, and that night I was happily battering the body at my first capoeira class in Brazil. I remember it well because during the partner practice I was paired with a woman who, whenever I would attempt a move, shook her head and exclaimed, *"muito fraco"* ('very weak'). The class was conducted barefoot, as most capoeira classes are, and the combination of rough boards and spinning kicks served to abrade most of the skin off the balls of my feet. A little physical pain was not enough to affect the euphoria of my successful start, however, and though I was to experience many similar discomforts during the course of the next two years, I was lucky never to be laid up by injuries for more than a few weeks. With minor exceptions, my welcome in the capoeira world of Brazil was enthusiastic, and the fieldwork period was one of the happiest times of my life.

As capoeira moved into schools and studios under the influence of Mestre Bimba, the importance and prestige of street games steadily declined in the eyes of most players. This reciprocal relation reproduces a significant distinction in Brazilian culture between *casa* ('house') and *rua* ('street'). Da Matta has shown the importance of this distinction in patterning interactions in many areas of Brazilian life, arguing that it is even operant, in somewhat modified form, during the apparently chaotic period of Carnaval (1984: 209–12; also 1987). Therefore moving capoeira inside, off the street, was a crucial step in the domestication of the sport, especially for middle-class sensibilities, and explains why Bimba made his students promise not to play on the street under any circumstances. In this case, the academy becomes a kind of surrogate *casa* within which activities are supervised, and are therefore safe and healthy, as opposed to the dangerous and unruly street games.

The distinction between academy (house) and street, which became operant in capoeira at the time of the divergence of the two styles, has an interesting counterpoint in disagreements as to appropriate dress. The standard uniform of most capoeira play was described in chapter 1 as a self-conscious evocation of the costume of plantation field slaves: plain white pants and shirt (the latter sometimes optional) and bare feet. In fact, this garb only became standard with the development of the *Regional* style of capoeira and its spread into the rest of Brazil from Bahia. The dress code of former times was quite different. Although early styles in capoeira dress varied somewhat over time and regionally, it is clear that shoes were always required. This is because the games were outside and, following da Matta's analysis, no self-respecting Brazilian would go out in public (*rua*) without shoes on, and the same is true, to a lesser extent, of shirts. To go out on the street without shoes and shirt (with some exceptions) is to admit publicly of the direst poverty and lack of regard for social decency. In fact, traditional *Angoleiros* would frequently show up at games all 'duded up' in their fanciest clothes. So the development of the *Regional* uniform was clearly only appropriate to the indoor academy setting and helped to reinforce Mestre Bimba's injunction for players not to participate in street games at all. But *Angola* style players, even in the academy setting, never gave up the older tradition of dress, and even today they always wear shoes (and shirt) while playing. Only rarely do they play in fancy dress (though it still can be seen in some games), and frequently they now wear tennis shoes, to aid in mobility. The fact that the conservative style in capoeira adheres to appropriate street dress is further evidence for the importance of the urban setting on the development of the game.

These days, anyone who is serious about learning the sport will train for at least some time in an academy (*academia,* as they are usually called), which is where I spent most of my time. It is customary for a student to choose one master and train with his group exclusively, but it is not uncommon for students to move around and sample several different approaches, especially as they become more proficient. Masters tend to take a dim view of this, for obvious reasons, but there is little they can do about it except cast aspersions on the skill and competence of others. Unfortunately, this kind of disparaging talk is common practice, not unusual in the martial arts in general, which hinders greatly efforts to unify the sport. Since it was my intention to train with and interview as many masters as possible, there was no way I could remain loyal to any one school, but most teachers made allowances for me as a special case and encouraged me to work out with them, even if only for a single session.

Classes are usually held at least three times a week, and this is generally acknowledged as the minimum intensity needed to develop skillful play. Formats vary from school to school, but a typical workout begins with warm-up exercises, followed by group practice in named capoeira moves, frequently a period of partner practice, and sometimes sessions end with a practice game (*roda*). From time to time, each academy will open its doors for an open *roda*, and on that day any player can show up to participate, under the direction of the academy *mestre*. In the *Regional* schools, these open games are intermittent and have the character of a special event, whereas it is the practice of many *Angola* academies to have an open game every week. These weekly *rodas* (usually held on Sunday) are a reproduction of the regular neighborhood games of former times, except they are now held indoors in the shelter of a given academy. This gives the master (or group of masters) additional control over events, since anyone who doesn't conform to house rules can be ejected.

Only two *rodas* of this type were meeting regularly in Salvador during my fieldwork period, one of which began while I was there. The older one, already mentioned, was that of Mestre Virgílio in the outlying *bairro* ('neighborhood') of Fazenda Grande. As noted, he is carrying on the tradition begun by his teacher, Mestre Waldemar, who passed away in 1990. I was fortunate to be able to work extensively with Mestre Waldemar before his death, and his loss will be felt for a long time in the capoeira community. Virgílio's academy functions primarily as a grade school during the week, and the desks and chairs against the walls are convenient for the many spectators at his events, a large number of whom are local kids. It was in this setting that I first began to understand something about how different the *Angola* style of play was from what I was used to seeing elsewhere. At the time of my arrival in Salvador, this kind of game seemed like an endangered species, but during the fieldwork period, and in recent years, *Angola* style has experienced a strong resurgence.

A major influence on this revival was the renovation of an old seventeenth-century fort in the neighborhood of Santo Antonio além do Carmo, which the city converted into a community arts center. Space was provided there, at a nominal cost, for local artists to work and display their wares, and one of the rooms was taken over as a capoeira academy. This school was inaugurated in 1982 by Mestre João Pequeno (João Pereira dos Santos), a student of Mestre Pastinha, and was conceived as a continuation of Pastinha's academy in Pelourinho, where the first indoor *Angola-*

style *rodas* were held. Recall that before starting the original *Angola* academy, Pastinha too had hosted outdoor *rodas* in various parts of the city. João Pequeno ('Little John') named the academy Academia João Pequeno de Pastinha e Centro Esportivo de Capoeira Angola in homage to his great master, who died in 1981. Because of its central location, the Sunday afternoon *rodas* in this academy attracted many *capoeiristas* from all parts of the city, a number of whom had been in virtual retirement and welcomed the opportunity to begin playing regularly again. Soon after the academy opened, another master began teaching upstairs, and on my last visit (1988) there were three functioning capoeira schools in the fort of Santo Antonio. This site has clearly become a major center for the resurgence of *Angola* play in Bahia, which in turn has influenced the development of the modern synthesis of capoeira styles I call *atual*.

Most academies do not have open games on a regular basis, however, but only on occasions which mark the significant progress of the students through various stages of mastery. These formalized stages evolved as part of the institutionalization process in Mestre Bimba's academies, and they can be seen as liminoid transitions, in Turner's terms (see Turner 1982 and discussion in chap. 1), since they are named after, and patterned to copy, rites of passage. A *batizado* ('christening') is a celebration of initiation into the capoeira world given to a group of new students who have demonstrated their dedication by attending classes regularly for a period of time (usually a month or two). In *Regional* academies, this event marks the first time a student is allowed to play in a *roda* to the music of the *berimbau*, and the student must begin by demonstrating his or her knowledge of the *seqüências*, set sequences of required moves done with a partner. The focus of the event in all academies is when a student to be initiated plays capoeira with a master, usually not his or her own but one of those invited specially for the occasion, and is ceremonially 'taken down' in the course of play. After this, the student may be given a 'war name' (*nome da guerra*) to be used in capoeira circles. At some academies, the newly christened student may receive his or her first belt ranking, and a 'godparent' may even appear to offer a kiss and/or a flower. After all new students have been initiated, there is an open *roda* for everyone in attendance and there may be food and drink offered to participants and guests.

A *formatura* or 'graduation' ceremony is often held together with a *batizado*, which can be part of an *entrega de cordel* ('awarding of belts') at academies which use belt rankings. Another of Bimba's innovations, colored belts are not confined to *Regional* academies, but are also found in most middle-ground, *atual* academies. *Angola* academies do not use belts, but they may still have *batizados* and graduations. When a master decides that a student is qualified to start his own academy, when he has learned most of what the master has to teach, he is called a *capoeirista formado*. To celebrate the achievement of that status at a *formatura*, the candidate is required to play against all the masters at the event, often in succession. If he survives, he has graduated. This is a rare event compared to *batizados*, since many more students begin practicing the sport than ever achieve mastery; in fact I only witnessed one official *formatura* in my fieldwork period.

The ceremonies of initiation and graduation were not part of early capoeira practice, but they fit in so well to the academy setting that they have been adopted by most teachers. In the days of street capoeira it was unusual for masters to have more than one or two students at a time, since there were usually no regular classes. Also there was no formal payment, in most cases, but a more general reciprocity which took various forms in each relationship. With the advent of academies, it was common for a master to have many paying students, indeed it was desirable to have as many as possible to pay the rent and recompense the master for his time. Thus these ceremonies serve to capture the interest of students by giving them definite goals, to create solidarity among groups who undergo the transitions together, and to reinforce loyalty to the academy and to the master in charge. This kind of structure may also foster a certain competitiveness between the students, however, to see who progresses faster. In the next chapters, I will argue that the contrast between these immediate, fixed goals and what seems to have been a more nondirected process of immersion in the world of play characteristic of former times is emblematic of a fundamental esthetic opposition that manifests itself in a host of other stylistic and structural differences.

In addition to games in the academy setting, and on the street, I should say something more about two other contemporary subtypes of capoeira performance: folklore shows in theaters and cabarets and organized tournaments. These two occasions both differ dramatically from other capoeira events, but in diametrically opposing ways. In folklore shows, players are paid to display flashy moves, night after night, to an audience which doesn't understand the game and on whom all subtlety would therefore be lost. The result is a style of play which risks nothing and in which danger is mostly illusory (although accidents can happen). Nonetheless, the movement qualities of capoeira are exciting enough by themselves to engage popular interest, and the stage offers a regular (though small) source of income to younger players who are not ready or able to teach the sport. There were five regular, nightly folklore shows in Salvador during the fieldwork period, which, besides capoeira, usually included versions of: *maculêlê, candomblé, samba,* and *puxada da rêde.*

As early as the turn of the century there had been challenge matches between capoeira players and other martial artists, for which rules were developed and admission was charged. For instance, Rego retells a celebrated story of the victory of a *capoeirista* named Ciríaco over a Jiu Jitsu expert, Sada Miako, around the turn of the century in Rio (Rego 1968: 263). Organized tournaments between capoeira players did not begin until the 1960s with the growth of the institutional sport, and the first national tournament was held in 1972. I witnessed four tournaments, including the Brazilian nationals in 1983, and in this setting the style of play tends toward pure aggression, the exact opposite of show capoeira. I will have more to say about both these extreme types in the next chapter, where patterns of physical interaction are examined in detail.

SOCIAL AND ECONOMIC FACTORS IN CAPOEIRA PLAY

Salvador was the first capital of Brazil and for several centuries one of its largest cities, but by the beginning of the twentieth century its population was still only about two hundred thousand inhabitants (Faria 1980: 29). By 1950, this figure had doubled, and the current population is approximately one and one-half million people. Along with this accelerating growth has come an increase in urban poverty, inadequate housing, and a general lack of social services. These problems are typical of many cities, especially in the so-called 'third world,' but they have been exacerbated in this case by the decline of Salvador as a major center in Brazilian economic and political life. The focus of this power in contemporary Brazil is in the south, especially in the cities of São Paulo and Rio de Janeiro, which have become the industrial and media centers of the country.

It is beyond the scope of this study to compare the social position of capoeira players in the northeast to those in the south, or even to carefully delineate the socioeconomic situation of current players anywhere in detail. I have conceived this work to be an initial investigation simply into what the phenomenon of capoeira is, how it is played, and what these practices mean and have meant to players and spectators in Brazil. Although some material has been available on these questions, the answers seemed to me superficial, and my hope was to take the understanding of the game to a depth sufficient for further comparative work. Of course, I have not been able to ignore questions of class and race in Brazil as they impinge on the study of capoeira, and in this section I try to give a general account of the current situation, as well as some preliminary indications as to where future studies might lead. The issue of race is particularly perplexing for a North American in Brazil, and therefore I have chosen largely to leave it aside rather than provide an unsatisfactory, possibly inflammatory, account. I will say that I experienced almost no opposition to my work in Brazil as an apparently white male among the poorest and darkest sectors of society, although I frequently felt snubbed by members of the elite (though probably not on racial grounds).

The size of the average capoeira class in Salvador is about a dozen students, but I observed classes with a range of two to forty-two students in them. Special events like *batizados, formaturas,* and tournaments may attract over one hundred participants from many different academies. Fees at the academies are hard to calculate, given the many changes in Brazilian currency and the problem of relative value, but at the time of fieldwork they ranged from approximately five to fifteen dollars a month for two to three lessons a week, plus an initial enrollment fee.[5] In addition, students were usually required to buy T-shirts with the academy logo and training slacks. Material costs and fees are often negotiable in the poorer academies, as d'Aquino points out (1983: 64), but at the upper end of the scale there is less flexibility.

Academies in the poor neighborhoods are those at the lower end of the fee scale, predictably enough, and have few amenities, often simply consisting of a room with a concrete or wood floor and an adjoining changing room. Restroom facilities at such sites are nonexistent or rudimentary, as they would be in many of the neighboring houses. At the other extreme are those classes held in dance and exercise studios, usually in middle-class neighborhoods or downtown. Here one pays the highest fees, but the rooms have mirrors and barres, tiled bathrooms with showers and lockers, and sometimes even saunas. Clearly the students in these two types of class setting vary enormously in socioeconomic background, age, and sex. Students in the cheaper academies are almost exclusively male and are on average darker-complected and younger than those in the expensive dance studios.

In general, very few women study or play capoeira in Salvador, as compared with other cities in Brazil and the United States, but those that do (estimated at less than one percent of all students) are found overwhelmingly in the dance studios and wealthier academies. D'Aquino reports similar figures and notes that even when women do participate, they tend not to stay with it as long as the men do (1983: 64). In Rio and São Paulo, where as many as five to ten percent of the players may be women, capoeira is generally considered more socially acceptable by middle- and upper-middle-class people. Even in the south, however, female instructors are rare to nonexistent, and I never encountered a female *mestre*. This situation is probably a legacy of the all-male tradition in the capoeira of the recent past and may alter in the near future.[6]

Since capoeira in southern Brazil is generally 'imported' from

Bahia, it has more acceptance with the middle classes, because there is no recent tradition of street toughs playing the game. In Bahia, many middle-class youths look down on the sport because of this long, and continuing, association with poverty. The general pattern is that when capoeira is played by the middle classes, and thus has an acceptably high social status, some women participate at least on an occasional basis; when capoeira is a lower-class activity, as it is predominantly in Bahia, it retains its traditional all-male aspect. One might predict that, if this pattern is consistent, even more women might play capoeira (as a percentage of those who play) in the United States than in southern Brazil, and that does seem to be the case. Bira Almeida reports that during the first large-scale encounter between U.S. and Brazilian players, his U.S. female contingent frequently won tournaments while the males usually lost (1986: 60).

In Salvador, boys may start playing capoeira at a very young age, as early as five or six years old, but the most common pattern is to begin as a teenager, or older pre-teen. Many young men in the city, with the percentage increasing in the poorer neighborhoods, have had some practice in capoeira by the age of twenty. Of those who have formal instruction, most take classes for a few months to a few years and then give it up as the responsibilities of jobs and families begin to assert themselves. Very few stay with it to become masters, and masters usually begin to refrain from physical play in their middle to late forties. Of the living masters, only three in their sixties, João Pequeno, João Grande (João Oliveira dos Santos), and Gato (José Gabriel Goes), were still actively playing at the time of this fieldwork, while others like Waldemar and Caiçara limited themselves to teaching and/or leading the music. I estimate the average age of capoeira students in Bahia to be about seventeen to eighteen years of age; this figure is probably somewhat higher in Rio and São Paulo, where university students, especially in physical education, often become interested during their courses of study.

The largest classes I attended were those of Mestre Camisa in Rio, with approximately 150 to 175 students, and I have heard reports of large classes in São Paulo as well. In total number of formal academies, these southern centers also lead the way: Mestre

Suassuna estimated that there were over a thousand capoeira academies in São Paulo alone. Although this number may be somewhat inflated, the official registry of the Federação Paulista da Capoeira listed about sixty affiliated academies in 1983, a figure which they admit represents only a small percentage.[7] Both military and police in Brazil have been teaching capoeira as part of their self-defense training for about the last twenty years, and these programs are expanding. Many universities offer capoeira courses in their physical education and dance programs, and as the demand for teachers in North America, Europe, and Asia increases, this creates more avenues of opportunity in Brazil as well.

In spite of these advances, few masters are able to make a living in Salvador exclusively by teaching capoeira, and that is one of their constant complaints. It is somewhat easier (but still not easy) to achieve this goal in Rio and São Paulo, which is one reason why, beginning in the 1950s, many masters from Bahia moved south to open academies. This was part of a general migration toward economic opportunity, but it also had to do with the lack of capoeira in those cities, which presented an opportunity for Bahian masters. In Rio this lack was recent, presumably due primarily to the effective police repression of the sport in the early twentieth century, whereas there seems to have been very little capoeira in São Paulo before the mid-twentieth century, or anywhere else in Brazil except Recife.

Most instructors who stay in Salvador augment their incomes with other jobs and teach capoeira on the side. Those who don't do this struggle to make ends meet and are frequently reminded by their colleagues of the examples of Mestre Bimba and Mestre Pastinha, both of whom died in poverty because they tried to survive solely on capoeira. The range of occupations masters have adopted is as varied as the economic profile of their students. At one extreme, there are professionals, a medical doctor who offers free classes to poor youths and a dentist who teaches in dance studios, for example. Some instructors have degrees in physical education, and these are the ones who usually teach university classes and/or military and police self-defense. Other masters are soldiers or policemen who teach on the side, or security guards, either municipal or private. The list could extend indefinitely: car mechanic, instrument maker, civil servant, cult leader (*babalo-rixá*), carpenter, and construction worker, but the majority fall on the lower end of the economic scale. I noted that some of the younger players, and even a few masters, make money appearing in folklore shows, and some of them are also hired to tour with traveling shows. I have also made reference to the few players who still try to make money on the street, performing capoeira in front of the public market or in the Terreiro de Jesus (a central plaza in front of the cathedral). Many of the latter are true street toughs who hustle for any kind of gain, legal or illegal—modern versions of the *malandro*.

It is clear that in Salvador a majority of capoeira students come from the poor sectors of the society, but that a significant minority come from the middle sectors as well (and a very few from the upper levels). Although I have no hard data, it is my impression that the proportion of lower- to middle-class players is more evenly balanced in other cities such as Rio and São Paulo. It also seems that lower-class players in all areas tend to start training earlier and continue longer, since the majority of current masters came from humble backgrounds.

Slavery ended late in Brazil (1888), in comparison with the rest of the New World, and its legacies are still very much a part of Brazilian society, especially in the northeast. One manifestation of this is the frequent use of metaphors of slavery by poor people to express dissatisfaction with current conditions of inequality. For example, in Bahia one commonly hears the phrase, "Slavery never ended here." I took this to mean that the system of actual slavery has given way to a kind of 'wage slavery' based on racial discrimination, entrenching black people in poverty and sustaining the wealth and social domination of the white elite. Like most metaphors, the saying relies on a certain hyperbole to reveal an underlying or unexpected truth. The truth in this case is that poverty in Salvador correlates strongly with color and that wealth and power are still concentrated in the hands of a light-skinned oligarchy of influential families (see Hasenbalg 1985; Faria 1980). The underclasses are forced to seek support in the form of patron/client relationships with these powerful individuals if they want to survive, and opportunities for upward social and economic mobility are minimal for people of color. Capoeira is rich in such metaphors of slavery; indeed from a certain perspective the entire game is a metaphor, a representation of the struggle of slaves against oppression. In the nature of signs, 'slavery' now has a different set of interpretations than it did during the colonial period, but capoeira still offers a much-needed message of hope: that liberation (in a number of senses), even against great odds, is a living possibility.

A student enters the capoeira world by grace of the master, and the *mestre/discípulo* relationship is a complex one. As became clear in the scenario of the *bênção* ('blessing'), the master cannot afford to be merely a friend, but must sometimes, even frequently, take the role of adversary in order to teach the harsh lessons of *malícia*. In this case, if the metaphor of slavery holds, the *mestre* has 'become' a slave master for the moment, reproducing a version of master/slave relations as a lesson to his students. In chapter 2 I observed that, for some slaves at least, relations with the master were highly ambivalent, involving both strong negative and strong positive emotions at the same time. This kind of ambivalence is likely to be even more common in contemporary patron/client relations, as gratitude for favors wars with resentment against an intransigent system. It follows that, if the capoeira master is to do his job well, he must also become an ambivalent figure, both respected and feared, and no better example of such a figure can be found than Mestre Bimba himself. In many stories recounted by his students it is apparent that they saw him this way, indeed his fearsome qualities stand out in high relief, yet he also inspired intense loyalty (see Almeida 1986: 127–29; de Almeida 1982: 65–69).

Therefore the *mestre/discípulo* relationship can and does serve as a kind of template, an icon available for rehearsing several key relations in the Brazilian social system. Especially important are power relations, both past (master/slave) and present (patron/client), for which strategies of domination and liberation developed in the game have special relevance. These include the ability to deceive and unmask deception (the 'kick behind the handshake'), and a basic willingness to accommodate oneself to others, always tempered by the readiness to resort to violence when necessary. The capoeira ideal of *malícia* is a value that summarizes many of these strategies, which are useful for survival inside and outside the ring, especially in the urban ghettos, the *invasões* ('squatters' settlements'), and *favelas* ('slums') of Salvador.

Although a good capoeira *mestre* must sometimes adopt the role of a dominator, his primary character should be that of a liberator, since he is, after all, working with his students to help them achieve their goals. In other words, there are other lessons besides *malícia* to be learned in the sport, especially the value of comradeship. This kind of positive feeling grows naturally between players who love the same game, who strive, suffer, and triumph together. Such emotional bonds are strong between a student and his master and between fellow students in the same academy (and/or neighborhood). In the songs of capoeira, reference is frequently made to fellow players as *camará* (from *camarada*, 'comrade,' 'pal,' 'buddy') or *camaradinho* (diminuitive form, signifying endearment), as well as *mano* (from the Spanish *hermano*, 'brother').

These terms refer not just to one's own close companions in the sport, but ideally should extend outward to include all capoeira players. There is a definite ethos of equality for all within the ring, similar in spirit to what Turner has called "ideological communitas," since it should ideally transcend all social boundaries of class, color, age, and the like (Turner 1977: 132–40). This ideology springs from, and is reinforced by, "spontaneous" experiences of harmony and kinship with others in the course of play. Of course, such experiences may or may not happen in a given encounter, and in practice this kind of solidarity often breaks down in the face of individual and group rivalries. The fact that players usually express regret over such incidents, however, and see them as departures from the correct standard, reinforces the view that comradeship is seen as an overarching principle, a kind of communitas, even when honored by the breach. Although the values of *malícia* and solidarity might seem to be in conflict, in practice they serve to complement each other, to aid in maintaining the central creative tension between aggression and harmony.

PLAY SPACE, SOCIAL SPACE

The real challenge for a close analysis of any expressive genre is how to relate detailed patterns to the cultural world of shared meanings. Since signs are (at least) doubly embedded, within local and global contexts, researchers seek out interpretations which seem to satisfy criteria in both domains. This still remains a highly problematic undertaking, of course, but it seems to be unavoidable if understandings are to be communicated within and between cultural groups. Some suggestions have already been made as to the cultural significance of capoeira play, and the discussion of relationships and roles previews one kind of strategy which seems useful. To provide a transition from the social to the physical sphere, the object of the next chapter, I want to examine three more ideas that suggest ways of linking these two domains, the play space and society at large.

Since I took buses almost everywhere in Salvador, I had ample time to observe patterns of interaction on those vehicles, a subject for a dissertation in itself. One habit of the drivers which used to 'drive' me crazy was that frequently, when they met a fellow bus driver coming from the opposite direction, especially one from the same route or a friend, they would stop in the middle of the street, window to window, and have a chat. While this comradely banter was going on, of course, all traffic came to a complete standstill, since the buses were stopped in both lanes. It used to amaze me that rarely, if ever, did the motorists caught behind the buses bother to honk, nor did the people in the bus ever make comments about this practice. Having lived in New York City, I would often speculate about the mayhem that would be inflicted upon such offending drivers were they to attempt this practice there. Over time I began to realize that people were accommodating the bus drivers, perhaps because they were sympathetic to the difficulties of the job (at low pay) and did not begrudge them this little social diversion. A common idea in Salvador seems to be that social life comes before work, and if efficiency suffers that's too damn bad, let the boss worry about it. Also, I noticed that when car drivers did occasionally get annoyed and honk their horns, the result was that the bus drivers continued talking even longer, delighting in the frustration of those too impatient to wait!

While showing some film footage of capoeira to an LMA (Laban Movement Analysis) class at the University of Washington, an intriguing case of convergence occurred with regard to this idea of 'accommodation.' In the Laban system, 'shaping' is one of three general categories used to account for the ways a body can orient itself in space. Shaping is frequently defined as the way a body adjusts or molds itself to available space: for instance, the way it can be made to 'accommodate' or 'adapt' itself to any objects in that space, such as another body (Dell 1977: 54–58). When the word 'accommodation' came up during that class, in response to the quality of movement in capoeira games, I was struck by the memory of a phrase I heard so often in Bahia, "*O Baiano é muito acomodado*" ('Bahians are very accommodating'). This refers to the easygoing quality of Bahian people (as in the case of the bus drivers above), their acceptance of the quirks and idiosyncracies of others, and the vagaries of life in general, without apparent irritation or complaint. This linguistic coincidence may be historically arbitrary, but upon reflection it seemed to me that at an underlying level there was a true metaphoric (iconic) relation between 'accommodation' in capoeira play and the temperamental 'accommodation' of Bahians in general.

In the confining ring which the players choose to enter, they are always testing each other by intruding into the close "kinesphere" of their opposite number.[8] This intrusion takes the form of an attack, which means that it is intended to contact the body, and the player being attacked responds by trying to escape, which preserves his spacial integrity. The interplay of attack, escape, and counterattack is one way to interpret this basic dynamic of the physical dialogue. Although they take the form of attack/escape, these moves need not be intended or regarded martially, but can also be seen more neutrally as movement initiatives and responses. From this perspective, the physical interplay becomes a generalized give and take, a "to-and-fro movement" in which one player no sooner seems to vacate a space than the other obliges by filling it up. It was this kind of intimate spatial intercourse which suggested to the dance students the idea of 'accommodation' in the LMA sense. Often during capoeira play, especially when more congenial moods prevail, there are extended periods with little or no actual contact, as the two players accommodate smoothly to each other's moves.

This kind of accommodation is more apparent because of the limited, almost confining, space of the capoeira ring. The absolute limitation on the play space is an essential and acknowledged part of the esthetic of the game. The relatively small size of the ring forces a certain proxemic closeness, which is then accentuated further by the 'choice,' really a stylistic imperative, to move closer still. The best players take pride in playing as close to their partners as possible, and it is only beginners who tend to stay away from each other. Yet within these confines, adepts regularly engage in huge, sweeping flights of acrobatic movement. It is often said that a good *capoeirista* always has enough space, no matter how small it is, to do what needs to be done. For instance, one master had us practice cartwheels (*aú*) in place, so that we ended up exactly where we had begun. In self-defense, if a capoeira player is backed into a corner, he claims to have an advantage! This was demonstrated convincingly time and again in training sessions.

Patterns of accommodation, therefore, depend upon and are highlighted by an esthetic of closeness in capoeira, which can also be related to Bahian and Brazilian social patterns, in this case proxemic habits. Edward Hall's classic works have repeatedly demonstrated the intimate links between spatial and cultural organization in many societies throughout the world (1959; 1969). An analysis very like his work on France (1969: 144–48) could be done to show that Latin American people are used to an intimate or close proxemic distance in ordinary interaction, and Brazil is no exception. On the beaches, in bars and clubs, during numerous festivals, close proximity and physical contact are encountered routinely, and many Brazilians seem to enjoy and seek out such experience. Situations which can be extremely traumatic for North American or northern European tourists, such as being unable to move in the crush of a Carnaval crowd, are no problem for most locals, though of course there is substantial individual variation in this (see Wafer 1991: 8).

In an ethnography on the construction of Brasília, Holston (1989) has argued convincingly that, other things being equal, space correlates with class, so that poor people are forced to tolerate crowded conditions, whether they like them or not. From this perspective, one might argue that, in their love of crowds, poor Brazilians, at least, are making a virtue of necessity. But it is extremely hard to avoid ethnocentrism here, since the tendency for middle-class North Americans is to see more space as 'better' than less. An alternative view is that closeness provides warmth and security, while distance promotes isolation and loneliness. Brazilian friends repeatedly expressed versions of the latter view in their criticisms of life in the United States.

For whatever reasons, proxemic closeness and accommodation to others seem to capture essential aspects of Bahian life, and they are expressed as esthetic and stylistic patterns in capoeira play. One of Hall's main insights was that spatial relations are frequently latent or tacit patterns that have become so habitual as to be ordinarily beneath notice. Although some capoeira players are articulate about the importance of closeness, others are less so, and the idea of accommodation in the game is my synthesis, culled from many observations but never expressed in just those terms by any informant. Very few social scientists would, I hope, argue with the fact that tacit or subliminal forms, habits, patterns, rules—call them what you will—exist and strongly influence behavior. An obvious example are phonological and syntactic rules in language which all speakers 'know,' since they follow them, but almost none can articulate. The real problems arise when researchers attempt to make these latent forms explicit, especially if the investigator is commenting on the cultural practices of another group. Yet the anthropological theory for some time has been that it is precisely the outsider who is most likely to be able to reveal tacit knowledge, since insiders tend to be too caught up in those habits to recognize them. Recently, this doctrine has been called into question (see Clifford and Marcus 1986; Clifford 1988), but the critics of ethnographic representation have made few alternative suggestions relative to the problems of understanding and interpreting tacit knowledge.

Let me conclude by considering one more movement pattern

in capoeira, in order to problematize the various ways it might be interpreted culturally. One of the most distinctive aspects of capoeira movement is body inversion, time spent upside down with the weight mostly on the hands and the feet in the air. This characteristic makes the game an acrobatic exhibition, especially appropriate to young men with flexible bodies and strong arms. The head may also be used to support the body in a three-point headstand using the hands and the top of the head, or even all by itself as in the head spin, *pião* (a 'top' [spinning toy]). Common inverted moves are the cartwheel (*aú*), the handstand (*plantar bananeira;* literally, 'to plant a banana tree'), and the *queda de rins* ('fall onto the kidneys'), a kind of headstand using the side of the head with one elbow bent into the kidney area for support. The goal seems to be for the capoeira player to be as comfortable on his hands as on his feet, to be able to move freely from one support system to the other.

Why develop a sport with this emphasis on bodily inversion, adding a degree of difficulty that insures few will ever master it?[9] A number of possibilities suggest themselves. Since this is still primarily a sport for young men, one might think of the African continuities and characterize it as a kind of initiation ritual, many of which are reported to involve acrobatics on that continent. In that case, its degree of difficulty is in line with the trials frequently inflicted on young men undergoing initiation. Since participation in capoeira was never a mandatory rite of passage for young men, however, one might speculate instead that slaves in Brazil wanted to invent a sport which was impossible for whites to do, thus proving their physical superiority, since as laborers they were far stronger than their masters. Though it requires great strength, capoeira also demands extreme flexibility, especially in the back, so the acrobatics might be seen as a kind of physical therapy that prevents backs and limbs engaged in heavy lifting from stiffening.

Semiotically, I am tempted to see this physical inversion as a sign corresponding to the desired inversion of the social hierarchy: to elevate the slave to master status and lower the masters to the bottom. In this sense the game could be said to represent a kind of 'anti-structure' of society, in Turner's terms (1977), which correlates well with the value of communitas between players, and there are many other aspects of the game which can be captured by the model of structural inversion. The idea that social inversion corresponds to physical inversion could be seen as a kind of sympathetic (iconic) magic, like causing like, or as a kind of Freudian wish fulfillment, a play in fantasy for what could never be the case in reality. Some have also suggested that going upside down is connected to African evocations of the spirit world, which is pictured as a total inversion of the everyday world in several cultural traditions (Thompson 1988).

The players themselves see in the acrobatics a form of physical liberation, a freedom of motion which gives them a sense of flight, of transcendence. The acrobatic demands of the sport are a constant testing of the physical limits of the body, and they seem to create correspondingly liberating mental sensations as well. Mestre Nô, for instance, was fond of saying, "*Dou um pulo sem saber, sem querer*" ('I take a leap without knowing, without caring'). Yet the masters simultaneously insist that the moves are also always effective as self-defense, a factor which keeps them grounded and focused.

To a greater or lesser extent I believe that many of the above elements are in play when a *capoeirista* goes upside down, depending on the player and the game: some are made explicit and others remain tacit, and the problem is to isolate which range of interpretations is appropriate to a given context. Here the Peircean model can be of some initial help. As an icon, the idea or image of inversion is fraught with potential, since it can be taken to stand for status reversal, spiritual contact, personal liberation, and so forth.[10] For Peirce, iconicity is a mere "may be," which correlates well with Turner's view of liminoid states as "subjunctive" frames: worlds of "as if," in contrast to the "indicative" mode of normal social life (Turner 1988: 101). As these potentials are constrained within various contexts (indexically), some meanings are selected for, others factored out by the concerned participants. Insofar as certain interpretations are articulated, and become routine, they then can be called symbols and, in this form, are capable of entering fully into belief and value systems. In this conception, iconic and indexical modes of signification are more likely to be left tacit by participants in an event, and symbolic ones more likely to be conceptualized. It is in grasping latent patterns that the trained observer sometimes has an advantage, but only if he or she is careful to situate these interpretations in actual interactive settings and within local systems of articulated symbolic significance.

In this regard, I argue that the basic themes of liberation and domination, of freedom and slavery, of cooperation and deception, are the general symbolic preconditions within which images of accommodation, closeness, and physical inversion are usually at play in capoeira. Within such constraints, these icons can be evoked over and over again in various semiotic channels, with varied effects. During the era of slavery, liberation was not merely a metaphor, or was less of one, since active battle against the forces of oppression was a real possibility. Given the example of Palmares, the potential for total social inversion, for example, was actually on the horizon for some Afro-Brazilians. In contemporary Salvador, and throughout the poor neighborhoods of urban Brazil, people are much more sanguine, even cynical, about the possibilities for dramatic social change. As a result, the ideal of liberation has been reduced to the status of 'mere' metaphor, and the icon of inversion is commonly taken as a sign of the potential for personal liberation, as above. Because of the fluid interchange between tacit and overt, between semiotic and social, the meaning of capoeira play can change in response to historical conditions while still 'conserving,' in latent form and iconic potential, older interpretations for the future. Yet the past is always new when it comes into future being, and it may well be that what seem to be completely new interpretations have unsuspected continuities with the past.

Jogar—Body Play

During the fieldwork period, I observed approximately one hundred and fifty capoeira performances of many types and participated in perhaps one-third of them, sometimes only in the music. The shortest *rodas* are those which end a normal class workout, when the instruments are brought out and the students learn in a practice game of perhaps fifteen to forty-five minutes duration. The longest games are those accompanying traditional festivals, such as the one in Santo Amaro described in the Preface. The regular Sunday *rodas* in Salvador, at the two *Angola* academies mentioned in the last chapter, generally lasted from three to six hours, depending on how many players showed up.

Capoeira is always played in a circle, sometimes marked on the ground, as in tournaments, and sometimes simply formed by players and audience. Figure 4.1 diagrams the basic layout of a typical ring, showing the distribution of players and spectators around it.[1] In chapter 5 I will discuss how the musical ensemble can vary in different types of games. D'Aquino makes a distinction between primary and secondary audiences in capoeira: the primary audience are all fellow players who will take their turn in the ring, while the secondary audience are usually only interested spectators (1983: 38). This means that any physical contest is being evaluated, and supported, by experts as well as bystanders. Only potential entrants to the ring (primary audience) have the right to take up an instrument or to begin a song. It is their responsibility to support the play in the ring, to create an atmosphere conducive to an excellent game. But the secondary spectators are by no means passive: it is permissible for them to yell comments, to clap their hands in rhythm, and to respond on the chorus of the songs, if they know them. Occasionally someone

Figure 4.1 Capoeira Ring

will cross the border: a spectator will spontaneously decide to go into the ring for a bout. This happens frequently at public festivals, especially in Bahia.

As I have indicated, capoeira is always played in pairs and only two active contestants are allowed in the ring at any time. The partners usually play close together, so that the movements of one force a response in the other, in the now familiar interchange I have been calling physical dialogue. As a kind of 'conversation' in movement, capoeira can be hotly aggressive or coolly detached. When the conversation is polite and respectful, the movements invite maximum accommodation, there is an orderly alternation of turn-taking, and moves seem to flow effortlessly together. When the play becomes aggressive and violent, a *jôgo duro* ('hard game'), capoeira borders on actual fighting, even wrestling, and can turn into a real brawl at a moment's notice.

A pair of prospective *jogadores* ('players') must begin by squatting at the 'foot' (*pé*) of the lead *berimbau*, and they will return to the same place at the end of their bout. Sometimes players will 'line up' waiting for a chance to enter the ring. In this case they will squat behind the two at the foot of the bow(s), forming a second curved line immediately inside the ring of musicians (see fig. 4.1). As the pair directly in front of the lead *berimbau* move into the ring to begin play, those behind them in line move up, so that the next two are ready when those in the ring finish their bout. In other games, and this was more common in the past, players will wait outside of the ring for one pair to finish before they move to the foot of the *berimbau* for their turn. There is one other way to enter the ring, which is for a new player to cut in on one of the two contestants and begin to play with the other. This is called *comprar o jôgo* ('to buy the game') and can sometimes result in extremely short confrontations when people are impatient to play and don't want to wait for others to finish.

The average length of a bout, the interchange between two players, varies considerably, limited as it is by the stamina of the opponents and how hard they are pushing themselves. Generally about two minutes is an estimated average, though in some *rodas* it can be much shorter, perhaps thirty seconds or less, when many players are buying the game. This is especially true at outdoor festivals or whenever large numbers of players are present. Extremely long encounters, like the one described in the Preface, may last ten to fifteen minutes, with several pauses in the action which themselves can be a kind of game. Even so, this degree of stamina is exceptional and such long bouts are quite rare. For comparison, imagine a ten-minute round of boxing!

A fundamental value in capoeira play is improvisation. In training one practices a repertoire of named movements and learns how to defend against given attacks, how to attack given defenses. But in the course of actual play it is up to a player to respond to each situation as he sees fit, even creating a new move on the spur of the moment if necessary. The emphasis on improvisation is related to the ethic of freedom or liberation central to the game, and changes in the amount of improvisation allowed or desired are important in distinguishing stylistic trends in capoeira.

The Object of the Game

Since I have repeatedly referred to capoeira as a game, it might be asked, "What is the object of the game?" or "How does one win or lose?" The first and easiest answer is that the object is to cause one's opponent to fall down, to score a *queda* ('fall'). That is, one should knock him off his feet or hands, causing him to land on some part of his torso, preferably his butt. In the recent past it was common for *capoeiristas* to play dressed in fancy white suits (see fig. 4.2). This was partly so that after the match their pristine clothes would be elegant testimony to their skill, since outdoor games were the norm and clothes were easily stained. This is an expression of the rule that the only parts of the body to touch the ground during play should be the feet, the hands, and the head. Although practice in many academies still requires white uniforms, mistakes in play are no longer 'inscribed' quite so clearly on wood or concrete floors. Even today, some of the *An-*

Figure 4.2 Antique photo of capoeira, probably from the 1930s. Players are all dressed in white and relatively "fancy" clothes, although dress shirts have been removed in some cases. Photo by Weldon A. da Costa.

gola players will show up at a *roda* and play in fancy street clothes, though not necessarily white ones.

The classic way to knock the opponent over is to sweep his feet out from under him, a move called *rasteira*. The easiest way to do this is when only one of the opponent's feet is on the ground, usually because the other is kicking. Another way to cause a *queda* is to trip the opponent using a variety of *banda* (literally, 'flank' or 'rear'), which usually requires pushing him over one's outstretched foot. In addition there are the so-called 'scissors' moves (*tesoura*) in which one traps the adversary's leg or legs between one's own and brings him down by twisting one's body, using the hands as support. Finally, one can knock an opponent over using any of the kicks or by butting him with the head (*cabeçada*). The *cabeçada* is especially appropriate when the opponent is on his hands, since it is considered bad form to kick an adversary when he is upside down.

In general it is prohibited to push an opponent, except as part of a *banda*, or to hit him with a closed fist. There are a couple of open-handed blows practiced, but these are usually employed as feints to distract an adversary. Sometimes one may make a fork of index and middle fingers and jab it toward an opponent's eyes (*forquilha*), but this is also usually a feint or even a joke, just to keep him on his toes.

The lack of hand strikes and consequent reliance on kicks in capoeira has been remarked on many times. The most frequent explanation of this, mentioned in chapter 2, is that the slaves' hands were frequently chained together and they developed a way of compensating for this. However, in practice it was at least as common for a slave's feet to be chained, indeed more so, since a slave could still work with feet chained and hands free (an impediment to escape), whereas the reverse would prevent most work. If one imagines a person with both feet and hands chained together, it would still be possible for him to use some of the capoeira moves, including the mule kick and the head butt. Nonetheless, it is clear that in the development of capoeira most of the slaves and freedmen who played the game were unchained most, if not all, of the time and could have made use of all their faculties had they wanted to.

Other hypotheses for the predominance of the feet have been proposed: for instance, the idea of disguising the martial aspects of the game, making it look like a mere dance. This persistent oral tradition accounts for other aspects of capoeira as well, including the use of music. It should be noted that by restricting the use of the hands to a defensive or support role, more total body movement is required, thus creating a more dynamic style and also making the game safer for participants. It is much easier to see a kick coming than a punch, and thus easier to avoid it. Likewise the game is easier to control if punches are prohibited. Since mock battles can easily deteriorate into real ones, it is important to introduce restraining measures against this possibility. At the present time it is not uncommon to see players become angry with each other and begin fighting in earnest. One sure sign of this is when they begin using their fists to strike blows.

The ways of causing one's opponent to fall are informally graded, as being more or less perfect. The ideal seems to be not to use force, but timing and knowledge: to apply a gentle pressure at the right time to unbalance the opponent and cause him to fall. The best way is the *rasteira* applied to a base leg while the adversary is kicking, and the second best is a gentle *cabeçada*, knocking him off his hands. It is up to a player to get out of the way of all kicks and it is his own fault if he gets hit. Nonetheless, it is considered bad form to batter one's opponent rather than simply taking him down (see table 4.1). One can also throw a hip into an opponent or hit him with the buttocks (*bundada*) to knock him down. In addition, one can sweep an opponent's foot with one's hand (*rasteira de mão*) and even grab both his legs with one's arms (*arrastão*) to pull them out from under him. When this latter tactic is used too often the match can degenerate into a kind of wrestling, and this is generally thought of as ugly capoeira.

The question of winning or losing has only recently been quantified and formalized (rules, point systems), especially in tournament settings. In more traditional contests, the crowd watching the match decided the winner informally among themselves, with differences of opinion being standard. This consensus approach is also common in African martial arts like wrestling and may represent influence from that esthetic tradition,[2] although a

TABLE 4.1 Some Capoeira Rules for Physical Play

A. Normative Rules

1. Active play is between two contestants inside the ring.
    1.1 Obey the conventions for entering and leaving the ring.
    1.2 During play, don't move outside the ring.
    1.3 Shake hands with your opponent before and after the bout.
2. Try to take your opponent down.
    2.1 Only feet, hands, and head should touch the ground.
    2.2 Don't try to injure opponent physically.
        2.2.1 No strikes with closed fist are permitted.
        2.2.2 No pushing allowed, except as part of a takedown.
    2.3 Emotional, psychic, and/or prestige damage are okay.
3. Always be ready to defend against an attack.
    3.1 Don't turn your back on an opponent.
    3.2 Keep your hands up for protection.
    3.3 Keep your eyes on your opponent at all times.
4. There is no play without music (*berimbau*).
    4.1 Music starts before physical play.
    4.2 When music stops, play stops.

B. Pragmatic Rules

5. Don't block attacks (except before they mature, or *in extremis*).
    5.1 Escape, then counterattack.
    5.2 Be prepared to escape from most common attacks.
    5.3 Be prepared to attack most common escapes.
6. Keep moving (*ginga*).
    6.1 Try to increase your freedom of movement while decreasing
        that of your opponent.
    6.2 Never come to a complete stop.
7. Try to deceive your opponent into becoming vulnerable.
    7.1 Establish patterns, only to break them.
    7.2 Pretend to do one thing, then do another.

NOTE: Normative rules are not usually written down, except for tournament settings, when they are much more explicit and point awards are specified. This distinction comes from Bailey (1969), but the boundary is extremely fuzzy in capoeira (see chapter 7).

similar informality is widely found in folk contests generally. In the case of a fall, of course, the result is visible for all to see, but frequently evenly matched players cannot take each other down. In this case, there are other criteria for judging superiority, and the object of the game becomes merged with the style of play.

When discussing tactics at a capoeira retreat in California, Mestre Acordeon (Bira Almeida) expressed the ultimate object of the game in terms of 'control.' He said that a player should attempt to control his adversary, while not letting himself be controlled. One way this can be done is by denying one's opponent space to move. Forcing a player out of the ring, even throwing him out, is a clear way to assert control over the play space. In tournaments, if a player steps out of the ring, he loses points. Bira accordingly counseled his players to take the center of the circle away from the adversary, forcing him to the periphery of the ring, or outside it altogether. The other extreme of spatial control is to 'surround' one's opponent within the ring, forcing him into complete immobility. This is done, at the highest levels, by being able to foresee what the adversary is about to do in order to neutralize that move before it gets started. As the trapped one (a position I have been in more than once), the sensation is that no matter where one turns, there is the opponent waiting; the opponent is always "in one's face."

The master most adept at surrounding and immobilizing me was also one who, appropriately enough, espoused an esthetic of capoeira in tune with this skill. When I asked Mestre Moraes what the object of capoeira was, his response was "*movimento só*" ('only movement'). He argued that the need for complete and total mobility, in any and all directions, was the key principle from which all other tactics and postures followed. For Mestre Moraes, the takedown is effective because it immobilizes an opponent, and in his view the idea of control reduces to providing maximum mobility for oneself and the minimum for the adversary.

The search for the object of capoeira turns out to be a complex one, involving esthetic as well as tactical principles. The importance of the takedown, the notion of spatial control, and freedom of mobility are complementary notions close to the essence of the game, and all are clearly related to the general themes of dominance and liberation. Note that these values all emerge from the player's perspective; they relate to tactics and feelings of genre-internal significance. But capoeira is not just for players—it also has an audience of spectators: it 'opens out' toward a wider social field. On the streets or in the fields, in academies or stage productions, adepts play to the audience and not just for each other. This means, as I have already suggested, that it is productive to view capoeira as a kind of drama, a theater of domination and liberation. This view is grounded on events within the ring, but it goes on to contextualize interactions on the periphery, in the circle of musicians, and among the spectators, ultimately including metacommentaries on the action before and after the games. At the most basic level, however, awareness of an audience influences how players interact, since the question of who has gotten the upper hand in a contest is often decided by the spectators.

Especially in the traditional *Angola* games that I witnessed in Bahia, there is an immense variety of tactics available to a player who wants to dominate an opponent. These tactics are evolved in the emergent context of play, but constrained by many preconditions as well, such as the history of past encounters between the two contestants. In addition to denying an opponent space to move, one can control the tempo of the game by throwing the opponent off his comfortable rhythm, causing his play to be jerky or hesitant while one's own remains smooth and seemingly effortless. One can play more slowly or more quickly than the opponent is able to (slowness being very difficult to sustain, especially while on the hands). A related tactic is intimidation, one form of which is simply to demonstrate one's physical prowess, dexterity, strength, and/or speed to an opponent, striking fear into his heart. This can be done by prestige alone, so that *capoeiristas* are sometimes known to cultivate reputations for being 'bad' (*mau*, in a sense very like that used in American Black English), 'dangerous' (*perigoso*), a 'dog' (*um cão*, thus ferocious, vicious), *maluco* ('crazy; unpredictable'), as well as *bom* ('good') or *excelente* ('excellent'). A weak player who knows that he is up against a strong one is usually defeated before he starts, and I have seen contestants intentionally fall down or show other signs of overt submission, as if 'asking' for mercy.

In addition to intimidation, another indirect method of gaining the upper hand is humiliation, which also can take many forms. For instance, a clever player can mimic the ineptitude of his adversary, thus making a mockery of him for the audience. Of course, it takes a lot of talent to convey one's intention to do this

without appearing inept oneself. In the same vein, one can feign
fear as a form of mockery. For example, a common practice is to
cast one's eyes up and cross oneself as if to say, "God protect me
from this dangerous player." When this is done after a weak kick
or other puny attack, the effect is clearly ironic, often provoking
laughter in the audience. However, the effect can be more complex when the attack was a good one which just missed. In that
case, the feigned fear in crossing oneself might be read as, "You
almost got me that time, but I'm still not shaking." This is the
implication because, if the crosser were truly afraid, he presumably would not want to take the time, nor have the presence of
mind, to cross himself in the first place.

Humiliation can take extreme forms as well, including such
tactics as pulling an opponent's pants down or sitting on him.
I remember a particular bout which had turned nasty and degen-
erated into angry grappling, an occurrence by no means infre-
quent. After a struggle, one player ended up lying on top of the
other, both of them face down. The player on top gave a few
pelvic thrusts on the buttocks of the other in imitation of homosexual intercourse. As the player on top, he was in the 'dominant'
position while the one on the bottom was forced into the 'passive,' or 'submissive,' role. In a culture that still retains aspects of
traditional *machismo*, this represents degradation in the strongest
terms.[3]

At this point it should be clear that interactions in capoeira
can be truly theatrical, in the sense that they are capable of expressing great complexity of meaning and a wide range of emotions. Also, the integral role of the audience is evident in the use
by players of frequent gestural 'asides.' To communicate to the
reader possible 'readings' of these asides and gestural 'dialogues,'
in order to facilitate analysis, I will sometimes take the liberty of
literalizing the metaphor of 'body language.' As I have already
done above, I will occasionally translate gestures into speech,
since it seems to be the easiest way to communicate their pragmatic force. All such translations are intended solely as suggested
glosses, not as semantic renderings of the 'meaning' of the gestures. I take it as given that such gestural signs 'mean' in different
ways to different people (they receive various interpretants) but

that there is often a consensus among observers as to what their 'significant effects' are in given cases.[4] This consensus can be verified, in part, by discussions with players and audience after the event and by pragmatic cues: responses such as laughter or singing during the performance.

All of the related objectives discussed so far are concerned with competition between two adversaries in the ring, and indeed that is the main point of the capoeira encounter. There is a sense, however, in which one can demonstrate mastery of the game without even contending, merely by embodying dynamic qualities like balance, grace, poise, and harmony. It might even be argued that the point is not necessarily who 'wins' a bout (or was not until recently) but whether the contest is beautiful or not. Mastery of the sport involves expressing one's potential with great style, whether doing the simplest movement or the most complex. A great player should also bring out the potential for greatness in his opponent and should manifest his atunement in the music.

Demonstrating this kind of mastery is in perfect accord with traditional African esthetics. In the Afro-Brazilian cults, such excellence flows from the heavens in the form of *axé*, the energy of life (cf. Thompson 1983: 5–9), and in Bahia, *capoeiristas* also are measured in these terms. Chernoff reports that African master drummers are not praised for taking flashy solos, for standing out, but because they are able to keep the ensemble functioning well together, for making the musical event "sweet"(1979: 139). From this perspective, the role of the *mestre* ('master') in capoeira might be seen not as someone who does the best acrobatics or even defeats all opponents, but rather one who is responsible for the success of the entire event, the orchestration of the *roda*. From his commanding position holding the lead *berimbau*, he controls the tempo of the game, initiates most of the songs, and enters the ring to play the most beautiful games at the propitious moment. In the fullest sense, therefore, it is the achievement of this ideal of mastery that is the true object of the game for many players.

THE MOVEMENT REPERTOIRE

One characteristic aspect of capoeira movement is that, rather than a set of static stances, or bases, from which kicks and punches are thrown, as is the case in most Asian martial arts, capoeira has a moving base called the *ginga*. This 'step' is usually the first thing taught to beginners, insuring from the outset that they will keep in motion. The word '*ginga*' is a technical capoeira term, but it derives from the Portuguese verb *gingar*, one meaning of which is: "to sway from side to side while walking; to waddle" (Taylor 1980: 320). The word also occurs in common Brazilian usage, frequently in its participle form *gingada*, referring to the way a person walks or dances, especially in relation to footwork.

An alternative meaning is 'to scull,' as in rowing, thus *ginga* can also be a sculling oar. Some versions of the capoeira *ginga* seem to resemble the actual motion of sculling or rowing, as the torso leans forward and backward alternately. Many of the songs refer to the ocean, encouraging the player to imitate waves or the bobbing of a boat:

c:	samba no mar	dance in the sea
	samba no mar, marinheiro	dance in the sea, sailor
s:	samba no mar, marinheiro	dance in the sea, sailor
	samba no mar, estrangeiro	dance in the sea, stranger

Here the song is referring to a specific dance, the *samba*, which is so universal in Brazilian culture that it can easily become synonymous with dancing in general, as in this case. Since capoeira is also (partly) a dance, its identification with *samba* is entirely appropriate. Dancing in the sea can be an image of freedom of motion or, alternatively, a description of wallowing, slow-motion movement, if the song is used satirically. Obviously, sailors have learned a lot from observing the ocean:

s:	marinheiro, marinheiro	sailor, sailor
c:	marinheiro só	lonely sailor
s:	quem t'ensinou a nadar?	who taught you to swim?
c:	marinheiro só	lonely sailor
s:	foi o tombo do navio?	was it the plunging of a ship?
c:	marinheiro só	lonely sailor
s:	ou foi o balanço do mar?	or was it the rolling of the sea?
c:	marinheiro só	lonely sailor

The part of the *ginga* most suggestive of this rocking motion of the water is the *balanço*, used in this and other songs to link seafaring and swimming with capoeira. The names of several other

basic movements also come from lore of the sea (or the bay), like
rabo de arraia ('stingray's tail') and *bôca de siri* ('crab's mouth').
These correspondences reinforce the importance of the role that
sailors, fishermen, and dock workers played in the development
of modern capoeira.

According to Bira Almeida (1981: 133), the *ginga* can be
divided into three aspects: the *passada* or footwork; the *balanço*
or bobbing front and back; and the *jôgo de corpo* (literally, 'play of
the body') involving the torso, head, and arms. (For a transcrip-
tion of the *ginga* into Laban notation, see Appendix A.) The *balanço* involves a shift of weight from a front foot to a back foot
and back again (LMA: sagittal plane), which may or may not be
accompanied by the torso sway described above as similar to a
rowing motion. The *jôgo de corpo* involves twisting one's torso
from side to side and moving the hands and arms in such a way
as to distract the opponent while also protecting oneself, especially one's head. Some teachers, especially in *Regional* style, are
very strict about positioning hands, feet, and body in the beginning and others are less so, but most agree that eventually the
ginga should be varied and personalized. *Angola* masters emphasize that the qualities of a player should be expressed in his *ginga*,
whose variations correspond to the improvisations of the game
itself. The *ginga* turns out to be the *alpha* and *omega* of capoeira,
the first thing learned and the ultimate signature of the expert.
This aspect will be explored further in chapter 6, but for now it is
enough to say that all moves flow from the *ginga* and the qualities
of the *ginga* inform all moves a player makes.

Capoeira teachers usually divide the repertoire of moves into
three or four basic types. The scheme I will describe here was
given to me by Mestre Nô (see Appendix B), but it is fairly typical
of other breakdowns I have seen (for example, Almeida 1981:
134–35). He begins by distinguishing attacks (*ataques*), defenses
(*defesas*), and the *ginga*, which is called the 'base' (*base*), or the
'fundamental movement.' Right away there are serious problems,
however, in using a taxonomic format of the sort commonly employed in cognitive anthropology. Many of the named movements
can function *either* as attacks or defenses, or even as *both* at the
same time! As will become clear, this is because the distinction

between attack and defense often becomes lost in the flow of the game. The category *desequilibrantes* (movements that 'unbalance' one's opponent), for instance, which includes the most common counterattacks (*contragolpes*), was listed by Nô under both attacks and defenses. Even a seemingly straightforward attack like the 'blessing' kick (*bênção*) can also become an escape when executed by an advanced player.

Accordingly, an alternative way to understand Appendix B is not as a taxonomy, but as a list of ideal types or 'prototypes.'[5] Typical attacks are *golpes* ('strikes'), typical defenses are *esquivas* ('escapes'), and counterattacks are somewhere on the border between the two. The typical counterattack is a *desequilibrante*, although *golpes* and *fugas* can also be counterattacks. Like the *desequilibrantes*, the *ginga* can be either attack or defense, but usually it is neither. Almost anything can be classified with anything else in the scheme, which underscores the freedom and fantastic movement potential of the sport. There is a tremendous amount of controversy about the names of capoeira movements, with different teachers using different names, therefore Appendix B should only be taken as one representative, but in no way definitive, scheme.

In some naming schemes, all defenses are called 'escapes' (*esquivas; fugas*); or, alternatively, 'escapes' form an important subcategory of defense types. This is in line with Rules 5 and 5.1 in table 4.1, which capture a central tendency of the game: attacks should not be blocked directly, but rather the player should escape from an attack first, then counterattack. This does not mean that there are no blocks in capoeira, but rather that they have reduced importance relative to escapes. A good player will divert the force of a blow with a block in order to protect himself while escaping, or he will block an attack before it is fully formed, to prevent that attack. Such a player will not counter the full force of a blow with a block unless there is no other alternative. This is partly because the emphasis on kicks makes many attacks so powerful that they are difficult or impossible to block effectively, but just as important is the maintenance of the give-and-take, the flow of the game. The emphasis on escape and counterattack reduces body contact and makes possible the dancelike interplay characteristic of beautiful capoeira. This is also the key to establishing the kind of 'turn-taking,' typical of normal interchanges, that makes the dialogic, discourse model of the game especially productive. Finally, escape/counter is in tune with the general pattern of indirectness, central to the esthetic of *malícia*.

As players become skilled, the time between escape and counterattack is progressively reduced, so that the counter follows hard upon the escape. At the highest levels of play the two eventually become unified into one continuous movement. When this happens there is really no distinction between escape and counterattack, and even the attacks themselves begin to contain within them their own defenses. Therefore, advanced play cannot easily be analyzed in terms of attack and defense, but becomes a seamless flow of mutual interpenetration. This is the sense in which the *ginga* 'takes over' play altogether, and the game moves from *both* (attack) *and* (defense) to *neither* (attack) *nor* (defense), as the agonistic element becomes buried in the ludic. This kind of high-level play is characterized by a kind of 'flow,' which is beautiful but can be deadly if suddenly interrupted.[6] Bodies in flow at the level of physical discourse are signs (icons) of communitas in social discourse, and interrupting the flow is a frequent sign of *malícia*.

To the breakdown in Appendix B, another category is added in the *Regional* method, called 'throws' (*golpes ligados* ['bound throws'], or *golpes cinturados* ['belt throws']). These moves are controversial, since some say all the throws were added to capoeira by Mestre Bimba under the influence of Asian martial arts such as Jiu Jutsu. It seems likely that some of these throws were invented by Bimba (from whatever source) as training moves (especially the 'belt throws'), since I never saw them used in regular capoeira play. Sometimes in folklore shows or street (money-making) games, I observed players take time out from the flow of the action (presumably by prearrangement) to do a couple of these throws as crowd pleasers. However, certain other throws *are* used in regular play, even in more traditional *rodas*, such as the *cruz* ('cross'), in which one player grabs the other between the legs with one arm and across the shoulder with the other, lifting his entire body off the floor in order to throw him down head first. Therefore it seems reasonable to suppose that at least some throws have always been used in capoeira, at least in the recent past, but that Mestre Bimba may have added some new ones for training purposes.

Another way to subdivide the movement repertoire needed to play capoeira is to consider a distinction known in the LMA system (from the domain called 'shape') as 'spokelike' versus 'arclike' movements of the limbs (Dell 1977: 49–53). Spokelike movements are those which go straight out from and/or back toward the torso like the spokes of a wheel, the torso being the hub. Arclike movements are those in which a limb describes an arc or curve through space, relative to the body, like the rim of a wheel or any segment of it. This alternation exists as a tactical option in capoeira and some masters are fairly explicit about it, but usually without making the distinction systematically. Examples of spokelike attacks in capoeira would be: *bênção, chapa, cabeçada,* and *coice;* while arclike attacks include: *meia-lua, rabo de arraia, armada,* and *queixada* (see Appendix B).

One common tactic is the artful alternation of spokelike with arclike attacks: one establishes a pattern of arcing play, for example, and then suddenly breaks through with a direct, spokelike blow. This idea of setting a pattern and then breaking it, of creating expectations and not meeting them, is perhaps the essential capoeira strategy and a prime example of *malícia* at the microstructural level. As noted above, there are many other patterns that can be established, including such variables as tempo, height, inversion (hands versus feet), and so forth, but in all of these the player with *malícia* is one who can fool the opponent by the creation of unfulfilled expectations, the breaking of an established pattern.[7]

Another way to think about these practices of deception involves the notion of 'indirection.' In the tactics above, a player tries to direct his adversary's attention one way so that he can lull him into a pattern which can then be interrupted. In microinteraction, this reduces to a feint, the most basic form of indirection: fake x to open up the opponent to y. A player who feints achieves

success if he can appear to be directing his body one way when
he actually intends something completely different. Once again
the LMA system can aid in understanding this kind of interaction:
in that scheme an effort quality is said to be 'direct' if the body is
tending toward a single point in space, and 'indirect' if it has
no definite, but rather a diffuse spatial orientation (Dell 1977:
28–30). A basic feint can thus be understood as a quick change
in directional orientation, but capoeira players sometimes go further. Some subtle players fool their opponents by an artful alternation between direct and indirect effort qualities: that is, they
are able to give the impression that they have no direct intentions,
that their attention is wandering, as a lure to tempt an adversary
to attack. At the moment of truth, however, they are easily able
to shift back to a direct spatial mode and catch their opponents
by surprise.

A specific example is the use of eye contact. A central principle of capoeira play, drilled into students over and over, is never
to lose sight of one's adversary in the ring (see Table 4.1, rule 3.3).
Players are told to practice this in every variety of acrobatic position. However, many master players avoid looking one directly in
the eye; in fact, they almost always use peripheral vision so they
can appear not to be watching! This is indirectness in action as a
form of feigning. Masters will sometimes turn their heads away
or even turn their backs, as if to assert that they have eyes in the
back of their heads. That they constantly tell their students not to
do this, and then proceed to do it themselves, is a further illustra-
tion of perhaps the most basic lesson of *malícia:* rules are made to
be broken.

These tactics illustrate how *malícia* can work at the body level,
the ground for its functions at the conceptual level. To return to
the discourse model, two players frequently begin normal play by
establishing a movement 'conversation' based on an orderly alternation of turn-taking, as follows:

a & b	a	b	a	b
[ginga]	attack	escape/ counter- attack	escape/ counter- attack	escape/ counter- attack

Malícia then consists in an interruption of the conversation, one player doesn't wait but takes two turns, usually by faking one attack and making another, or by attacking twice in a row. Interrupting physical patterns goes together with interruptions in the alternation of turn-taking, both attempts of one player to fool the other by artful indirection. This provides a more detailed example of how, as at the end of the last chapter, signs seem to 'propogate' from one semiotic domain to another. In this case, the tactics of pattern interruption and indirection in physical play can be seen as similar to (iconic with) scenarios of deception (like the blessing) dependent on cultural and psychological expectations.

Note that *malícia* cannot function without at least some cooperation in establishing a pattern in the first place. If no pattern is set up, if no conventions are in force, there is nothing to interrupt, and there can be no expectations to foil. Therefore, in addition to the overt themes of competition and struggle, capoeira play depends on more covert norms of cooperation, related to the values of comradeship previously discussed. The argument will be that the domain of physical interaction foregrounds combat and *malícia,* in most cases, while the aspects of harmony and cooperation, no less necessary to the ethic of deception, usually remain in the background. In the next chapter, I will show that this configuration of patent/latent tends to be reversed in the musical domain, where solidarity is necessary for the normal interaction of instrumentalists and singers, and *malícia* recedes into the background except under special circumstances. Another way to express it is that competition is unmarked in the physical interaction while cooperation is unmarked in the musical channel.

Capoeira Styles Revisted: *Angola,* *Regional,* and *Atual*

No movement description of capoeira would be complete without accounting for the variations between styles of play. This means first distinguishing more traditional forms of *Angola* play from the newer *Regional* innovations, and then discussing how the recent synthesis I call *atual* mediates between those two extreme types. When one observes capoeira classes today, the session will invariably start out with calisthenics, usually including

an aerobic workout and stretching. The only exceptions to this
I have seen are one or two very traditional *Angola* teachers who
start immediately with capoeira moves.

The widespread use of calisthenics is probably due as much
to the advent of European physical education practices in Brazil,
starting in the 1920s (Marinho 1945), as to any specific innovations made by Mestre Bimba in his academy; although, as a self-
conscious modernizer, Bimba was open to these practices. Several
students of Bimba reported that he would make prospective
trainees pass a physical 'test' before he would even accept them
into the academy. After their introduction from Europe, physical
education exercises were quickly adopted by the army, the police,
and in public schools, so that these influences were probably de-
cisive for their inclusion in capoeira training as well. Mestres Nô
and Paulo in Bahia were trained traditionally by *Angola* masters,
for instance, but both of them now have their students *fazer física*
('do [warm-up] exercises') before beginning the capoeira training
per se.

An innovation by Bimba that has heavily influenced training
procedures was the invention of the *seqüências,* set 'sequences' of
movements practiced by two players together to prepare them for
the give and take of the game. These *seqüências* must be learned
by anyone wishing to advance up the ladder of expertise in *Regional* academies. It is in the teaching of these choreographed sequences that standardization of movement is emphasized, not
only of individual movements, but of responses to movements.
This does not mean that in an actual game a player must respond
to attack *x* with defense *y,* but it does mean that his tendency,
especially as a beginner, is to do so, since he has practiced it that
way repeatedly in a *seqüência.*

Since the emphasis in *Regional* academies is strictly on self-
defense, aspects of physical interaction which were not deemed
sufficiently martial were often discarded. The result is that even
though some *Regional* players boast about how many more moves
their style has than the *Angola* style (cf. d'Aquino 1983: 153–
54), in fact the latter has much more variation, since it fosters
playful activity which is not necessarily directly combative. *Regional* masters and others concerned with competitive capoeira

have spent much effort trying to standardize terminology and catalog all the moves. Almeida discusses such an attempt, which resulted in a list of about eight hundred moves (1981: 131). Contrast this with an interview by Mestre Pastinha, mentor of *Angola* players, shortly before his death.

> Q. "Master, tell us how many strikes there are in capoeira."
> A. "Young man, it isn't possible to say; they are without number. For every strike which is launched, there are two defenses already prepared, and for those two defenses, four more strikes. One is [always] improvising and thinking while fighting." (*O Globo,* December 1963)

As previously noted, Bimba also required his players to promise not to play in street *rodas,* thereby removing another source of free variation from the game. To this day, many masters, especially students of Bimba, forbid their students to play in the streets. If it is true that *Angola* is the more improvisational style, that it exhibits greater variation and is less standardized, it follows that it should be harder for players in *Regional* style to practice *malícia.* Indications that this is true come from the fact that *Regional* players tend to play down *malícia* as a value in favor of technique and skill (d'Aquino 1983: 102–6). That is, they strive not to be sneaky and tricky so much as to be faster, stronger, and more effective.

By now several scholars have written about stylistic differences in capoeira (Frigerio 1989; Evleshin 1986; d'Aquino 1983; Dimock 1976), but the majority of those accounts tend to follow 'commonsense' generalizations made by players themselves, most of whom are arguing for the superiority of their own style. Close analysis reveals that many of these characterizations are extremely oversimplified, and others are simply wrong. Perhaps the most frequently heard description is that *Angola*-style capoeira is played 'lower' than *Regional* style, closer to the ground. This is generally true, but it is an oversimplification. The tendency in both *Regional* and *atual* games, the newer styles, is for players to stay on their feet most of the time, going to their hands only occasionally, and often in a perfunctory manner. This is because the low, hand-supported positions are perceived to be more vulnerable, less effective in a self-defense context. Sometimes this perception is rationalized, sometimes merely tacit, the product of imitation. This tendency for 'high' play is especially evident in street players whose style may be influenced as much by Kung Fu movies as by any formal capoeira instruction. I have frequently heard Mestre Moraes, an *Angola* traditionalist, admonish young players as follows: "How can you play capoeira without touching a hand to the ground?" *Angola* players can use both high and low positions, though initial training emphasizes low postures in order to develop strength.

Masters of all styles should be equally comfortable high or low, though this may not always be the case, and *Regional* masters especially tend to avoid the low game. Tournament players tend to stay high in competition—indeed some formal capoeira matches resemble karate sparring or even Greco-Roman wrestling—but may be comfortable going low in open *rodas*. Students of the influential Mestre Suassuna (Reinaldo Ramos Suassuna) in São Paulo are equally comfortable high or low, and I would characterize his capoeira style, though consciously conservative, as *atual*. In short, there *is* a tendency for *Regional* to be a 'higher' game, and *Angola* to be 'lower,' but differences correspond as much to individual teachers, and to the contexts of play, as to style per se, especially in the expanding realm of capoeira *atual*.

D'Aquino asserts (1983: 152, 155) that *Angola* is played at slow and *Regional* at fast tempos, but I don't believe this to be the case. It is true that in some *Regional* events the very slow game is omitted, since it is not thought to be as effective for martial training, but all the masters I interviewed agreed that the game can be played at any tempo, led by the *berimbau*. *Angola* games definitely may be fast, since some of the fastest tempos I experienced accompanied those *rodas*. The normal practice in *Angola* games is to begin slowly and then gradually speed up. When the tempo gets too fast, the master may stop play and begin again at a slow tempo. In general it seems fair to assert that the full range of tempos is more often used in *Angola* style than in *Regional* or *atual* play, where tempos tend to vary less.

One of the ways that *Angola* players characterize the *Regional* game is as a lot of "*vup, vup, vup.*" This sound is an imitation of the way legs and bodies 'swoosh' through the air. The import is to suggest that there is a lot of flashy but meaningless movement in that style. They say there is much high kicking but no contact is made, as if the players were putting on a show of how high they can kick regardless of where their opponent is. "Why should I raise my leg up to here?" Mestre Canjiquinha (Washington Bruno da Silva) once said to me, lifting his hand over his head. "I'm not doing a ballet dance." *Regional* masters respond by saying that kicking high gives them more flexibility, thus more versatility in attack and defense. They often assert that their physical training is more complete than that of *Angola* players, many of whom have serious weaknesses in their game.

Not only are *Angola* kicks usually no higher than the waist, some teachers say that one shouldn't kick at all except to actually hit one's opponent. Rather one should rely on the feint. "I avoid throwing blows," said Mestre Moraes, "even the head butt can be dangerous." A kick well faked can cause the same reaction in an opponent as a kick thrown, with the advantage that the feigning player is in a better position to neutralize his opponent's response. This is one important way that the *atual* style of capoeira tends to be like *Regional* rather than *Angola*. The young players like to throw those hard blows and kick high, making for a lot of "*vup, vup, vup.*" Mestre Nô, teacher of many of the best street players, encourages this. "You must go ahead and throw that blow strongly, with force," he often told me. However, true to his *Angola* roots, he prefers low kicks to high ones, and he is also able to play an excellent feinting game, when in the right company.

Another difference at the body level between the styles is one I noticed while training, then confirmed in observation: namely that *Angola* is played more 'on the toes' (actually the ball of the foot), while *Regional* is more of a 'flat-footed' game. This is especially noticeable in the low postures like *negativa*, but also comes across in the kicks, where the base foot is flat in most *Regional* training but the heel is usually raised in *Angola* style. Even this varies somewhat from master to master and should not be taken as a hard and fast rule, but only as a stylistic tendency. In

Figure 4.3 *Aú:* open position (unmarked), being done by Cacau, the player at left (background). This is a street game in front of the Mercado Modelo, near the waterfront. The player at the right is about to "buy the game."

the middle ground of *atual* play the student is usually allowed to do what feels most comfortable, with the result being a large amount of free variation in this detail.

Many of these differences in movement style follow from a principle often invoked in the *Angola* style, the need to "*fechar o corpo*" ('close the body'). If the body is open, it is vulnerable to attack, so it should be kept 'closed' (*fechado*) most of the time, thus protected. The only reason to open up is to lure one's opponent into a trap. One opens a specific target in order to provoke an attack there, having prepared a counterattack beforehand. In this case, one is practicing deception, *malícia*, by pretending to be open when one is not. This explains why *Angoleiros* do not kick high, since it opens up the body too much, and why they rely on feints, attempts to fool the opponent into opening while one remains closed oneself.

Two moves which illustrate this difference in the concept of openness between the styles are the cartwheel (*aú*) and the

Note that it would be unusual for players to do this back to back, as pictured. Compare with photo.

cocorinha, a squatting defense *(cocorinha* literally refers to the 'defecation' position). *Regional* players tend to do an open cartwheel with legs straight up (fig. 4.3), whereas *Angoleiros* favor a 'closed' cartwheel (*aú fechado*), with legs together, knees down toward the chest (fig. 4.4), protecting the body and preparing the legs for a counterattack against any threat. In most capoeira discourse, the open kind of *aú* is the basic type and is therefore lin-

Figure 4.4 *Aú fechado:* 'closed' cartwheel, demonstrated by the player on the left. The action takes place in the courtyard of the fort of Santo Antonio, now a community center featuring several capoeira academies.

Once again, orientation of torsos in this depiction is more likely to be reversed in normal play. Compare with photo.

guistically unmarked. As such it is opposed to several marked or special varieties of cartwheel, including the 'closed' version (*fechado*) and more specialized kinds, such as *aú folha seca* ('dry leaf cartwheel'—so named because the player appears to curl up and fall to the ground like a dry leaf). This usage differs somewhat for players in *Angola* academies, where the closed cartwheel sometimes becomes the unmarked form. The *Regional* style of *cocorinha* has heels flat on the ground, legs apart (fig. 4.5), whereas the *Angola* version is on the balls of the feet, knees together (fig. 4.6). Although protected from a high attack in the *Regional* position, one arm over the head, the crotch and torso are open for a low attack. The *Angola* version closes the crotch and crosses arms in front of the torso, completely protected except perhaps for a high attack coming down on the head. These differences reflect the tendencies for high versus low play in the two styles, as well as the *Angola* preoccupation with 'closing' the body.

The concept of closing the body is not merely a physical one, however, but relates to an older, spiritual notion which, although largely vestigial, is still believed in and practiced by some *capoeiristas* today. In chapter 2 I mentioned the *mandingueiro,* a specialist in protective fetishes, a designation now virtually synonymous with *capoeirista.* There is a famous line from one of the songs which goes, *"Quem não pode com Mandinga, não carrega patuá"* ('Who cannot [make it] with the *Mandinga,* doesn't carry an amulet'). One function of the *patuá* is precisely to 'close the body' in a spiritual sense. If one's body is protected spiritually, then no harm can come to it physically. This kind of protective fight magic is common throughout Africa, for instance among wrestlers, and seems to have been integral to the practice of capoeira in the past. Few capoeira masters will openly admit to this form of belief today, but the *patuá* is still used by some in secret, and there are still ritual specialists, called *feiticeiros* ('sorcerers') who claim to know how to make them (Almeida 1986: 122).

One way to summarize an essential aspect of the difference between the two extremes of capoeira style is to turn once again to Huizinga's distinction between ludic and agonistic. In general I believe it is appropriate to characterize *Angola* as the more ludic

Figure 4.5 *Cocorinha: Regional* style, as demonstrated by Pica-pau, playing with Mestre Almiro. (Photo by Cecile M. Hansen)

Figure 4.6   *Cocorinha: Angola* style. When players are both in the same position, as here, they are usually preparing to enter the ring (*saída*).

style, while *Regional* is fundamentally agonistic. The claim is that the former is usually more playful, of the nature of a pastime, while the latter is primarily a competition, a martial contest. This means that contest, in the *Angola* mode, is contained within a framework of more nondirected play, where the event itself and the quality of play are (or should be) seen as primary. The *Regional* innovations, on the other hand, came from the desire to make capoeira more effective as self-defense, a true martial art, like the famous Asian systems. Combat and competition are the focus in these games, which is why the first formal tournaments were organized by Bimba's students. The *atual* style of capoeira is midway between the two extremes, some masters emphasizing fighting while others preserve more of the traditional ludic framework.

This does not mean that capoeira in the *Angola* style is not a deadly form of self-defense, nor that *Regional* players do not joke around and perform beautiful, dancelike movements, but it is an attempt to isolate the central tendency in each style. The object

of the ludic style is more in line with an African esthetic: to
make the game as beautiful as possible by harmoniously combining all the elements, by balancing competition with cooperation.
The object of the agonistic style corresponds more closely with
contemporary Western traditions: the emphasis is on individual
achievement more than group effort, competition is central, and
nonmartial aspects, such as the music, tend to recede into the
background. As an overarching framework, Huizinga's distinction will allow for the inclusion of elements from all the significant domains of expression in capoeira, and as evidence of stylistic
variation accumulates, the reader will be able to decide whether
or not it captures the essence of those differences.

The esthetic difference between the styles seems to be related
to socioeconomic and ethnic differences between the players. In
the previous chapter I noted that Mestre Bimba had drawn students preferentially from the middle- and upper-middle classes, in
effect excluding poorer students by charging hefty fees. When capoeira spread to the rest of Brazil in the 1950s, it was mostly
Bimba's students who led the way, and the type of players they
most readily attracted were from the same background. Accordingly, the agonistic styles are strongest outside of Bahia, especially
in the south, where more students come from the middle sectors
of society and are ethnically Euro-Brazilian. Such students are attracted to capoeira as 'the Brazilian martial art' and, until recently,
identified less with its African heritage.

In time capoeira was reintroduced to the poorer, darker
people in cities outside Bahia, though there are reports that continuity with the past seems to have been maintained in some cases,
especially in Rio de Janeiro (Moura 1983). As more ludic styles
began to reemerge, aided by a second wave of *Angola*-style masters from Bahia, some of Bimba's original students began to question the path of modernization, as described above, and the result
is the proliferation of the *atual* style of capoeira. Although it is
possible to distinguish both ludic and agonistic varieties in the
emerging *atual* synthesis, in general the distinction is losing its
efficacy as both tendencies are reunified into "just one capoeira."
It is impossible to know how capoeira will be played in the future,
but at present it seems unlikely that many of the *Regional* inno-

vations will pass from the game, especially those closely associated with the requirements of the academy setting. The new capoeira will most likely be a combination of both older styles, as *atual* already is, and cultural influences from many parts of the world may make past changes seem minor by comparison.

THE STRUCTURE OF CAPOEIRA PERFORMANCE

Just as figure 4.1 represented the ideal or typical physical configuration of players around the circular space of the game, it will be useful in describing the order of events in a capoeira performance to provide an ideal or typical sequence, a 'syntagm' of the action.[8] Unlike the model of the players in space, which requires (at least) two dimensions for descriptive adequacy, the performance syntagm can achieve fairly accurate representation in one dimension, as an ordering of events in time. The formal model offered (in table 4.2) does not account for all possible sequences, partly because the rules of the game are not always fixed or explicit, but it will establish the basic pattern of play and adequately describe the variations between styles. Notice that the *Angola* sequences are the most complete, while the typical *Regional* syntagm is generated by omitting some events. As usual, *atual* performances fall somewhere between these extremes. By examining which aspects of the syntagm are altered or omitted in *Regional* and *atual* play, it will be possible to elaborate further on the differences between styles.

Strictly speaking, an *Angola*-style *roda* begins with the *ladainha* ('litany'), a solo sung by the master of the *roda* or by a

TABLE 4.2   Syntagm of Capoeira Performance

A. Musical Events
(warm up)   1. *ladainha/chula*   2. *corridos*
B. Movement Events

1a. gestures	3. *saída*	4. *Jôgo*	5. shake hands	
		4a. *comprar o jôgo*		
		4b. Inner Games:		
		—*chamadas*		
		—circling		

Simplest Sequence (*Regional*): 2–3–4–4a–5
Fullest Sequence (*Angola*): 1–1a–2–3–4–(4a)–(4b)–5

visiting master. Although it is not necessarily the first event, since there is often a sort of informal 'warm-up' period, no serious play begins until a *ladainha* has been sung. Often the 'warm-up' period is a time for the music to get swinging and for beginning students to practice a few moves. With a cry of "*ié,*" the master stops the music, and thus the play, since there is no play without music. After a short pause, the lead *berimbau* begins to play a rhythm known as *Angola* at a slow tempo (see chap. 5). When all the instruments have come in, the master cries "*ié*" again, and begins to sing a solo, the *ladainha*.[9] The players are arranged around the ring as in figure 4.1, the two who will begin the game crouched at the 'foot' of the lead bow, listening to the solo, since traditionally it was directed primarily at them. The singer is usually playing the lead *berimbau*, although sometimes he may be playing a different instrument, or even be one of the two squatting players preparing to enter the ring. The *ladainha* always concludes with a call and response, the *chula* ('verse' or 'song'), led by the soloist, which takes a standard form and serves as a kind of an invocation.[10]

Both the *ladainha* and the *chula* are accompanied by gestural activity, especially on the part of the two about to enter the ring. For instance, if God is invoked during the *chula*, with "*Viva meu Deus*" or "*Viva Deus do Céu*" ('Praise to my God' or 'Praise God of the Heavens'), those squatting (and sometimes other players) raise their hands and faces to the sky. When they sing "*Viva meu Mestre*" ('Praise to my master'), they can indicate with their hands their own master, if he is there, or the master of the *roda* if they want to honor him. Sometimes the *entrada* contains phrases like, "*ele é mandingueiro; ele é cabeceiro; sabe jogar*" and these may be accompanied by gestures between the squatting players, who point at each other to indicate: 'he is a *mandingueiro;*[11] he is a head-butter; [he] knows how to play.' After the *chula*, the soloist begins one of the regular call and response songs called *corridos* (literally, 'running' songs), which will continue intermittently until the *roda* ends or until play stops for another *ladainha*, whereupon the sequence repeats.

The beginning of the *corridos* is the signal for the squatting pair to enter the ring and start play. Before this *saída* ('exit' from the foot of the bow), the players bless themselves by touching the ground, then touching themselves, sometimes on the forehead, sometimes the heart, sometimes crossing themselves. After this blessing they'll shake hands and 'offer' each other the floor. The latter gesture is an open hand or hands in the direction of the ring, equivalent to the classic formula, "After you." "No, after you." Moving into the ring is done slowly and cautiously, the players keeping low to the ground.

Mestre Nô told me that in the old days a *capoeirista* would bless himself three times before entering the ring: once when he first knelt down at the foot of the bow, once at the end of the *ladainha* or when the chorus sings "*Viva meu Deus*" during the *chula*, and once right before starting play. This is an indication that the game had increased ritual significance in the past. There is also a final blessing marking the end of the physical interaction: the players return to the foot of the *berimbau* and touch the ground one last time. This can be done formally before the next pair go out, or informally while play continues.

Mestre Bimba taught his students that the proper time to enter the ring in a *saída* is not after the *chula* at the beginning of the *corridos,* as I observed it being done in *Angola* games, but rather during the *chula*, after a certain phrase which was a signal: "*dá volta ao mundo*" ('take a turn around the world'). Although the *chula* has a standard musical structure, the actual phrases chosen (from a set of traditional verses) may vary freely at the whim of the soloist, and it is difficult to imagine that the *saída* was ever keyed rigidly to any one phrase. In any case, it is rare that even Regional players adhere to Bimba's convention today, especially since they often don't bother with the *ladainha* (and therefore the *chula*) at all.

To begin play, *Regional* players always cartwheel into the ring (*aú*) while *Angola* players usually use some form of *rabo de arraia* ('stingray's tail'), also known as *meia-lua de compasso* ('half-moon in a compass'). Actually, true to form, the *Angola*-style *saída* can be almost anything, including a 'closed' cartwheel or a back flip, as long as at least one hand is on the ground, whereas the *Regional* standardization requires an 'open' carthwheel. Frequently *Angola* players begin with very difficult strength moves in order to intimidate their opponents.

The *saída* leads directly to the *jôgo* ('game'), the main physical interaction which is the heart of the capoeira performance. Pauses or diversions in the flow of the *jôgo* will be examined below, but to complete the syntagm, each bout ends with a signal from the master, telling one pair their time is up and preparing the way for the next pair of contestants. Traditionally, the signal was given on the *berimbau* and was simply a series of beats on the open string accompanied by a lowering of the bow to the horizontal position. This signal is still used in João Pequeno's academy, though it frequently goes unnoticed by the players until verbal cues get their attention. Some other masters signal by whistling, and I saw one teacher who used a police whistle. At the signal the players should return to the foot of the *berimbau,* shake hands, and bless themselves one last time, retiring to the edge of the circle to help out with the music. The players can also decide to end before any signal is given, simply by stopping play and shaking hands. This I call the 'conclusion,' since it marks the end of a bout, although as far as I know there is no standard term for this closing practice.

The two contestants should always shake hands after a bout, as they did before it, and they may even embrace each other. I saw cases where the players ended up so angry at each other they didn't want to shake hands, and the masters made it their business to calm them down until they did. There is a real sense in which, if they cannot shake hands in good faith, the fight is still in progress, even if the action has (temporarily) stopped.

Another aspect of *malícia* is that, if one is out for revenge, one should never let one's enemy know, nor should one attempt an immediate reprisal. Rather, one should plan and wait for the proper moment, making the enemy feel nothing is amiss, then get him when his guard is down. A story was told to me about a master who thought a player had insulted him in a *roda*, not showing him the proper respect. The master didn't let on that he was angry, pretending that nothing had happened. Two weeks later he went out for beer with that man and some others, and when the offending player lifted his glass to his mouth, the master smashed it into his face. He then lectured the surprised and bleeding player about proper behavior in the ring. This and other stories (for example, Almeida 1981: 119–20) about surprise attacks are consistent with the themes of *malícia* already developed, though perhaps representing its darker side.

Notice that several elements of the syntagm, especially those marked with parentheses, are optional in any given case and that some elements co-occur with others. For example, the *corridos* are sung initially to signal the *saída* but continue intermittently throughout the *jôgo*. The syntagm for an entire *roda* is essentially a repeat or iteration of the sequence for each single bout, since the *roda* is simply a sequence of bouts strung together.

The most common pattern today in *Angola* events is for a *ladainha* litany to be sung three to four times during the course of a *roda*. The games begin with a *ladainha*, and the action is stopped each time for a fresh beginning in an event lasting several hours. This gives the masters a chance to cool down the action if it is getting too intense and/or to highlight an important bout between accomplished players. The *ladainha* is always sung at a slow tempo and, as a measure of respect, physical play should not begin until the *ladainha* has ended and the *chula* verse has been sung. Occasionally there is only one *ladainha* to introduce the proceedings, and frequently in *Regional* and *atual* games the invocation is omitted altogether. In those cases, one of the *corridos* is usually sung to get the action going, but players do not need to wait before jumping into the ring. I have even witnessed games where there is no singing at all, or only very sporadic singing. The presence or absence of the *ladainha/chula* invocation at a *roda* is a clear diagnostic for distinguishing ludic from agonistic styles, and in later chapters I will discuss the implications of this difference.

During the *jôgo*, action is continuous, except for transitions when one pair of contestants is finishing and another pair begins. The ideal case is that a couple of players will wait for the previous pair to finish, then squat down at the foot of the bows to enter the ring in a *saída*. More common these days, especially in street *rodas*, is for an entering player to 'buy the game' (*comprar o jôgo*) by cutting in on another player, as described above. Ideally, when cutting in, one replaces the weaker player to challenge the stronger, but in practice this is impossible to determine with certainty in every case. Sometimes when a strange player comes into a roda, others will gang up on him by always cutting in on his opponent, thus forcing him to play with everyone in succession and wearing him down. One rule of respect is that one is never supposed to cut in on a master, but rather let him play as long as he wishes. Like most rules in capoeira, however, I have seen this violated and, even though most of the players and the knowledgeable audience members may disapprove, there is really no way of enforcing it. However, I have also seen masters simply push away the would-be intruder and go on playing, ignoring his attempts to cut in.

The end of the *roda* event is sometimes marked by a change in the pattern. The *Angola*-style *rodas* of João Pequeno, for example, were ended with a traditional song,

s:	Adeus, Adeus	goodbye, goodbye
c:	Boa viagem	pleasant journey
s:	Eu vou m'embora	I'm going away
c:	Boa viagem	pleasant journey

which has been widely used as a closing theme (Rego 1968: 56). While singing this the players (with or without instruments) would parade around the room in a circle, the music finally ending with a final cry of "*ié!*" Mestre Virgílio would not necessarily use this song to end, but after his closing "*ié*," the musicians would often start playing a *samba* beat and some of the players would dance. This practice is one of several indications of the close association between *samba* and capoeira, perhaps a legacy of their common origin from the *batuque* circles of the slave era. Aside from the shouted "*ié*," *Regional* and *atual* games do not usually end with any specially marked event.

GAMES WITHIN THE GAME

In *Angola* style, the *jôgo* is by no means a seamless flow of continuous action, but is usually broken up by several types of 'inner games' or subroutines. The most common kind of diversion is called *chamada de mandinga* or *chamada de bênção* (*chamada* means 'call,' thus this is a 'call of the *mandinga*' or 'call to the blessing').[12] The signal for the beginning of a *chamada* is for one

TABLE 4.3   Syntagm of *chamada de bênção*

Events [my terms]	Indices [see table 4.1]
1. the call	1. violate rules 3.1, 3.2, 6.2
2. the response	2. one player stopped, other does *floreios*
3. the approach	3. one stopped, other enters near kinesphere
4. the waltz	4. hands joined (truce)
5. the separation	5. violate rule 6.2 (sudden attack)
6. resume normal play	

player (henceforth 'the caller') to stop moving and spread his arms wide, leaving himself open (see table 4.3). He can do this either facing his opponent or with his back turned. The latter option seems more radical, given the capoeira rule (appropriate also to most martial arts) that one should never turn one's back on the adversary (see table 4.1, and discussion below). Other possible interruptions in the flow of play include 'circling' the ring (*dá volta ao mundo;* literally, 'take a turn around the world') and returning to the foot of the *berimbau,* not to end the contest but for another *saída* with the same partner. Of these, the only one still used in the *Regional* style of capoeira is circling the ring, which in that context is usually done because the players are tired and want a breather. Often such circling effectively ends the bout, since another player will take the opportunity to cut in and 'buy the game.'

When asking about the loss of the *chamadas* from the *Regional* game, I was often told that they are just resting periods, and that strong players don't need such rest. A close examination of the *chamadas,* however, reveals that they are actually an important aspect of the traditional game and that for the *Angola* player, even circling the ring is not principally a breather (cf. d'Aquino 1983: 143). In my analysis, all of the 'games within the game' represent an opportunity to develop and explore *malícia,* since they set up a field of low-level rules or expectations which can then be violated. While it is true that in capoeira rules are made to be broken, some rules are clearly more important than others, and the creation of a tacit hierarchy of rules, habits, and expectations enables the players to explore their *malícia* without destroying the very fabric of the game. In order to demonstrate how this

Figure 4.7 *Chamada de Bênção.* Mestres João Pequeno and Moraes at Little John's academy in Santo Antonio. (Photo by Kenneth Dossar)

works, I will describe the operation of the *chamadas* in general, followed by some examples of how these subroutines provide opportunities for *malícia* in action.

   When a player sees his opponent open himself in an invitation to a *chamada,* he might respond by attacking immediately, since it would seem to be a prime opportunity. I have seen players in *Regional* or *atual* games do exactly that when confronted with a 'call,' because they were unfamiliar with the conventions of the inner games. An *Angola* player will rarely attack immediately, both because he is aware that a *chamada* is being signalled, and because direct attacks are foreign to the esthetic of deception, which celebrates indirectness. The convention is for the one being 'called' to put on a solo demonstration, to 'show his stuff,' partly in order to prove that, far from being tired, he is still able to perform the most complex acrobatics, called *floreios* ('flourishes'). Such exhibitions are also entertaining for the spectators, of course. After a few acrobatic moves, the soloist cautiously approaches his opponent, who has not moved the entire time, but is still in his stationary, open posture. The task of the moving player is to come close to the 'caller' and join hands with him,

always on the alert for an attack. The closer he gets the more the tension heightens, since in the near range a sudden elbow or knee is hard to avoid. The stationary player is also on intense guard since he is vulnerable as well, and if his back is turned he usually turns his head to the side in order to watch his opponent out of the corner of his eye. The players join one or both hands after they come together and, side by side, step backward a few paces and forward a few, in a kind of walk or dance (fig. 4.7). They can either be front to front or front to back, depending on which direction the caller was facing when he opened himself. In another variation, the soloist can place his head on the stomach of the caller and they can 'waltz' back and forth in that position (fig. 4.8). After a few steps in each direction, one player offers the other the floor, in the same gesture used for the *saída*, and the tension heightens again as the players separate. Usually the first player to make a break for the open floor receives a kick from the other, or sometimes the kick itself will be the signal to break and resume normal play.

The *chamada* activities serve as subroutines which intensify the action by forcing the players into close proximity, thereby heightening the tension. They also serve as tests for both players, to see if they are able to approach and separate while remaining protected against attack. Often the *chamadas* are accompanied by many small feints, almost like fidgets, to feel out the opponent, to see if he is guarding a certain point. Likewise, these routines provide a set of conventions which then may be manipulated in the search for *malícia*. For an *Angola* player, the circling of the ring is another such opportunity. In this case, one player simply breaks off play and starts walking or jogging around the inside of the ring in a counterclockwise direction, and the other player follows behind him. One way to be *malicioso* in this 'circling' (d'Aquino

Figure 4.8 Variation of *Chamada de Bênção*. Mestres Nô and Curió at the academy Grupo de Capoeira Angola Pelourinho in Santo Antonio. (Photo by Michael Goldstein)

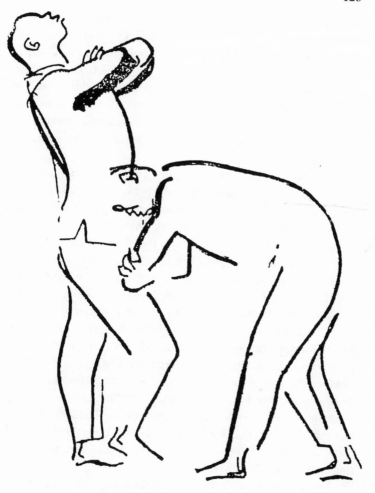

1983: 121) is for the lead player to simply kick straight behind him at the follower, hoping to catch him off guard. Likewise, the follower can catch up to the leader and try to kick or trip him while his back is turned. The fact that most of the time neither happens—the lead player merely turns to the follower when he is ready and starts to *ginga,* signaling that normal play is resumed—simply provides the expectation which makes the occasional breach more exciting.

Finally, a player can break off play and return to the foot of

the *berimbau,* only to begin again with the same partner in another *saída.* Sometimes in this case there is a special *saída,* rarely
used as an initial opening, in which the players join hands squatting and frog-jump sideways into the ring (fig. 4.6). This jumping
ends when one player lifts a foot and kicks the other one, the
signal to break and resume normal play. All these terminating
kicks (as in the *chamadas* as well) are expected, though one
never knows who will initiate them or when, and have standard
defenses.

One other game within the game I have not discussed is the
'money game,' mentioned previously, because it is mostly a thing
of the past. There were special rules and songs associated with
this subroutine, but much of the lore concerning it has been lost
and is a subject of disputes between the older masters. The basic
idea is for money to be placed in the center of the ring where it
must be picked up with the mouth, by a player who is on his
hands. Since both players are trying to get the money, considerable strategy is required. Versions of this play can still be seen
today, as described in the Preface, or in the games by the market in Salvador on Saturdays. Exact details of how the money
game should be conducted are controversial, however, including:
whether the money should be placed on a scarf, how the players
maneuver for position, whether coins can be picked up or only
paper money, and so on. The interchange described in the Preface
was the single most elaborate money game I ever witnessed, and
many times players simply ignore the presence of money in the
ring until the game is over.

One key question with regard to these inner games is, when
should one decide to initiate one? The most general response is,
when one has demonstrated an advantage over an opponent. If
one has taken one's opponent down, of course, this provides a
natural break in the action, and one is free to do what one wants
until the opponent regains his feet. If one returns to the foot of
the bow or begins circling the ring, however, it underscores or
indexes what has just occurred, in case the audience missed it.
This indexing is even more important if one's advantage was less
marked and more easily overlooked. So these routines not only
serve to heighten tension, they also serve to dramatize play, to

highlight the action, and to give a player a chance to say "I am in control."[13]

One Sunday I attended Mestre João Pequeno's *roda* at Santo Antonio, one of my habitual haunts. The climax of the event was an encounter between Mestre Curió, also a teacher at the academy, and Mestre Moraes, a young *Angola* master. After several minutes of heated play, Curió turned his back and spread his hands in a *chamada*. As usual, Moraes backed off and went into a short routine of acrobatic moves, the *floreios*. As he was about to execute a particularly difficult move called *relógio* ('clock': one tucks one's elbow into one's side and spins the entire body on one hand; so named because one's body then resembles the hands of a clock),[14] Curió saw what he was up to, ran over and stomped on him, causing Moraes's body to touch the floor. Then Curió dashed back to where he had been and spread his hands in the *chamada* as if nothing had happened. This was a 'dirty trick,' since the convention is to remain in one spot once one has initiated the *chamada*, until the adversary approaches to join hands (table 4.3, numbers 2 and 3). Yet the audience loved it, and even Moraes was forced to smile, since, although Curió had violated a convention of the subroutine, it was a clever application of higher-order rules (table 4.1, 3 and 7–7.2) and thus a good example of *malícia*. After that, whenever Curió went into a *chamada*, Moraes was wary of the same trick. From time to time Curió would test him by faking a sudden break from his open position and Moraes would immediately turn his *floreio* into a defense. This interplay was greatly enjoyed by the audience and demonstrates how the rules for the subroutines provide a framework that can be violated without destroying the game itself.

THE LANGUAGE OF THE FACE

Facial expressions are also important in the communication of meaning in capoeira and, like the other gestures, they tend to be stylized, exaggerated for the benefit of the audience. When I first began to study capoeira in the United States, it was impressed upon me that the game should be played with a smile, that one should keep smiling as a way to overcome pain and fear, and that even if he were to kill someone, a *capoeirista* should kill with a smile on his face! After many months in Brazil, I began to realize that this was only a partial truth, that the situation was more complex and subtle, especially in the highly expressive *Angola* games. The understanding I finally arrived at, after much observation and conversation, was that capoeira should be played with a light heart, with an 'internal smile' (my phrase), although outward expressions might vary to suit the moment. That is, the best players (in my view) did not simply paste an unchanging grin on their faces, but rather they frowned, they laughed, they grimaced, they feigned anger and fear, in short they acted many roles but always in the spirit of play. Underneath there was something like a child's delight in acting, having fun, laughing off adversity, shrugging off pain, smiling ruefully at mistakes.

One of the joys of watching beautiful capoeira is discovering that one has been taken in by one of these consummate actors. One 'reads' face and body to mean that the player is really angry or hurt or upset, only to be pleasantly surprised when he throws off the mask with a laugh. This kind of dramatic pretense is another aspect of *malícia*, of fooling one's opponent, and often the audience can be fooled as well.

Trained movement observers, and my training has only been slight, might notice several outward signs which indicate, for instance, when a player is beginning to become truly angry and aggressive. I used to practice this regularly in Brazil, since anger is one of the ever-present dangers of capoeira, a game which constantly foregrounds icons of combat.[15] Nonetheless, I was sometimes fooled, maybe because the threshold between simple 'hard play' (*jôgo duro*) and actual fighting seemed to be higher in Brazil, and perhaps even higher in Brazilian capoeira, than it would have been here in the United States. I would sometimes be convinced that a contest was an all-out, angry brawl only to watch in amazement as the players shook each other's hands and retired from the ring as if nothing untoward had happened.[16] Other times, however, one player would so successfully imitate anger that everyone, including the audience and his adversary, would believe it, only to drop the pretense and leave the crowd amazed. Usually such an imitation, involving a controlled mimesis of the icons of anger, including a red and frowning face, would provoke a corresponding emotion in the opponent which the latter would be unable to control, leaving him exasperated when the other player laughed his off. Making one's opponent angry while staying calm oneself is another way of dominating him, humiliating him, and/or frustrating him, since it is recognized as bad form to *perder controle* ('lose control').

Accordingly, capoeira teachers say that one should play with a 'cool head' (*cabeça fria*), which may be the survival of another African value, as Thompson has argued using his notion of an African-American 'aesthetic of the cool' (1966; 1979). Notice that superior emotional control is an example of a kind of one-upmanship available to the slave, through which he could demonstrate his power over the master by making him angry and frustrated while the slave smiled inwardly. A similar dynamic is valuable in contemporary power relations as well, as the dominated sometimes succeed in getting back at their social superiors by manipulating their emotions.

This kind of inversion of the signs of power was brought home to me in a capoeira bout in Massaranduba (a Salvador neighborhood near the church of Bomfim) on the occasion of a *formatura* ('graduation'). During a bout, one player had snuck a kick in through the guard of his opponent, stinging him, and the offended player became angry, attempting to retaliate. The more he tried to hit the first player back, and could not, the angrier and more frustrated he became. The sneaky kicker responded with a series of mock cringes, each of which served to emphasize the other player's emotional state and telegraph to the audience the fact that he had landed a blow, which most had not seen. These cringes angered the attacking player even more, since they highlighted both the fact that he had been hit (which he could have covered up if he hadn't lost his temper) and that he was impotent to counterattack. I suddenly realized that I was witnessing the cringe being used as a weapon! This dramatic reversal of the physical signs of domination and submission is a scenario appropriate to many power relations, especially in cases where the subordinate cannot retaliate directly. The frustration of the angry player is reminiscent, for instance, of the powerlessness felt by a master that cannot punish a slave who has goaded him, because

to do so would demonstrate the slave's power over him, and thus
the latter's superiority. Workers in Bahia who delight in frustrating their bosses are employing the same kind of power reversal in
the modern setting. In the slave case, the risks are greater (torture
or even death), but the constraints on the master are also greater,
since slaves were expensive and hard to replace. In the contemporary world, the risks are reduced to losing a job or a patron,
but given widespread poverty, employers have little worry about
replacing their workers.

PRETEND TO RUN AWAY

An excellent example of an iconicity between the microstructure of body movements in capoeira and social interactions in
general can be found in a set of movements whose similarity I try
to evoke under the heading of 'pretend to run away.' There are
two versions of this kind of move which I have seen in the *jôgo*.
In the lower variation, often known as *recuo* ('retreat'), a player
runs away from his opponent keeping one hand on the ground.
This means that his feet actually follow a circular path, with the
hand at the center, and the player inevitably returns back where
he started. The upright version usually has no name, and in this
case a player simply turns his back on the opponent and starts
running away from him, only to turn back suddenly and attack.
The latter sequence is also found in the subroutine of 'circling the
ring,' described above, when a player may demonstrate *malícia* by
starting to circle, only to trick his opponent with a sudden kick.
In one case 'circling' is a named subroutine of the game, while the
other two versions occur during the *jôgo* itself, with no break-off
of play to mark the beginning of a special interactive frame.

Once, in the interior of Bahia, a capoeira player told me that
'pretend to run away' was a tactic frequently employed by thieves,
escaping slaves, and others being chased. He pointed out that
while fleeing they could lash back in a sudden kick and that pur-
suers would be powerless to stop themselves in time. Here is an
example of a movement strategy that is a miniature scenario of
malícia applicable to three different contexts: first, in its most
compact version, a quick diversion in the capoeira *jôgo*; second,
slightly more elaborated in a named subroutine that interrupts the

flow of the *jôgo* by 'circling' the ring; third, in actual practice outside the ring where it has a self-defense application. This demonstrates that similar physical signs can link events both in and beyond the capoeira world and shows one very concrete way in which lessons from the game can be applied to outside life.

However, there is even more to this seemingly simple scenario. Conceptually, this set of physical interactions may be interpreted, and intended, in a number of ways. In the *jôgo*, they can be done mockingly, by feigning fear when 'running away.' In practice, they can be done with deadly intent, the perfection of execution literally a life or death matter. What gives this kind of move so much potential significance, it gradually occurred to me, is its powerful indexical quality. That is, running away from anything serves as a break in the flow of events, a break which indexes both what has happened immediately prior to the flight and what will happen immediately after. For example, a thief steals a woman's handbag and starts to run. The running itself galvanizes the attention of the passersby: they look to see what is being run from and discover the distressed woman, now screaming, then they look to see what will happen to the fleeing thief. Often many will take up the pursuit (especially in Bahia, where they are much more diligent in such attempts than in the United States), not so much to engage in catching the thief, perhaps, as to be able to watch him being caught (or escaping). Their curiosity is drawn to know the outcome.

The dramatic power of this movement complex is utilized indexically in normal social interactions in Brazil as well. For a North American whose gestural repertoire is relatively small, Brazilian conversations are a marvel of kinesic elaboration. This is often remarked on by foreigners, some of whom will try to imitate the complex hand gestures which normally accompany speech. Toward the end of my fieldwork period, I began to notice that speakers, especially males, were in the habit of walking away from a group a few steps, only to return immediately to continue the conversation. This behavior was especially marked when there was any heat or anger in the debate. Because I was so steeped in capoeira interactions, I began to think about the similarity between this conversational gambit and 'pretend to run away.' As I observed conversations more closely, I realized that the speakers who employed this device were trying to gain or regain the attention of their fellows by use of this dramatic index.

Sometimes a man would further emphasize his turn away from the group by spitting before he turned back to the fray. The use of spitting in conjunction with the walk-away behavior was brought home to me at a festival when a group of people were sitting with me in a small open bar. One of the men would say something, walk over to the door and spit, then return to say something else. If no one paid attention to what he had to say, which was frequently the case, he would return to the door of the bar, spit again, then return to try once more. He was forced to do this partly because it is impolite to spit on the floor of a room, but also he was trying as dramatically as possible to get the attention of the group by use of these indexes, and frequently that is how this gestural complex is employed. This explains why it is common in arguments, when people tend to stop listening to each other, and also why it may be used more by those who are insecure of themselves. The abbreviated form of this behavior is simply to turn one's head and spit, and I have seen some people in Brazil (primarily men) who were hard-pressed to say anything without prefacing it in this way.

I believe it is useless to argue that there is any causal connection of influence between 'pretend to run away' as it is used in capoeira and the similar behavioral complex employed in everyday conversation, except to note that they are both employed as dramatic indexes. Yet the extreme similarity of form argues for a cultural unity of expression, evidence for the existence of something called cultural style, which links everyday life with folk art like capoeira in a deep way.[17] These links can often be verified by locals when called to their conscious attention, but, because of their subliminal nature, they are hard to make explicit and even harder to document. Cultural styles are composed of signs which are semiotically related, but functionally and pragmatically diverse: able to function in many ways, mean many things, but all in the same 'way.' Many such signs are preserved in physical habits, which are at once resistant to change and subliminal in action, therefore excellent vehicles for stylistic expression.

Tocar—Musical Play

Capoeira music is a complex system in itself, involving an instrumental ensemble, solo vocals, and a chorus. The system merits a separate study of its own, so the approach here will be to give an overview and basic outline of the most important forms, especially those related to key values like deception and solidarity. In the presentation of the syntagm of a capoeira *roda*, it was already necessary to refer to musical events, just as it has been helpful to refer to the song lyrics from time to time in the exploration of fundamental values. This illustrates the interdependence of the semiotic channels in capoeira, all of which must operate together for the art to assume its characteristic form in practice. In the same way, distinct levels of analysis in linguistics cannot be understood in isolation: there can be no adequate phonology without reference to syntax and no correct syntax independent of semantics.[1]

There can be no capoeira without music. Although some practice sparring is done without music in academies, this is merely training for the action in the ring, which is the event such training is designed for. During a performance, there is an intimate interplay between the musicians and the contestants in the ring, a relation of interdependence. As physical play changes, the music should change accordingly, and if the music changes, the contestants should take note and respond in kind. Thus there should always be communication between music and movement, and maintaining this relation is part of the job of the master or masters in charge of the *roda*. If the music stops, the action in the ring stops. If the music isn't right—for instance, if someone is playing out of rhythm—the contestants should stop to wait for it to be corrected. The musicians, all of whom are *capoeiristas* themselves, create the atmosphere within which the game comes to life; they make the game possible, and the game, in turn, gives meaning to the music.

In addition to this general interdependence between music and motion, there is reputedly a more specific kind. That is, many accounts of the sport relate the existence of distinct rhythms or 'beats' (*toques*), each of which has a name, although there is tremendous disagreement about which names refer to which *toques* and also about how many different *toques* exist. According to some sources, each named beat supposedly corresponds to, or calls forth, a different type of physical play. I went to Brazil believing this to be the case, but after learning to play the instruments and sing the songs, I began to doubt it. My current view, which I will attempt to document below, is that there is really only one basic capoeira rhythm, a meter in two (or some multiple), and that the named *toques* are all variations on it. Changes in the style of physical play attributed to rhythmic variation instead seem to me to be due mostly to changes in *tempo*. However, *toques* are generally associated with certain tempos. For instance, the *toque* called *Angola* is usually played at slow to medium tempos ($\quarternote = 84-108$), while *São Bento Grande* tends to be played fast to very fast ($\quarternote = 119-182$). These two are by far the most common *toques* and, in my experience, if one can play only these two, one can accompany ninety-nine percent of the *rodas* in Brazil.

I mentioned in chapter 4 that the typical progression in *Angola* games is for the tempo to start slow and to gradually increase. At any time the master may stop the action and begin again. He will usually start again by singing a *ladainha* litany, after which (following the *chula* verse) play will resume slowly, since *ladainhas* are always sung to slow tempos. I believe that this is the only way to reduce the speed of the music, since I never observed a case in which the tempo slowed while the musicians were playing, except when inexperienced students began unintentionally 'dragging.' In a typical event lasting several hours, the music may be stopped and restarted several times, and usually this is because the master wants to sing a *ladainha*, not because the action is 'too fast.' Some masters resist the general tendency to speed up the tempo and say that the mark of a good ensemble is when they can maintain an even tempo for a long time. Tempos vary less in *Regional* and *atual* games, as previously discussed, partly because they rarely sing *ladainhas,* and thus there is no occasion for slowing down.

The singing takes the form of call and response, characteristic of African and African-American music, and in theory any player can initiate *cantigas* ('songs' or 'chants') by yelling out a call, even those engaged in the ring, though the latter is rare. Ideally, all players should respond to the soloist, and keep responding until he stops. In some *rodas* there is very little singing, especially in the more agonistic styles, and older masters frequently complain that the youngsters are not interested in learning the songs. However, even today a capoeira student would be hard-pressed to call himself a *capoeirista,* no matter how excellent his physical prowess, unless he is able to play all the instruments and sing at least a few songs.

The Ensemble

The following instruments may be found in contemporary capoeira *rodas: berimbau* (a musical bow), *pandeiro* (tambourine), *agogô* (a two-toned clapperless bell), *reco-reco* (a notched bamboo scraper), and *atabaque* (a large drum resembling a conga) [see fig. 5.1]. Rego noted that, instead of the round tambourine, a square frame drum, called *adufe,* was formerly used, but it apparently has disappeared (1968: 83). Although I saw some *adufes* in the Recôncavo of Bahia, they were never used to accompany capoeira. The *reco-reco,* though rare,[2] is still being used in some of the more traditional *rodas,* though I never saw them in capoeira outside of Bahia.

Many masters say that the *atabaque* is a recent addition to the capoeira ensemble, and I believe this is true, since it is too heavy to carry easily. Capoeira was traditionally played outside, on the streets and in plazas, so only relatively light and portable instruments were preferred, especially in the days when the police might show up to arrest the players and they had to flee. On the plantations, the making of drums was usually prohibited, since their sound could carry long distances, and it was known that they

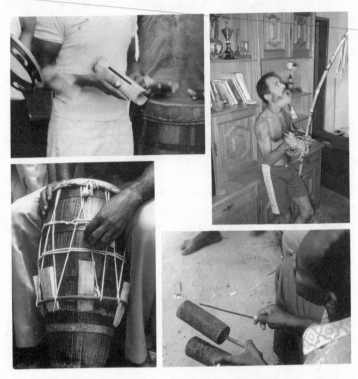

Figure 5.1   Capoeira ensemble. Clockwise from upper right: (1) Mestre Nô plays *berimbau* at home; (2) homemade *agogô*, Santo Amaro; (3) *atabaque* (wedge tuning), Santo Amaro; (4) *pandeiro, reco-reco, atabaque* (bolt tuning).

could be used for semantic communication. Today *atabaques* are frequently found in the academy setting, but almost never in street games.

If this is true, how is one to explain the painting by Rugendas (see fig. 2.2) showing capoeira being accompanied by a drum similar to an *atabaque*? I believe that during the slave era, when capoeira and other Afro-Brazilian musical forms were in development, instrumentation was quite variable. Since blacks rarely had the luxury of time and place, many *batuques* happened on the spur of the moment, and people used whatever instruments were available. Evidence for this comes from the use of pots and pans, plates and knives, and plenty of hand clapping in traditional *samba* groups. Over time, as the various musical genres became well established, the ensembles became more fixed. Even as recently as the 1950s, a photo of capoeira was taken in which one musician was playing a guitar (Ott 1955: 160)! For the same reason, it is possible that the *berimbau* itself was not even used with capoeira from the beginning. There is an oral tradition which relates that the *berimbau* was added to the martial training in order to disguise the self-defense as a dance. If this is the case, what was being done before the addition of the bow was arguably very different from the capoeira practiced today.

Originally all the instruments were handmade, of course, another reason to keep them small and simple, and even today many masters make their own *berimbaus,* although professional *berimbau* makers exist. The popularity of factory-made tambourines was probably one reason why the *adufe* became extinct, and it is the rare blacksmith who bothers to make an iron *agogô.* Most bells today are factory produced of aluminum or steel (but see fig. 5.1 for an exception).

The lead instrument in capoeira groups is the *berimbau,* and it is by far the most important. Without the *berimbau* there can be no capoeira, and if there is just one bow, and nothing else, it is enough for a game. Older masters say that traditionally there were three sizes of *berimbau* at an event, a small one called *viola,* a medium-sized one called *médio,* and a large one called *gunga.*[3] This is quite probably an African continuity, since sacred drum sets from Yoruba and Ewe traditions also come in sets of three, often referred to as the father, the mother, and the child. Such matched sets of *atabaques* are still found in Bahian *candomblé* and in Cuban *batá* and *conga* ensembles, for example.[4]

I never observed any contemporary event in which this traditional arrangement of three bows was strictly adhered to, however, though most players know the names of the different sizes. In practice, the number of *berimbaus* at a *roda* varied in my observations from one to seven, but most commonly there were three or four. Even when exactly three bows were used for a *roda,* I never saw a case in which they were deliberately arranged according to size, partly because few people bother to make the largest size any more. Nor was much effort expended on tuning the bows to each other, in most instances, though it may be that closer attention was paid to such details in the past.

There are always fewer of the other instrument types than *berimbaus,* so a typical ensemble might consist of three bows, two tambourines, one bell, and one *atabaque,* as in fig. 4.1. When games are held outdoors, *atabaques* and even bells are rarely seen. The music is begun by the lead *berimbau,* usually in the hands of a senior master, and the other instruments enter in the following order: first the other bows, then tambourines, bells, scrapers (if present), and drums last. After all the instruments have established the rhythm, the audience and other players may clap hands. These days young male *capoeiristas* in Bahia rarely clap, a tendency which is expressed in the song lyric, "Who plays tambourine is a man, who claps hands is a woman." This is a reference to the fact that any audience member (many of whom are women) may clap hands, but anyone who plays an instrument is also expected to go into the action and be tested. In the past, men who restricted themselves to clapping and never dared the ring were thought of as cowardly, therefore 'like women,' though this type of gender stereotyping is losing its point in a world where women are now entering the ring as *capoeiristas.*

In my analysis of the structure of capoeira music, I will focus on the *berimbau,* since it is the lead instrument which the others merely accompany. This is further justified by the fact that, unlike some other Afro-Brazilian forms, the supporting instruments do not play cross rhythms, but are restricted to doubling the beat of the bows, with a few fill-ins and improvisatory flourishes. Therefore it will be necessary to describe the form of the *berimbau* and how it is played in some detail.

THE *BERIMBAU*

Knowledge of how to build and play the *berimbau* was probably brought over from Africa, especially subequatorial Africa. Musical bows of almost identical design have been reported from Angola, South Africa, and Mozambique, although bows of different types are found throughout West Africa (Maraire 1982; Kubik 1979). Although musical bows are also found in aboriginal

South America, their form and mode of play are somewhat different, and it seems unlikely that there was influence from that direction (Izikowitz 1935: 205). Nonetheless, there seem to have been certain innovations in the style of play (as well as in external decoration) when the bow came to the New World. Perhaps the most important change is that in traditional Africa, the musical bow is primarily a solo instrument, used mostly for private entertainment, due partly to its soft sound compared to most drums (Maraire 1982: 55). In Brazil, the bow developed into an ensemble instrument, employed in public performances of capoeira and *samba*, although it still is sometimes hard to hear over the other instruments and crowd noise.

The word *berimbau* itself is a Portuguese word (though of uncertain origin) which in the past referred to the mouth harp (or Jew's harp), also called *guimbarde*. It came to be associated with the African type of musical bow because some of the early bows were played using the mouth as a resonator, like the mouth harp. Putting one end of a musical bow in the mouth (*berimbau da bôca*) is a style of play often seen in Africa. To distinguish between mouth bows and gourd resonated ones, the latter were called *berimbau da barriga* or 'stomach bows,' since the open end of the gourd is pulled on and off the stomach. Kubik points out that the sound of the word *berimbau* is phonetically similar to southern Bantu names for the bow, such as *mbulumbumba* (1979: 33), which would facilitate the convergence of terms. Rego reports that Brazilian bows are sometimes called *bucumbumba*, among many other names, and cites Ortiz on the Cuban *burumbumba;* however, he also offers the possibility of *kimbundo* (Angolan), *mbirimbau,* and even a *Mandinka* word *bilimbano* (1968: 73–74). The term *gunga*, the name for the mid- or large-sized capoeira bow, is almost certainly a Bantu word, probably derived from *Umbundu* (Angolan) *urucungo,* variations of which are also reported throughout Brazil and in Cuba, or from the unspecified Angolan *hungu* (cf. Shaffer 1977: 14; de Oliveira 1958: 19).

The Brazilian *berimbau* is a wooden pole (*vêrga* or *vara*), usually about fifty-six inches long (seven hand spans or 120 cm.), bent by a single metal string (*arame*), with a gourd resonator (*cabaça*) tied around both pole and string near one end. The bow is held in the left hand (by right-handed players) and the string is struck with a small stick (*vaqueta*) in the other hand (see fig. 5.2). The stick hand also holds a small rattle (*caxixí*) made of woven grass or vine, filled with seeds, shells, or pebbles. Between thumb and index finger of the bow hand, the player holds a coin (*moeda* or *dobrão*) or stone, which is used stop the string, thus producing two main tones (stopped and unstopped). There are reports of the *berimbau* being used in other ensembles, such as *samba de roda* or some types of cult activity, especially in the past, but today the bow is virtually an index of capoeira, since it is associated exclusively with that sport. *Capoeiristas* sport *berimbau* tatoos or jewelry and its image appears frequently on academy shirts and logos.

The best wood for the body of the bow is said to be *biriba* (probably either *Rollinia deliciosa* or *Annona lanceolata*), which has the requisite hardness with just the right amount of flexibility. The shaft should bend just slightly, not overbend, and should re-

Figure 5.2   Technique for playing the *berimbau*.

tain most of its straightness when unstrung. Because *biriba* is so heavy, some bow makers prefer *taipoca* (unidentified). Some say that in the past *pau d'arco* ('bow wood') was popular (*Tabebuia serratifolia* or *T. impetiginosa*), but now it is too expensive, since the plant is exported as a medicinal herb. Another good wood, also very heavy, is *pau-ferro*, 'ironwood' (*Caesalpinia ferrea*). One wood that should not be used is bamboo, which is too flexible, has a tendency to split, and since it is hollow it doesn't have the right sound. If someone has a bamboo *berimbau*, he is at once marked as a buffoon who doesn't understand the game.

Various species of gourds are used, the most common being *Cucurbita lagenaria*. Gourds with the thinnest skins make the best sound but are also the hardest to work, since they break easily when dry. Steel wire is salvaged from old truck tires by most *berimbau* makers in Bahia today, since it is free, but the tire cannot have been burned, since the heat makes the steel brittle. Steel or other iron alloys were probably used aboriginally in Africa, since metallurgy is quite old there, but both animal and vegetable fibers were also used, both in Africa and Brazil, in areas where metal was unavailable. The gourd and the wire are tied to the bow with cotton twine, though sometimes leather is used, and a piece of leather is placed over the top of the pole to keep the wire from cutting the wood. Two holes are drilled in the gourd through which cotton twine (sometimes waxed) is looped, and this loop is pulled over both pole and wire, kept on by the tension of the wire. If the bow is properly bent, the gourd should be no more than a handsbreadth from the bottom. The *caxixí* is woven of various kinds of vines or grasses, with a gourd bottom. One traditional coin used to stop the string is a copper *quarenta mil-réis* (literally, 'forty thousand royals'), a 'thousand royals' being a standard old-style monetary unit. Sometimes a hole is drilled in the coin and it is attached to the bow with a cord, so it won't get lost or stolen.

From the wealth of detail above, even more of which could be provided, it is evident that the *berimbau* is an instrument upon which much attention and love have been lavished. The lore of the *berimbau* is truly enormous, the instrument being very nearly sacred to capoeira players. For example, Bira Almeida, a master of the *Regional* style and former tournament player, nonetheless has a long, detailed account of how to make a *berimbau,* including injunctions that the wood "must be cut from a live tree in the forest on the right day and under the proper moon" (1981: 72). In describing the making and use of the stone for stopping the string, he continues, "Depending on you and the magic work involved, this stone can be a real *patuá* [amulet] and will protect your body against evil eyes" (p. 74). Fear of the 'evil eye' is common in many areas of the world and in Brazil is syncretized with similar beliefs about witchcraft and sorcery which came from Africa. Here is the idea of 'protecting' the body again, with the use of the *patuá* fetish, this time from one of the most modern and innovative of masters.

De Oliveira records an African myth relating to the origin of the musical bow, which he says comes from east and north Africa:

> A young girl went out for a walk. Upon crossing a
> stream, she knelt down and drank water with cupped
> hands. At the very moment when she had avidly satis-
> fied her thirst, a man dealt her a strong blow on the
> nape of the neck. As she died, she immediately trans-
> formed into a musical bow; her body became the
> wood, her limbs the cord, her head the sound box,
> and her spirit the melancholy and sentimental music.
> (de Oliveira 1958: 7)

Compare this with what I heard Mestre Nô say about himself one day at a capoeira event in Bahia: "I am capoeira. My body is a *berimbau.* My skeleton is the pole [*vêrga*]; my tongue is the coin [*dobrão*]; my head is the sound box [*caixa de som*]. One of my arms is the stick [*vaqueta*], one of the strands of my coiled hair is the string [*arame*], and my rattle when I was a baby is the *caxixí.*" What seems like an African continuity in the image of the bow as a body serves to demonstrate the strong identification between *capoeiristas* and the *berimbau* and emphasizes the spiritual aspect of the game latent in these beliefs, which is sometimes overtly expressed. For example, in the Brazilian religion of Umbanda,[5] some members associate the seven parts of the *berimbau* with the seven deities or 'lines' (*linhas*) of their pantheon.[6]

Berimbau part	*Spiritual correspondence*
1. bow wood (*vêrga*)	1. Oxóssi
2. wire (*arame*)	2. Oxalá
3. stick (*vaqueta*)	3. Ogûm
4. gourd (*cabaça*)	4. Pretos Velhos
5. stone or coin (*moeda*)	5. Xangô
6. rattle (*caxixí*)	6. Yemanjá
7. two cotton strings	7. Ibeji

All of these 'lines' derive from the names of Yoruba deities except the *pretos velhos,* who are said to be the spirits of deceased slaves. The reasons for the connection between the bow parts and the spirit beings are esoteric, having to do with shared qualities (iconic relations). For instance, the two cotton strings, one of which fastens the gourd to the bow, while the other keeps the top of the wire attached to it, are related in their 'twinning' to the *ibeji* who are the spirits of twins. It is not clear if these correspondences are relatively recent creations or are based on some earlier, little-known lore. None of the capoeira masters revealed to me anything like this scheme in connection with the instrument, but they do attribute a general aura of the sacred to it, which may have been more elaborate in the past.

The sound of the *berimbau* is often compared to a melancholy cry and frequently related to the moans of slaves longing for their African homeland. Once again, the words of the master capture something of the intensity of the music for adepts of the game: "The *berimbau* can pacify the soul when played in melancholy solos; the rhythm is black and strong, a deep and powerful pulse that reaches the heart. It inundates mind, space, and time with the intensity of an ocean tide. The dense aura that emanates from the single musical bow slowly envelopes [*sic*] you. Without your realizing it, the powerful magic of the *berimbau* has tamed your soul." (Almeida 1981: 63).

BERIMBAU MUSIC

Capoeira rhythms on the *berimbau* sound at first like an alternation between two basic tones: a high note produced by coin or stone pressed firmly against the string (stopped) and a low note on the open string (unstopped). Just as there is turn-taking in the game, for example in the alternation of initiative (attack) and response (defense), the high and low tones also 'take turns' sounding in a musical dialogue. One way to view this musical alternation, then, would be as an analogue to the interplay of attack and defense, the give and take of the physical dialogue. In the ring, there is also deception, the breaking of patterns, which might involve a player attacking twice in a row (or more), turning dialogue into aggressive physical diatribe. *Malícia* in the ring is echoed by 'deceptive' bow playing, in which the ear is 'tricked' into expecting a high tone and a low one is produced instead (or the reverse).

Such deceptive music relies on a third major tone of the instrument, which I call the 'buzz' tone, produced by holding the coin lightly against the string and hitting near it.[7] The result is really a non-tone if done correctly, but it sometimes sounds like a note halfway between the other two. Actually, there are two buzz tones, one struck with the stick and the other made with the coin alone, just brushing it lightly against an already vibrating string. By lingering on the buzz, a player may move at will to the higher or lower notes (usually about a whole tone apart), providing the flexibility necessary for deceptive playing.

Practically speaking, a musician lingers on the buzz note, which acts as a drone, and from which he can move to the high or low tones, forming patterns. In this guise, the drone buzz can be seen as midway between the two tones, as the link between opposing forces. This is emphasized by the fact that a player usually strikes the high tone above the coin with the stick and the low tone below it, the buzz being physically produced in an intermediate position. Since the buzz itself has no clear pitch, it can be seen as mediating between noise and tonality, perhaps as the pretonal matrix from which pitches are born. The sound of the buzzing *berimbaus* thus creates a diffuse field out of which the discrete tones and therefore the rhythmic beats seem to emerge. In this sense, the buzz is at once a mediator of rhythmic and tonal values and the undifferentiated ground which transcends those values: the matrix from which the very possibility of musical form itself, in this genre, may be born.[8]

In the physical domain, the analogue of the buzz note is the *ginga*, out of which all attacks and escapes are born. The *ginga* is neither attack nor escape, but it contains both. It is said that the advanced player never uses the *ginga*, but from another perspective everything he does is *ginga*. Likewise, the *ginga*, for most players, provides continuity between interchanges, a recovery position from which one is not obliged to either attack or defend (at least for a moment). Both the buzz and the *ginga* insure the flow of the game—one the musical flow, the other physical flow—providing the smoothness characteristic of capoeira that distinguishes it from many other martial arts. Scholars of play emphasize the feeling of flow in describing how one can 'lose' oneself in the activity. This also relates to an altered sense of time, which many agree is an important characteristic of play states (for example, Grathoff 1970: 78–79, 109, 150). Many *capoeiristas* report that they experience altered states during play, and they relate these states specifically to the music, but they are not often consciously aware of the structures which help to create, for example, the sense of flow.

In summary, the *berimbau* player can express *malícia* by artfully creating and breaking rhythmic patterns, which involves the alternation of the two opposing pitches. This alternation is iconic with the opposition of the two adversaries in the ring, which is mediated by the *ginga*, just as the tones are mediated by the buzz note. Both these mediators are necessary to the maintenance of the flow of the game, and it is out of this mediation that the possibility of opposition emerges. As signs of flow, both the *ginga* and the buzz can express the comradeship between players, the cooperation necessary for a successful game that also marks the limits to aggression.

Physical play stops and starts as players enter and leave the ring and when the inner games are called, but the music continues throughout, except when the entire game is stopped to begin again by singing another *ladainha*. Therefore *malícia* in the music cannot be so extreme as to interrupt the flow completely, since then it would be disruptive to the game. As a result, I will argue that music is the privileged domain of comradeship (communitas) relative to the physical interaction, which tends to fore-ground competition and *malícia*. Both values can be expressed through either channel, but the instrumental music is preferen-tially weighted toward the expression of cooperation, as a check against the violent tendencies of physical play. If this is true, it provides structural evidence for why the agonistic styles should be weaker in music, the ludic styles stronger. More evidence for this contention will be provided when vocal patterns are exam-ined below and in the following chapter.

TOQUES

Thus far I have distinguished four sounds that can be made on the *berimbau,* the two main tones and two types of buzz note. Since all four of these can be played with the gourd on or off the body, the result is a basic inventory of eight notes. This does not exhaust the possibilities of the instrument, but is complete enough to allow the major beats or *toques* to be notated (see fig. 5.3). Given a basic cycle of two beats, the *toques* vary melodi-cally, according to whether a high pitch or a low pitch is struck on a given beat, and rhythmically, according to whether a beat is accented or unaccented. If a beat is accented, one of the two clear tones is usually played with the gourd open (off the body); if a beat is unaccented, a buzz note is played with the gourd closed (on the body). This is the normal way these notes are played, but not the only way, since all of the eight possibilities are sometimes used. Unaccented beats can also be played with the *caxixí,* which can substitute for the buzz notes. This has the advantage that a tone can be sustained while the rattle plays over it.

The *toques* take the form of a theme with variations. The theme is usually one 'measure' of two beats and the variations can last for several measures before the theme is heard again.[9] A few of the themes are four beats long and the longest one I recorded is eight beats (four 'measures'). There are some standard varia-tions for each theme, but it is also permissible to improvise varia-tions at will, as long as signature theme is maintained. The result is that many of the same variations are heard with several themes, which is one reason I believe that all *toques* are variations on each other.

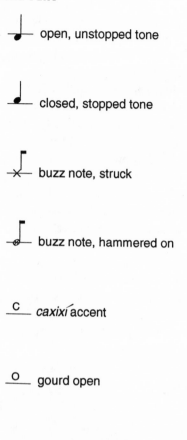

open, unstopped tone

closed, stopped tone

buzz note, struck

buzz note, hammered on

caxixí accent

gourd open

gourd closed

Figure 5.3   Key to *berimbau* notation. In general, the gourd is open on all sounded tones (●) and closed on all buzzed tones (x). The bottom two diacritics are only used when this is not the case. There are no examples of the closed gourd on a sounded tone in the following *toques*, but this pattern change is sometimes used, for instance, in many versions of *Iuna*.

I mentioned that the traditional *berimbau* ensemble consisted of three bows, and the masters who affirm this also say that when they played together each bow played a different, complementary pattern. This is in accord with many African drumming styles that have interlocking parts played by different instruments. In this view of the tradition, there were originally three *berimbau* patterns—theme on the lead bow, countertheme on the middle bow, and improvised variations on the high bow—played together to form one *toque*. At some point the ensemble of three bows stopped being strictly adhered to, and I believe it was at that time that *toques* which had formerly been supporting patterns began to be thought of as independent. This would explain (1) the proliferation of named *toques*, many of which are only known by one or two masters; (2) the confusion as to how these *toques* are to be played; and (3) the fact that many, if not all, *toques* can be played together as complementary varations. The third point also accounts for how *capoeiristas* today are able to play music together without the games being lost in musical confusion. This is only a hypothesis, to be sure, but one which helps explain an otherwise puzzling situation, and one which is in line with the reports of the oldest and most conservative masters.

In traditional games the *ladainha* solo is always sung to the *toque* called *Angola,* appropriately enough. As mentioned above, this pattern is usually played at a slow tempo, gradually speeding up to a medium tempo:

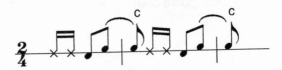

Figure 5.4   *Toque: Angola*

This is the signature theme of the *Angola* pattern and, to make comparison easier, I will leave out the variations in this and the other *toques* to be notated. But the reader should bear in mind that no theme is ever played in practice without a host of variations as well. In general, there is agreement about how this *toque* should sound (Onori 1988: 56; Shaffer 1977: 47), but some masters also report another version of the same *toque* which is an inversion. This *toque* is also called *Angola* by some, but most masters know it as *São Bento Pequeno* ('Little São Bento'):

Figure 5.5 *Toque: São Bento pequeno*

A comparison of the themes makes it clear that one is the mirror image of the other and that it would be quite possible to super-impose the two to form a kind of crossing pattern. In addition, some masters record *toques* called *Angolinha* (the diminuitive form of *Angola*), *Angola dobrado* ('Doubled' or 'Folded *Angola*'), and even *Angola Pequena* ('Little *Angola*'). Since there is not much agreement about how these should sound, I won't attempt to no-tate them, but the names themselves strongly suggest that they are variations of each other. Mestre Bimba was the only master in recent times who apparently didn't know the *toque Angola* (or wouldn't admit to it), but his version of *Banguela* is virtually iden-tical to what the others call *Angola* (Shaffer 1977: 52). I conclude from this and other differences in Bimba's nomenclature that he attempted to rename most of the *toques* to suit his purposes in restructuring capoeira. Since he wanted to distance himself from traditional *Angola*-style capoeira, he decided to rename that *toque Banguela*.

The most widely known and agreed upon *toque* is *São Bento Grande*, played at fast and very fast tempos in *rodas* throughout Brazil:

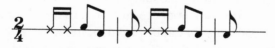

Figure 5.6 *Toque: São Bento grande*

Notice that this is a simple variation on *São Bento Pequeno* (above), substituting two eighth notes for a sustained quarter note. Once again there is virtually universal agreement on this *toque*, except by Mestre Bimba and some of his students. Bimba plays an inverted version of the above, sometimes known as *São*

Bento Grande Regional, to distinguish it from the more common version, which is then renamed *São Bento Grande de Angola* to avoid confusion (in his scheme!).

Figure 5.7   *Toque: São Bento grande Regional*

Others know the above *toque* as *São Bento Pequeno* (instead of the one shown in fig. 5.5) and still others know it as *Santa Maria.* From this point on, the confusion increases with the number of *toques,* but I believe my main point is clear. All the above can be played together as variations of each other, though they usually aren't due to tempo conventions, and so can most of the other named *toques.*

Variation around a central rhythmic structure seems to be the common pattern for capoeira playing, and the constraints on this variation apparently have been loosening since the beginning of the twentieth century. Additional evidence of this is provided by the fact that masters feel free to invent new *toques* which are variations on old themes. It is said that Bimba invented the *toque* called *Iuna,* to be used as background for games between masters or *capoeiristas formados.* Some dispute this origin, but *Iuna* has caught on in the capoeira community. Usually played at a slow tempo, this *toque* is also used at wakes for dead capoeira masters to show them respect. Mestre Canjiquinha invented at least two *toques: Samongo* and *Muzenza,* both of which are versions of the *samba.*

The fact that *samba* can be played on the *berimbau* by most *capoeiristas* is further evidence for the close association of the two pastimes in Brazilian life. Even though it seems quite different from the true capoeira patterns at first, upon closer examination it can also be seen as a variation on the standard pattern, with some shifts in accent:

Figure 5.8 *Toque: samba*

Two *toques* are said to have been used to warn *capoeiristas* of the approach of hostile elements, either the police or the plantation overseers: *Aviso* and *Cavalaria*. The first means 'warning' and the second refers to the mounted 'cavalry' corps used in the cities to catch *capoeiristas* and other nefarious types (see chapter 2). The pattern is said by some to be an imitation of the hoofbeats of the horses.

The longest named *toque* I encountered is associated with a particular song in such a way as to suggest the possible survival of a vestige of African drum language. The communication of praise names, proverbs, and other phrases is found in some African drumming systems, facilitated by an iconicity between the tonal structure of the spoken languages and the tones produced on the drums (see Nketia 1971; Stern 1957). Since there are eight basic tones on the *berimbau*, that is plenty for an imitation of spoken language in the African mode. One of the named rhythms known by several capoeira masters is called "'*Panhe laranja no chão tico-tico*," and one day Mestre Canjiquinha played it for me while singing a syllable for each note of the beat. Even though the song is in Portuguese, the one-to-one correspondence between notes on the bow and syllables in the phrase is extremely reminiscent of the way drum language works. Could this be the vestige of a formerly elaborated structural aspect of the music, now almost lost, or is it simply a playful imitation of that tradition? Actual drum language does survive in some of the Afro-Bahian cults but often it is not understood well, since the languages themselves are usually learned by rote and few initiates can translate phrases literally.

pan - he la- ran - ja no chão   ti-co tic(o)
("pick up the orange on the floor, sparrow")

se meu a-mor   fôr-s'em bor(a)   eu não fic(o)
("if my love goes away, I won't stay")

Figure 5.9   *Toque: 'tico-tico'*

VOCAL MUSIC PATTERNS

The sound quality of the voice in capoeira is distinctive and not easy to characterize. It is almost a yell or a sung holler, reminiscent of the timber of African-American work songs or 'field hollers.' As such the voice is loud and strident, but should be clearly melodic as well. Sometimes the melodic feel of the solo lines seems dissident or 'blue' to ears attuned to European pitch relations. This may be related to the uneven vocal skills of many of the singers, but at times it appears to be quite intentional and may have more to do with the tonal peculiarities of *berimbau* tuning, which are examined below.

The same oppositions and values are able to be expressed in the singing as are revealed in the instrumental music. As mentioned above, the vocal interaction in capoeira is basically call and response, with a soloist giving the call and a chorus the response. A soloist will usually initiate a song by singing the response line first, then the call line, after which the chorus should come in on the refrain. Sometimes the soloist will omit the initial 'prompt' of the response line and simply sing the call line, assuming that everyone knows the response already. This can be tricky, especially if the soloist switches suddenly from one song to a new one without a pause. In this manner he can 'fool' some or all chorus members into singing the wrong response. When a soloist discovers that chorus members are not paying close attention, he can shift rapidly from song to song, testing and challenging the chorus to keep up. This is one kind of vocal *malícia* on the part of the caller.

Since the soloist must initiate songs if there is to be any singing, he has 'power' over the chorus, in a limited sense. Structurally, the situation is analogous to the powerful master (soloist) and the mass of subservient slaves or clients (chorus). Is there ever a time when the chorus can turn the tables on the soloist, to complete the analogy of subordinate deception? The answer is yes. If the chorus withholds its response, the soloist cannot make music. This happens, for instance, when a young, inexperienced singer attempts the role of soloist and doesn't quite bring it off. Generally, the senior masters of the *roda* initiate the calls and the younger players respond, though it is increasingly difficult to get young people to sing at all. When an unknown voice begins a song, players may hesitate to respond if any of the following conditions occur: the call is weak or hesitant; the pitch of the response is not clearly indicated, or the rhythm is off; the song is inappropriate to the current action in the ring; the players are simply not inspired to respond. Thus the chorus tends to control who they are willing to respond to and who they aren't, which explains exactly why I was so nervous after initiating a call during the game described in the Preface.

A close examination of the structure call/response reveals a paradigmatic contrast between elements which has two main components: a numerical opposition—one/many—and a relation of precedence or priority—initiator/respondents—since the chorus can neither start a song nor continue it if the soloist stops. In addition, there is a syntagmatic relation of alternation as follows: (a,b,a,b,a,b . . .) where 'a' is solo and 'b' chorus. The paradigmatic contrasts can be seen as iconic to certain kinds of power relations, such as master/slaves or patron/clients. In Africa there was slavery before the Europeans came, but in a different form and on a restricted scale, at least below the Sahara. Since the call and response structure was and is common in many traditional societies, it was more likely used (or available) as an icon of social relations such as: king/subjects, household head/household members, cult leader/

followers, and so forth. All of these relationship types combine both dimensions: the individual/collective opposition and various relations of power.[10]

It should be emphasized that there is no *necessary* correspondence between any structural pattern and a given cultural interpretation. Rather these structures are *potential* meaning vehicles, able to be used in a variety of ways. For instance, the opposition individual/collective could be used to stand for only one structural component, that of one/many, while ignoring relations of precedence or power (or the reverse). This is always an option in the generation of cultural meanings from significant relations: selectively 'focusing' on one structure while 'ignoring' others. In the same way the syntagmatic alternation cycle can come to the fore, highlighting the turn-taking aspect of both the singing and the physical dialogue. In that case the call and response could be taken as iconic with the alternation of attack and escape in the ring, and the relation one/many would be 'ignored,' or temporarily neutralized.

Therefore when a soloist initiates a call, it can be like a contestant in the ring initiating an attack: both provoke responses and in both cases the breaking of expectations can provoke an inadequate response. In the same way that call and response alternate vocally, attack and escape alternate physically. To increase the flow between call and response, a soloist can overlap the chorus, coming in before the refrain is over. This vocal overlapping can be seen as a mediating element similar to the *ginga* in the physical game and the buzz tone on the *berimbau*. It is neither strictly call nor response, but something in between, serving to drive the rhythm and increase the fervor of the response, in most cases. Usually the soloist overlaps by singing a descant or harmony line above the chorus, attempting to strengthen the response and create an ambience of cooperation, minimizing the structural opposition between call and response. Since, in general, any capoeira player can become (or aspire to become) a soloist, and since soloists trade off, alternately merging with and emerging from the chorus, the underlying commonality of participation tends to be thematized. Normal turn-taking is the rule in solo-chorus interaction, since, as I argued above, the solidarity of communitas is the chief message in that domain and relations of deception are only of secondary importance. This also explains why the soloist usually starts a call by singing the choral response, to aid in the successful creation of vocal solidarity. Predictably enough, there is very little overlapping call and response singing outside of *Angola* circles, since the importance of singing in general is reduced in those settings. If my hypothesis is correct, this is because the agonistic styles emphasize competition, which causes signs of communitas and cooperation to fall away because they are not as highly valued.

Although cooperation and comradeship are usually fore-grounded in the vocal domain, there are indications that this was less true in the past. In chapter 2, I alluded to the tradition of verbal dueling, which was quite common (and still is) in several performance genres closely related to capoeira. In *Angola* games one can still see some degree of rivalry over the question of who will be the soloist and initiate songs. This relates to the implicit convention that the senior master has precedence in the singing, so that when several masters are present at a game there can still be some 'jockeying' for priority. This kind of rivalry is often very subtle, when present at all, in contemporary games, but in the next chapter I will discuss some evidence that seems to indicate that verbal dueling, and therefore vocal *malícia*, are still part of the capoeira esthetic, even if their elaboration is largely a thing of the past.

In addition to the overlap between solo and chorus, there is another mediating element in the vocal domain, namely the silence between songs, when only the instruments (and the contestants) are playing. This is also like the *ginga*, a recovery period which marks a suspension of the main action, during which there is temporarily neither attack nor defense. The pregnant pause between one song and the next, like the buzz note, is the diffuse or empty space at the center of the sound, out of which the vocal dialogue will arise. An alert group of musicians will use this time to watch the action in the ring and wait for an interchange which inspires them to make a commentary in song.

Thinking of silence as a positive aspect of the semiotic structure of a communicative system perhaps seems unusual at first, until one notices that there are many uses for silence and that it can have several disparate, even contradictory, qualities. As Foucault remarked in relation to large-scale phenomena, "There is not one but many silences, and they are an integral part of the strategies that underlie and permeate discourses" (1980: 27). Even in the capoeira domain I have already distinguished two general types: the silence between songs and the silence between call and response. It is this second type which can be overlapped with singing, to produce a conceptual pause that can be seen as either silent or filled (or perhaps both).

In the movement domain, I showed how counterattacks could be classified as either attacks or defenses, whereas the *ginga* might be more clearly seen as neither. In the same way, overlapping call and response singing links both sides of an opposition, while the space between songs is neither call nor response. At the microstructural level, then, in at least two distinct semiotic domains, capoeira can express both the unity of oppositions and the sublation of those oppositions into a new category within which they are neutralized. The game can be used to express the idea that solo and chorus, attack and defense, extremes which seem opposed, are identical beneath the surface; furthermore, within that identity, the very notion of opposition itself becomes meaningless. Even if these structural forms remain latent most of the time, they form an important ground for the overt expressions of communitas and transcendence in the verbal discourse of the players.

LADAINHA AND CHULA

The *ladainha,* as we have seen, is a traditional solo sung before the most important bouts in *Angola* games and to formally begin the *roda.* It is always followed by a call and response sequence, the *chula,* which is unusual in that the response changes each time it is sung: the chorus simply echoes what the soloist sings (see chapter 6). There is, however, a limited set of calls from which the soloist can choose, and there are certain sequences of calls which tend to be sung in a specific order. The *chula* acts as a kind of ritual invocation, since among the calls are lines praising God, praising one's master, praising the game of capoeira, and so forth. The *ladainhas* contain some of the most profound capoeira philosophy, including expressions of *malícia* and of the comradeship between players.

Although there are a set of traditional *ladainhas,* one of which a master may elect to sing, it is also acceptable to improvise one on the spot, a practice rarely seen today. The point of this improvisation is to make a comment on the players about to start the action, to prepare them mentally and spiritually, to teach them something of the philosophy of the game and of life. At the same time, of course, the soloist expresses how he is feeling at the moment. One master who still improvises *ladainhas* for special occasions is Mestre Moraes, not surprisingly one of the most conservative *Angola* masters in Brazil. He does this out of a deep respect for the tradition, and because he is proud of his verbal ability and beautiful voice. At the same time, he is most resistant to any new songs among the traditional repertoire of *corridos* (normal call and response chants), since he considers them inappropriate innovations.

Indications are that improvised *ladainhas* were much more common in the past and that, in general, solos were used more often to begin new bouts. Even now, play is usually stopped for a new *ladainha* in *Angola* circles before important matches, such as when two masters confront each other. I believe that when the *ladainha* is omitted in modern *Regional* and *atual* games, this represents the final step in a long process wherein the solo has been used less and less often to introduce bouts and where improvised *ladainhas* have given way to standardized ones. Likewise, the solo calls in regular *corridos* can be freely improvised, if done well, but in this case also there is much more improvisation and even solo variation in the ludic styles than in the agonistic ones. Notice that the loss of improvisation in the singing seems to correspond to the loss of variation in the physical dialogue, if it is true, as I have argued, that modern, agonistic styles have become more routinized.

Song Melody

Although I will not provide an exhaustive analysis of the melodic structure of capoeira songs, which would have to include many notations, a few general observations about how melodies are constructed will reinforce some of the points made so far. As one might expect, solo lines are usually more melodically complex than choral refrains, but in both the general pattern is a stepwise jumping movement between a few primary pitches, often resembling a major or minor triad. Even in the long, improvised *ladainhas*, extended phrases are often sung on a single pitch before jumping to another, and most melodies hover around a small number of harmonically related tones. Intervals of thirds, fifths, and octaves are overwhelmingly predominant in these solos, with smaller steps sometimes ornamenting the passage between them. It is possible that the natural harmonics from the one-stringed *berimbau* have strongly influenced the melodic esthetic of the singers, although none of my informants was able to articulate this verbally.

Another interval frequently found in the chorus is a major second, or whole step, which corresponds approximately to the difference between a stopped and an unstopped string in the bow (but see below for qualification). Several choral responses are limited to that one interval, for example, *moleque é tu* ('the urchin is you'); or *Senhor São Bento* ('Great Saint Benedict'), while a host of others add just one pitch to the whole step relation. This means that the two-tone high/low alternation, or the three-tone high/low/buzz, both structurally resonant with physical interaction, are reiterated and played within melodic form as well. Even where the verbal phrase is quite long, it is common for only a few tones to be used and for long utterances to be sung on a single pitch. One example is the song *'Panhe laranja* notated above, one version of which has the whole refrain sung on only two tones, a whole step apart, exactly as the *berimbau* would play it. Likewise, there is a song with the refrain, "*é jôgo practicado na terra do São Salvador*" ("it's a game played in the land of São Salvador"), which uses only three tones, and most of the phrase is sung on a single pitch. I don't want to give the impression that this is the only melodic pattern in capoeira singing, or that all the songs conform to this format, but stepwise jumping does seem to be a fundamental way that melodies are constructed in the majority of the songs.

Vocal harmony is not always found in capoeira singing, but it is occasionally present, especially if masters are strong singers themselves. The most common practice is for soloists to sing a descant harmony over the chorus, or the last part of the chorus, as in the overlapping call/response described above. Sometimes the singers in the chorus will respond in two-part harmony, usually when the refrain has several variations that produce harmonies when sung together. When these combine with a descant from the soloist, the result can be a three-part harmony, at least briefly, which is the height of harmonic complexity in capoeira singing. The harmonic intervals are almost always thirds, fifths, and octaves, as above, and in this case seem to be confined to what I heard as a major scale.

For some time I assumed that the interval between stopped and unstopped strings on the *berimbau* was in fact a whole tone, but upon closer listening, and comparing several bows, I realized that the interval was usually somewhat less than a whole step but more than a half-step. In Western musical terms this kind of pitch is sometimes called a 'quarter tone' or (more generally) a 'microtone,' and the effect in this case is that the interval can be heard (by Western ears) either as a major second (whole step) or a minor second (half-step). In practice this means that *berimbau* music can be used to accompany songs in various modes or scales, with either a major or minor feel, but always with a slight dissonance. The result is a kind of harmonic ambiguity similar in many respects to the indeterminacy of the buzz tone. As Keil (1987) has shown, such dissonances are often neglected in musical analysis, but may be keys to understanding why music has a characteristic 'swing' or 'push.' They can also be important in enticing audience participation, which is why he refers to them as "participatory discrepancies" (see also Alén 1986). The fact that the voice of the *berimbau* is often identified by its peculiar 'moaning' sound could well be related to the unsettling but stimulating effect of this complex interval. The haunting quality of the bow's voice is said to 'call' (*chamar*) players to come and play, enticing them into the ring.

Musical Innovations

As I have shown repeatedly, changes in the musical structure of capoeira are a major distinguishing feature between styles of play. In general the newer and more agonistic styles, especially *Regional*, deemphasize the musical component, particularly the songs, since the main interest is in the physical contest. Even when there is singing in these events, it tends to be mere background, often lacking the sense of involvement in and interplay with the action.

In most *Regional*- and some *atual*-style *rodas*, there is no introductory *ladainha* at all, and therefore no *chula*, since these two are necessarily linked. Just as with the loss of the *chamada* subroutines, the absence of these forms reduces the power of the performers to comment on the action in the ring, to frame the action by highlighting or even interrupting it, thereby reducing much of the expressive potential in the game. Since they have little or no reason to stop the action, masters lose some measure of control over events, nor can they easily slow down the tempo of play.

One traditional role of an older master, when he is no longer physically able to challenge the young players, is to be a source of knowledge and wisdom. A primary channel for the expression of these gifts is in the songs, especially the *ladainhas*, since play is stopped and all attention focused on the soloist while they are sung. Sometimes in agonistic games *ladainhas* are sung by two or more people together while physical play continues, indicating that this function of the songs has been forgotten. As a result, respect for masters in general has dwindled in the agonistic styles, and younger masters must sometimes resort to force in order to keep their students in line. If an older master cannot compete physically with a younger player, and if physical competition is the focus of the sport, his role becomes secondary, even superfluous.

New songs are being written all the time for capoeira, which is fine in itself, but in many cases the traditional call and response structure is not adhered to. Long melodies, which might be appropriate for solos like a *ladainha*, end up being sung by more than one person at a time while action continues in the ring. The result of these innovations is that the structural oppositions between master and students (solo and chorus) and between rival soloists are lost. How can there be rivalry for solos when two rivals can simply sing the solo together? When these structural features disappear, certain aspects of potential expression are reduced, and the integral connection between the semiotic channels tends to be loosened. This is why the music in the newer styles of capoeira begins to take on a 'background' quality; young players in these games simply do not understand that the singing is supposed to comment on the action. In some arenas, therefore, the entire domain of vocal music seems to be weakening, falling out of popularity, as many young players are lax in responding to any song. To such players, focused on the agonistic interchange and how they might defeat some opponent, the songs may seem useless, even effeminate.

The recent trend toward reunification of the two styles into the current *atual* blend has, to some degree, resulted in a revival of interest in songs and singing. A major influence here has been the resurgence of *Angola* style capoeira itself, since the masters who self-identify with this approach make sure their students are schooled in all aspects of the music. Of course, one should be careful not to think of *Angola* style as merely preserving past traditions. It is clear that changes and innovations are part of all contemporary play, regardless of how it may be labeled, and there are significant differences between today's *Angola* practices and those of the era before academies, for instance.

As capoeira moves into arenas outside Brazil, linguistic barriers are obvious impediments to the dissemination of the singing. Students in the United States or Europe must learn enough Portuguese to be able to respond on the refrains, but only rarely will a foreign player feel confident enough to sing a solo *ladainha* litany, let alone improvise a new one. In summary, it seems clear that the importance of the *berimbau* and the instrumental ensemble to future capoeira play is assured, but the centrality of the singing and the form it will take in the future is very much in question. It may be that recent conservative trends and the interest in reunification of styles will combine to reinvigorate the vocal repertoire; alternatively, agonistic and martial interests may converge with linguistic boundaries to cause the singing to fade away or become vestigial to the practice of the game.

Brincar—Verbal Play

The song texts of capoeira reinforce the physical and musical play of the game, offering further semiotic possibilities, especially in the more direct fields of semantic and pragmatic meaning. Here continuities between the game and society at large can be made explicit, with specific references to sexual relations, economic facts, religious beliefs—in short, any aspect of culture the players choose to comment on. Most of the capoeira songs are in Portuguese, but once in a while there are words or phrases in African (or even Tupian) languages; though it is frequently hard to make definite attributions, since meanings are often in dispute or lost altogether. Scholars who have studied the influence of African languages on Brazilian Portuguese generally concur that few phonological or syntactic effects can be clearly documented, but that lexical borrowing has been significant (Megenney 1978; Mendonça 1973). Words of African origin are especially common in Bahian usage, and the songs of capoeira are no exception.

Sometimes the lyrics speak directly about social conditions, but more often, true to form, the allusions are indirect: couched in proverbs, metaphors, the many tropes of ambiguity. Capoeira players sing about comradeship and they sing about deception, but in language play, messages about harmony can imply treachery and songs about double-dealing can seem humorous. In other words, deceptive language as a form allows for a mediation between apparently contradictory values, and the creation of ambiguity becomes an appealing refusal to see things in simple, straightforward terms.

When is it appropriate to initiate a song, and what song should be chosen at any given time during the event? Criteria for the introductory *ladainha* are twofold: since this solo begins the event or any important match, the song should be directed primarily at the players about to enter the ring—preparing them for the contest—and secondarily to all the players at the event, invoking important ideas and values central to the game in general. The *chula* always follows the *ladainha* and functions in a similar way, except that the second function is usually primary. The phrases chosen (from a limited set) may honor any aspect of the game, including places, masters, and key values, but it is difficult within that fixed form to refer specifically to a given player or situation.

The regular songs, the *corridos,* should be sung in response to events in the ring or to provoke certain events. This was an essential aspect of singing in the past, still understood by *Angola*-style masters today, that represents part of the challenge of attaining complete mastery of the sport. The improvisation of solo lines is part of this skill, but an equally valuable talent is to use an old song in a new way, to introduce it at the right moment, such that the physical contest creates a new context for meaning with the song. In this way the traditional repertoire is constantly being pragmatically 'renewed,' while the semantic 'content' of texts remains essentially unchanged. Folk performers of capoeira have always understood that meaning is crucially linked to context. This is especially true of the *corridos* as a subgenre, and I will argue below that these songs differ significantly from the *ladainha/chula* complex in that respect.

The simplest kind of ambiguity in song texts is that of lexical polysemy. When examining the consensual meanings and etymologies of key terms from the song lyrics, I was struck over and over again by how often all of the potential meanings of a given term could be applicable, even those which seemed apparently contradictory. For example, the word *ligeiro* is frequently used to describe the quickness of players, as in this song (cited more fully below):

| s: | Esse nêgo é ligeiro | That guy is quick |
| c: | Dá, dá, dá no nêgo | Give, give, give it to him [1] |

One dictionary defines the word as follows: "**ligeiro -ra** (adj.) light, not heavy; slight, thin, slender; quick, agile, nimble; swift, fast; flighty; slippery, dishonest" (Taylor 1980: 388). It was quite a surprise to discover that a word I initially thought was a simple reference to speed, since that was the context in which I learned it, also had a metaphorical extension to 'slippery, dishonest,' linking quickness with the idea of *malícia*. Another example is the word *danado*, which can occur in exactly the same syntactic context as *ligeiro* in the song above: "**danado -da** (adj.) damned, cursed; mad; rabid; angry, wild, 'sore'; clever, smart" (Taylor 1980: 197). Once again an unexpected turn, this time allowing a cursed, rabid individual, perhaps a slave driven to distraction, to also be 'clever, smart.' This kind of ambiguity is found to some extent in all language, but is especially typical of the polysemy in black dialects in the New World, characterized by the positive valuation, sometimes privileged, of words with negative connotation in general use (for example, see Holt, pp. 140–51, in Kochman 1972). In capoeira songs, this polysemy allows for either positive or negative connotations to predominate in a given context, or for both to apply at once, creating ambiguity. Therefore a singer can highlight a specific aspect of a word, for instance, to praise or tease a player, or he may want to insult a player and praise him at the same time, in concert with the ambivalent feelings players frequently have about each other.

Since capoeira is a way of life to dedicated participants, not just an occasional diversion from it, the songs (cf. Rego 1968: 51, 48 for following songs) reflect this by portraying aspects of the entire life cycle:

s:	Eu naci no Sabado	I was born on Saturday
	no Domingo caminhei	on Sunday learned to walk
	na Segunda-feira	and then on Monday
	a capoeira jogei	I played capoeira

As in the North American myth of John Henry, who was born to drive steel, here we have a Bahian born to play capoeira.

| s: | naci dentro da pobreza | I was born in poverty |
| | não naci na raça pobre | not born of a poor race |

Here the pride of ancestry asserts itself over the circumstances of poverty and, by implication, slavery. In addition to mythic and naturalistic references to birth, there are evocations of mother love and to the period of infancy and youth:

s: chore menino	cry little boy
c: nhê nhê nhê	nyeh nyeh nyeh
s: menino chorão	big cry baby
c: nhê nhê nhê	nyeh nyeh nyeh
s: ele quer a mãe	he wants his mother
c: nhê nhê nhê	nyeh nyeh nyeh
s: porque não mamou	'cause he didn't get to nurse
c: nhê nhê nhê	nyeh nyeh nyeh

This song may seem incongruous in a sport for strong men, but it is often used in derision, perhaps directed at someone who is obviously frustrated and may be on the verge of losing his temper. In the case of a young boy or adolescent who has been stung with a kick, the song might be used to keep him from crying, by shaming him. One can make fun of an adult player by calling him a woman, as previously mentioned, or by calling him a baby or a boy.

s: é tu que é moleque	it's you who are the urchin
c: moleque é tu!	the urchin's you!
s: vai embora moleque	go away, urchin
c: moleque é tu!	the urchin's you!

'*Moleque*' was formerly the term for a little black slave boy (similar to 'picaninny'), which now applies to any young street urchin of the type so familiar in third world cities everywhere. Dressed in rags and old beyond their years, these urchins learn early how to survive with a minimum of parental or social support. Of course, calling someone a *moleque* is a strong insult in Brazil, especially if the person is an adult. Notice that the form of the song, like the one before, mimics the way children taunt each other: the first adopting the tone of a whine, and the second song typical of a childish verbal battle, with solo and chorus exchanging the very same insult. Both of these examples support the contention that verbal dueling is important to the esthetic of capoeira, since they employ taunts usually directed at one of the players. These songs can also be used to comment on an interaction in which both of the players have lost their tempers and the contest has become a 'childish' battle for direct dominance.

At the other end of the life cycle are old age and death, both of which also figure prominently in capoeira lyrics:

s: tamanduá   anteater
c: como vai, coroa?   how are you, old thing?

The old person is being compared to an anteater, probably one of the tree-dwelling varieties which moves slowly like a sloth (*Cyclothurus* or *Cyclopes didactylus*). *Coroa* means 'crown,' becoming associated with old age because of the 'crown' of hair around a bald head. This song could be sung while an old master is playing, but it need not necessarily be derogatory. If the master is still supple, it might be a kind of inverted praise, or it could be used to mock a younger opponent who is less supple than an older man. Older players can sometimes make up in knowledge and efficiency of movement what they lack in speed or strength, thus another song warns:

s: buraco velho   old holes
    tem cobra dentro   have snakes inside

Both European and African traditions are rich in proverbs, of course, but educated Europeans and Americans have often tended to look down on such 'folk wisdom' as trite and naive. In Africa, however, proverbs were (and are) considered to be an important source of deep wisdom and it is this latter attitude which prevails in the capoeira world today. Many lyrics of capoeira songs are in proverb form, and such sayings proliferate in the everyday speech of capoeira players. Deceptively simple, proverbs and sayings are often rich in polysemy and intentional ambiguity, facilitating a flexibility of application. I am aware of the extensive literature on proverbs, as well as the debates on how this term should be defined to apply to given ethnographic contexts (for a recent summary, see Briggs 1988: 101–4). Since this discussion is limited to sung versions, the problems of marking and context are similar to those found in other *corridos,* and proverbs do not seem to me to constitute a separate subgenre for singers. Accordingly, I will rely on a commonsense notion of proverb here and allow details to emerge in the course of the analysis.

The song above is typical of the form proverbs take in capoeira songs: literally, it describes a fact of nature—old holes have snakes inside. Metaphorically applied to the wiles of an older player, it can be used to warn young ones to beware of older players who often have tricks up their sleeves. A similar type of proverbial song makes the point that, in our terms, "the bigger they come, the harder they fall":

s:	siri botou	the little crab put
	gameleira no chão	the fig tree down

In this case, the literal account refers to the fact that *siri* crabs (freshwater crabs of the family *Portunidae*) like to build nests in the roots of *gameleira* trees (family *Ficus*) at the edge of swamps. After many crabs make holes, the tree can become unstable and fall down. The metaphorical application to capoeira is often fairly straightforward, as when a small player takes down a large one. Actually, smaller players frequently have the advantage in capoeira, since it is primarily a game of quickness and agility.

As noted in chapter 3, taking the opponent down is the clearest way to score a point in capoeira. Since this is the position of clearest disadvantage in the game, being on the ground becomes a metaphorical death, even if only a momentary demise from which one can rise again. So there are songs like:

c:	zum, zum, zum	zoom, zoom, zoom
	capoeira matou um	capoeira killed one

The *zum zum* is an icon of the sound of the *berimbau,* used in many songs, and similar references to capoeira 'killing' people are also common. It is true that people have died, on rare occasions, while playing the game, but this is almost always a tragic accident and not something one would routinely sing about. For the most part, I believe songs of this type refer to the metaphorical death of a fall, which is a common occurrence. A related phrase, also heard frequently, avows that capoeira is "*de matar*" ('to the death' or 'for killing'). This phrase is difficult to translate and has a more ambiguous sense. In some contexts, it may refer simply to the iconic 'death' of a takedown, but usually it seems to have a more serious intent. Capoeira is, after all, a martial art that can be (and has been) applied in life-or-death situations and should therefore be practiced with a 'killing intent.' This does not mean that one should try to kill one's opponent in the ring, but rather that one should be aware of the power of one's attacks, take the attacks of one's opponent seriously, and respect the power of the sport while practicing it. I believe this is the intent of the phrase "*de matar*" in most contexts, and in this it is similar to practices in other martial arts, in which students rehearse the techniques as if their lives depended on them.

Of the many songs about death and killing, none are more famous than those relating to the death of Besouro (literally, 'beetle'), a famous fighter who lived and died near Santo Amaro da Purificação, in the Recôncavo region of Bahia. Besouro was so named because, when surrounded by hostile police or soldiers, he was able to escape by seeming to fly over their heads, like a winged black beetle. There are many stories concerning his life and death (cf. Rego 1968: 263–65), some of which were popularized by his nephew, the late Cobrinha Verde, whom I was able to interview several times. Some say that Besouro was only slightly involved with capoeira as a sport, but became famous because he was a dangerous fighter who hated police and soldiers and took delight in beating and disarming them. Cobrinha told me that Besouro was a *feiticeiro* who knew how to protect himself with charms from bullets and knives and that the knife that killed him had been specially treated to counteract his magic. This is in accord with the entire *mandingueiro* complex associated with capoeira and explains one of Besouro's frequent praise names, *mangangá*. According to several sources, *nganga* is a Bantu word, denoting a specialist in herbal medicine and the spirit world in several subequatorial societies, especially in the Kongo region, now Zaire (MacGaffey 1986: 37, 293; Thompson and Cornet 1981: 37).

s:	Besouro antes de morrer	Besouro before he died
	abriu a bôca e falou	opened his mouth and said
	meu filho, não apanhe	my son, don't be defeated
	que seu pai nunca apanhou	since your father never was
	na roda da capoeira	in the ring of capoeira
	foi um grande professor	he was a great teacher

Quite apart from the historical actuality, then, Besouro has become a legendary figure in capoeira, embodying the ideal of perfect mastery. Thus another of his honorific titles is Besouro 'of the golden sash' (*cordão de ouro*).

s: Quando eu naci	When I was born
meu nome era Besouro	my name was Besouro
mas eu vou mudar meu nome	but I'm going to change my name
Besourinho Cordão de Ouro	Besourinho of the Golden Sash

As I mentioned in chapter 3, the custom of using colored belts for ranking is fairly recent in capoeira, so giving him a golden belt is obviously a posthumous and purely symbolic honor. The death of so great a hero as Besouro could only be accomplished by plotting and treachery, and it is usually blamed on the jealousy of a rich landowner who could not stand the fame of this poor black field hand. Here we have the themes of race and class struggle, which are so often the concerns, however obliquely, of capoeira songs. As I have argued, this tradition extends back to slave times and represents a perceived continuity in patterns of dominance in Bahia and elsewhere in Brazil, especially for those of Afro-Brazilian ethnicity. Within this framework, the plot against Besouro becomes a formative myth, along with the plot to kill Zumbi in the Quilombo of Palmares, for the injustice of the system. That is, valiant heroes, especially black heroes, are brought down by the superior force and treachery of the ruling classes who could not possibly have overcome them in a fair fight.

VERBAL DUELING

I have argued that the basic relation between chorus and soloist is one of harmonious cooperation, whereas the normal interaction between contestants in the ring is a struggle for mastery between players, a controlled interplay of dominance and submission. Struggle can be expressed in the structure of song performance by occasional tension between solo and chorus, as discussed, but sometimes *malícia* shows up clearly in the form of competition between soloists. Although overt rivalry is rare today, I witnessed it several times during *Angola*-style *rodas* in Bahia, and some historical accounts suggest that these duels may even have been standard practice in the past.

Many capoeira songs are taken (indexically) to refer to given players in the ring, being intended either as praise or as mockery (sometimes both at once). Some lyrics are syntactically 'open,' using the impersonal pronouns 'he' or 'she' (songs about women directed at men are often insults), and reference can either be indicated through gesture or indirectly by the context of the action. Other songs use standard names that, although perhaps historically specific, can be interpreted as generic names, applicable to any player. In these cases also, specific reference can be by indication or implication. One point of the improvised *ladainha* is to allow a master to praise or tease the two players crouched at his feet. A crouching player himself may also sing the *ladainha*, allowing him to direct certain lines at his opponent by pointing or otherwise indicating to whom he refers. This device of indication, using gestures toward a person with any part of the anatomy, can be employed by the soloist of any song, turning it into a form of address. The following cases will illustrate how this can operate in practice.

A master had just finished a physical contest and wanted to join the musicians in the circle. He went to one of the *berimbau* players and started to take the bow from him in a preemptory fashion. The other player, also a master, refused to give it up and started to sing:

s:	esse gunga é meu	this bow is mine
	esse gunga é meu	this bow is mine
	esse gunga é meu	this bow is mine
	foi meu pai que me deu	my father gave it to me

c:	esse gunga é meu	this bow is mine
	esse gunga é meu	this bow is mine

The master with the bow had cleverly used a traditional song to put the other one in his place, by vocally asserting his right to keep playing it. The other master was forced to grab a different instrument, but he did so with fairly good grace, since the song had turned the whole interaction into play. This is one way that potential hostility can be averted in the ludic styles. Note that this song illustrates the convention of the 'prompt,' as the soloist begins by singing the chorus and continues right into the verse. In this case it was necessary for him to adopt that pattern, in order to turn the song into a form of address, directed at the offending master.

Angola-style players dislike what they consider inappropriate body contact and especially dislike being grabbed or grappled with. One method of takedown, grabbing both legs of an adversary in order to pull him over (*arrastão*), is especially unpopular when used frequently. At a *roda* in Santo Amaro I saw several players forcibly eject a *capoeirista* who they thought was using this grab to excess, and a fight was narrowly averted. One Sunday at João Pequeno's *roda* in Santo Antonio (Salvador), there was a high contact interaction between two masters, habitual rivals, which was interrupted when one broke off contact and turned to the musicians, singing:

s:	Doralice não me pegue não!	Don't clutch me, Doralice!
	Não me pegue,	Don't clutch me,
	Não me arraste,	Don't pull me,
	Não me pegue não!	Don't clutch me, no!
c:	Doralice não me pegue não!	Don't clutch me, Doralice!

This song is ostensibly directed to a 'grasping' female who won't let a man alone. The singer left no doubt that he was calling the other master 'Doralice,' trying to equate him to a grasping female and thus playfully insulting him for doing too much grabbing. The opposing player simply ignored the jibe and smilingly returned to the foot of the *berimbau*. The anger with which the song was being sung to a certain extent reflected poorly on the singer, which was enough to satisfy his opponent, and the bout continued.

Once in the Recôncavo of Bahia I witnessed a fascinating interchange between two brothers at a capoeira event, who proceeded to playfully insult each other in rhymed quatrains, alternating solos, while the chorus interposed the familiar refrain, "*Eu sou Angoleiro*" ("I am an *Angoleiro*"). This formalized exchange of insults, sung in a most elegant style, lasted at least ten minutes until one of the brothers ran out of derogatory inventions. This was the only time I ever witnessed the competitive alternation of solos, certainly the most elaborate version of rivalry between singers, but several authors suggest that this kind of overt dueling was more common in the past.

Both Almeida (1981: 119) and Moura (1980: 47–48) provide examples of verbal challenges being exchanged between Mestre Bimba and his opponent before a physical contest. In these cases solos were alternated during the *ladainha* phase, when the players were both crouched facing each other before playing, and the competition was not a question of direct insult but more a test of poetic inventiveness. Thus there are indications, past and present, that verbal dueling forms a part of the capoeira esthetic. At present it usually takes the form of an informal rivalry between masters, frequently an extension of their struggles in the ring. It may be that in the past this rivalry was an established part of the formal sequence of the game and that it extended the skills of improvisation into the verbal domain.

There are numerous African and Afro-American examples of verbal dueling, including several closely related musical genres in Brazil.[2] For instance, throughout the northeast of Brazil, of which Bahia is a part, there has been a tradition of traveling troubadors, called *repentistas* ('improvisors'), who poke fun at the powers that be, the audience, and themselves, accompanied by a ten-stringed lute called a *viola*. They usually perform in pairs, singing alternate verses, each trying to outdo the other in wit and invention. Several of the capoeira *ladainhas* make reference to famous *repentistas* of the past, such as Riachão. In one common version, Riachão is asked to sing a *martelo* (literally, "hammer"), which is a rhymed song form with lines ten syllables long. There is also a capoeira kick called *martelo*, again suggesting a link between verbal and physical dueling.

Another genre with some similarities to the *repentista* tradition is a rare form of *samba* called *samba de viola* (Waddey 1980; 1981). Sometimes soloists in this style of *samba* try to outdo each other in improvised quatrains, while the chorus interposes a refrain. Given the fact that songs are often borrowed back and forth between *samba* and capoeira and that many of these Afro-Brazilian forms may have had a common origin in slave *batuques,* it is not unreasonable to suppose that shared elements are suggestive of past convergence. Further evidence comes from the fact that one size of *berimbau* is called a *viola*. This is not surprising, since both are stringed instruments sometimes used to accompany *samba*. In chapter 2 I cited Alves on the characters called *bambas* (masters of verbal and physical dueling) whose presence further emphasizes the importance of verbal competition in Brazilian musical culture, as well as the frequent link between physical and verbal dueling.[3] As I noted previously, similiar sorts of verbal and physical competition are practiced in many other African-American subcultures, and the two are often linked in those settings as well (for instance, Mohammed Ali's distinctive poetic approach to boxing).

THE BATTLE OF THE SEXES

Attitudes toward women in the traditional songs of capoeira can be summarized under the general heading of *machismo*, for the most part, reflecting the fact that men created and performed them in a manner characteristic of Latin American culture in general (Pescatello 1973).[4]

s:	Ela tem dente de ouro	She has a gold tooth
	foi eu quem mandei botar	it was I who had it put in
	vou te rogar uma fraga	I'll beg you for a rock
	esse dente se quebrar	to break that tooth
	casa de palha é palhoça	a straw house is flimsy
	se fosse fogo eu queimava	if I were fire I would burn it
	tôda mulher ciumenta	all jealous women
	se eu fosse morte eu matava	if I were death I would kill them

Women are frequently referred to as 'jealous' in capoeira songs, and perhaps this relates somewhat to the tradition of male *capoeiristas* having many lovers and frequenting the houses of prostitution. A reputation for this kind of behavior on the part of *capoeiristas* is well known in Bahia, and throughout Brazil, described, for instance, in the novels of Jorge Amado. Bira Almeida makes reference to this aspect of his past in his books about capoeira (1986: 120) and I have heard similar tales from many *mestres*, about experiences past and present. This lore of promiscuity among players is perhaps only an extreme form of the general *machismo* found in Brazilian culture. This is not to say that all men, or even all *capoeiristas*, participate in the *machismo* complex, but merely that it is still a dominant tendency in the society. I should add that it is not merely Latin American societies which exhibit these kinds of male attitudes toward women, of course, since they are to be found in many, if not most, societies in the world (including the United States), as feminists have been pointing out for some time. In Brazil and throughout Latin America, however, these attitudes and practices are more overt than in many other places and are often accepted as 'natural,' especially by male-dominated elites in the political and legal systems.

Given this kind of gender typing, it makes sense for *capoeiristas* to use songs about women in order to insult their male opponents. In one unusual case, this tactic was directed at me. The practice of clapping hands at a *roda* was something that I was used to from my training in the States, but it is by no means universal in Brazil. Once, at an *Angola*-style *roda*, I was busily clapping away when a young player came up and sang in my ear:

s:	quem bate pandeiro é homem	who beats tambourine is a man
	paraná	*paraná*
	quem bate palmas é mulher	who claps hands is a woman
	paraná	*paraná*

The intent was to make fun of the ignorant foreigner by calling him a woman. I had not really noticed until then that I was the only one clapping, so I stopped, abashed not because I had been insulted (to me there was no insult) but because I had violated a tacit convention I hadn't been aware of until then. It was only well after the fact that I deduced the probable origin of the custom and figured out approximately when and where it applied (see next chapter).

Although *machismo* has a very bad reputation in the United States, an outsider must be careful not to judge precipitously, without a considered study of the phenomenon in context. I do not wish to defend the excesses of male domination in Brazil or elsewhere, but living in Latin America has convinced me that even *machismo* is not a simple phenomenon and that appearances can be deceiving. Another variant of the *ladainha* which introduced this section, for instance, is a much less violent, melancholy remembrance of a lost love. This romantic kind of attitude is also common in capoeira songs and reflects an attitude that is virtually universal in love songs and not necessarily exemplary of *machismo* in particular.

It has been pointed out that many of the overt references to sex in African-American songs, in the United States and elsewhere, cannot be understood simply as male desires to reduce women to sexual objects, but can be seen alternatively as a kind of sexual play mutually understood as a harmless diversion (Kochman 1981: 74–88; Abrahams 1983: esp. chaps. 3 and 4). Some see in these games of innuendo an African esthetic of banter between the sexes in which the victor can emerge from either side, according to the skill of the talker or singer. Therefore, sexual references to women in capoeira, and especially in the *samba* repertoire where they are even more prevalent, might be seen as part of such a joking interplay, depending on how they are used in context. One could include such sexual stereotyping under the heading of *machismo*, but only at the risk of obscuring a complex interaction between the sexes that is often not taken too seriously and therefore may not reflect actual behavior too closely.

c:	Dona Maria de Camboatá	Dona Maria of Camboatá
s:	tira a saia e vamos deitar	take off your skirt and let's go to bed

The fact that capoeira players have reputations as profligate lovers (a reputation they are far from ashamed of, for the most part) has been something of an obstacle to the entrance of women into the sport. This is true because parents are reluctant to have their daughters work out with such types and also because previously women were not interested in being associated with such essentially male activities. Therefore some modern masters are trying hard to change the traditional image of the capoeirista as *malandro*, in order to attract students of all sexes and all social classes. Clearly this means that songs which employ standard *macho* attitudes toward women, or even those which employ teasing stereotypes, may no longer be seen as appropriate. This self-conscious change in image is one of the factors influencing the creation of new songs in the capoeira repertoire.

New Songs and Old

Since my emphasis throughout this book has been on the basic traditions of capoeira, I have not dwelt extensively on the newest innovations in the sport as it adapts to the modern world. One area in which this change is strongest is in the song repertoire, as I indicated in the last chapter. There I mentioned that in many of the new songs being composed for capoeira the basic call-response format is being altered. In addition, the content of the new lyrics naturally reflects modern attitudes and concerns, sometimes quite different from the older repertoire. I won't attempt a systematic analysis of the new material, but a few examples will give an indication of some directions these changes seem to be taking.

The key development that introduced the modern era in capoeira was the institutionalization of the sport, begun by Mestre Bimba, and the consequent introduction of large numbers of middle- and upper-middle-class players into the ring for the first time. These players brought with them new attitudes and ideas, which in time became expressed in the songs. It could be expected that songs of racial and class conflict, however disguised, would be softened and reinterpreted as the number of lighter-skinned and wealthier players grew. Songs of slave resistance are still meaningful to poor blacks in Bahia, but less interesting to middle-class whites in São Paulo. One of the newer songs, for instance, goes as follows:

capoeira não tem raça	capoeira has no race
capoeira não tem côr	capoeira has no color
ô, ô, ô, ô	oh, oh, oh, oh
capoeira é amor	capoeira is love

This clearly represents a new approach to capoeira, one that contrasts strongly with the tradition of race and class struggle which engendered the sport. How can this song be reconciled with the idea of *malícia* and related values, such as 'falsity' (*falsidade*) or 'treachery' (*maldade*)? The song above represents an emphasis on the normative communitas of capoeira while ignoring its competitive side, placing the sport in a world where class conflict and racism are obsolete. This kind of utopian vision is surely more appealing to members of a class where struggle is, at worst, a minor part of the daily reality than to those who are still victims of class domination and racism. Notice also that I don't indicate whether this part of the song is solo or chorus, since it is not clearly divided in that way. Sometimes it is sung by all players together, sometimes as a solo, and sometimes as call/response.

Still, some newer songs attempt to limit themselves to traditional capoeira themes or to reinterpret those themes in terms of a newly emerging mythos. For instance, none of the older songs refer, as far as I can discover, to life on the *quilombos* or to Zumbi of Palmares. Since the legend of the origin of capoeira in those republics of resistance is so popular today, despite the dearth of historical (epistemic) evidence, several recent songs have appeared celebrating Zumbi and his times. Attitudes toward escaped slaves in the older capoeira songs, however, are far from celebratory, as this old *ladainha* demonstrates:

s:	Riachão arrespondeu	Riachão replied
	não canto com nêgo desconhecido	I don't sing with an unknown guy
	êle pode ser escravo	he could be a slave
	andando por aqui fugido	around here on the run

Here the singer is demonstrating caution because the penalty for interaction with escaped slaves was severe. Later in the song, Riachão expresses satisfaction that he is a free man, although poor. This attitude of caution was one which had to be expressed in public, clearly, whatever one's private attitude toward escaped slaves. Cautious pragmatism seems to have been fairly common among freedmen of color in the last century, and the hero worship accorded Zumbi and the denizens of the *quilombos* is not generally found in oral texts until the mid-twentieth century.

These two examples of the contrast between older and newer capoeira songs give some idea of the changes in attitudes and values over the years in which capoeira has been played. It is difficult to generalize, even about the older material itself, since there is so much variation within the repertoire and in the way the songs are applied to contexts in the game. Of course, it is impossible to date the older songs, or even many of the new ones, but most masters are able to give a relative chronology that identifies the songs which were sung when they were learning to play.

SONGS OF THE SPIRITS

Although capoeira is not directly a religious phenomenon, the players use the songs to make reference to their spiritual beliefs, and there are indications that aspects of the game were quite highly ritualized in the past. This section will explore some of the religious aspects of the songs, especially the blend of African, Catholic, and native Brazilian elements which constitute the primary Bahian belief system now and in former times.

With all the discussion of *Angola*-style capoeira, I should note that *Angola* can also refer to one category or 'nation' (*nação*) of *candomblé* practice, as distinct from *Ketú* or *Gêge* types, for example. The *Angola* nation is distinct from the others in that there is generally less emphasis on interaction with the Yoruban *orixás* and more on the lesser spirit beings known as *exús* and *caboclos* (see Wafer 1991). This seems to identify both traditional capoeira and this kind of *candomblé* with a highly creolized set of practices, perhaps strongly influenced, as many think, by cultural concepts primarily derived from subequatorial, Bantu societies.

One of the most important aspects of Afro-Brazilian religious life is the process of trance induction. Although few masters believe that being possessed by a named spirit is (or ever was) part of capoeira play, most do believe that they experience some kind of altered state while playing the game.[5] In general, this state is vaguely described in terms of a sense of freedom, of flying, of losing track of time, and so forth. In this regard, there is a capoeira *toque* called *barravento,* which perhaps gives further insight into the altered states experienced in play. According to a dictionary of religious terms, *barravento* can be defined as a mild, preliminary trance experienced by initiates before they receive the actual spirit of a deity (Cacciatore 1977). Perhaps this is how one can understand the related capoeira song lyric:

c: valha-me Deus,   aid me God,
   Senhor São Bento   [and] Great Saint Benedict

s:	eu vou jogar	I'm going to play
	meu barravento	my *barravento*

São Bento, the saint most frequently mentioned in capoeira songs, lived in the sixth century and was the founder of the Benedictine order.[6] Although he is sometimes syncretized with Omolu in the Yoruba pantheon, a god of health and nutrition (Henfrey 1981: 58–60), in capoeira (and elsewhere) São Bento is often associated with snakes. Cascudo notes that charms to ward off snakebite, in general use throughout Brazil, frequently invoke the name of São Bento (1980: 119–20). It is unclear how this saint became linked to snakes, but Bastide notes that early stereotypes of *feiticeiros* (and *mandingueiros*) in Bantu-based performances like the *congada* or *cucumbi* always portrayed them as snake handlers and frequently associated them with Saint Benedict (1978: 123). Since *capoeiristas* were also associated with magical practices and called *mandingueiros*, the link seems fairly clear.

s:	essa cobra lhe morde	that snake will bite you
c:	Senhor São Bento	Great Saint Benedict
s:	ôi o bote da cobra	oh, the strike of the serpent
c:	Senhor São Bento	Great Saint Benedict
s:	o veneno da cobra	the venom of the serpent
c:	Senhor São Bento	Great Saint Benedict

In the modern context the song may be used, for instance, to compare the strike of a snake with the impact of a swift, stinging kick in the game, but, formerly, magical meanings may have been just as important. For instance, Cascudo notes that as a protection against snakebite, it was necessary to tie a knot in one's clothes or in a piece of straw, while invoking the saint's name. The idea was that the knot would act sympathetically (iconically) on the snake, 'knotting it up' and preventing it from striking (1980: 120). There are indications in the songs that similar magics were employed by *capoeiristas*, perhaps to immobilize their opponents (see Rego 1968: 110 for the following):

s:	Do nó escondo a ponta	In the knot I hide the end
	paraná	*paraná*
	ninguém sabe desatar	no one knows how to untie
	paraná	*paraná*

It is clear that a variety of syncretic cults developed in Brazil during the time that capoeira was evolving, and probable that many of the same people participated in both kinds of activities, just as today many capoeira players are familiar with *candomblé*. The practices of these early cults were kept secret from the authorities, and the uses of magic and sorcery even more so, which makes it especially difficult to make unqualified statements as to the origins and meanings of many of the phrases used in capoeira songs. The associations between African sorcery, the *mandingueiro* complex, snake magic, and Saint Benedict are clearly preserved in capoeira lore, but whether these represent influences from the Bantu-speaking peoples primarily, as Bastide claims, is difficult to verify. The association between snakes and Saint Benedict, for instance, can also be traced back to popular beliefs in Portugal (Cascudo 1979: 119).

The dominant Afro-Brazilian cults in Salvador today are those linked to the *orixás,* named spirits from the Yoruba tradition who enter the heads of initiates, causing them to dance and sing while in trance. Each spirit is associated with a Catholic saint, and one can refer to it either by its African name or by its Catholic one (cf. Wafer 1991; Omari 1984; Thompson 1983; Bastide 1978). Formal *candomblé* houses of worship date from the early nineteenth century in Brazil, and some of them practice a relatively 'pure' form of African ritual, especially those established in the direct Yoruban line. Trance possession is as old as slavery in Brazil, however, and the earlier cults, about which there is much controversy, are generally agreed to have been more syncretic, combining various European, African, and indigenous spiritual traditions. In general, capoeira seems more in conformity with these syncretic faiths, modern versions of which are still common, than with the formal African cult practices. Nonetheless, individual *capoeiristas* have been associated with *candomblé* since the nineteenth century, and today many players participate in cult activities, both formal and informal.

The *orixás* most commonly linked to capoeira are Ogun, the warrior god, also patron of metal workers; Oxôssi, the hunter, often pictured with bow and arrow; Xangô, a former king and husband to several female *orixás;* and Exú, the trickster, god of the crossroads and messenger between men and the spirit world. Of these, the first three are spirits to whom one may be dedicated if one is a *candomblé* initiate, and *capoeiristas* sometimes were (and still are) dedicated to one of them. Every initiate and every *orixá* also has a personal Exú who has specific duties and also possesses the adept from time to time (Wafer 1991; Omari 1984: 21). Members of Bahian society who do not approve of capoeira might cast aspersions on its players by linking them to Exú, who is often associated (erroneously) with the devil in popular imagination.

It is difficult to find many direct references to the Yoruba pantheon in capoeira songs, but this song in praise of Ogun is one example:

s: ê Ogunhê
    tata que malembê
c: ologué

There are indications that this chant was recently borrowed from the *candomblé* repertoire, since Ogunhê is one of the ceremonial greetings for Ogun used in that setting. The saint who corresponds to Ogun is Saint Anthony, and there are songs to him as well:

c: Santo Antonio, protetor   Saint Anthony, protector
s: da barcinha de Noê   of Noah's little ship

Saint Anthony is known throughout the Mediterranean world as the protector of fishermen and sailors, but Ogun has no such association, so it is unclear if there is any syncretism in this case. Given the importance of sailors and fishermen to the development of capoeira, that alone could explain the popularity of this song. As I mentioned in chapter 2, the word *paraná,* quoted in several of the previous songs and below, probably comes from the Tupian word for 'ocean' or any large body of water.[7] This word may have come directly into the songs by contact with indigenous people, or it may have entered the repertoire as a result of Brazil's war with Paraguay in the late nineteenth century. Many capoeira players are reputed to have participated in that venture, and there they would have become familiar with the Paraná River, on the border between Paraguay and Brazil, and the neighboring Brazilian state of the same name.

I want to use the example of *paraná* to end this section by evoking the diffuse feeling of sacredness which seems most typical of the attitudes of players toward their game. All of the elements mentioned above contribute to these feelings without defining them or limiting them to a single tradition. The ethos of freedom and the experience of liberation in play extend to the spiritual domain as well, allowing each player to find his or her own sense of the sacred within the ring. Most players do seem to find themselves in an altered state of consciousness while playing, whether it is the light trance of *barravento* or the 'mysterious leap' of Mestre Nô.[8] This state is greatly aided by the music, especially the 'magic' of the *berimbau,* which is permeated with the same ambient sacredness. In play, the *capoeirista* bobs up and down in his *ginga,* back and forth in an ocean of sound and meaning, losing himself in currents and tides of sensation.

s:	eu sou braço de maré	I am an arm of the sea
	paraná	*paraná*
	mas eu sou o mar sem fim	but I am the sea without end
	paraná	*paraná*
c:	paraná é, paraná é	*paraná* is, *paraná* is
	paraná	*paraná*

MALÍCIA AND COMRADESHIP: COMPETITION AND COOPERATION

I have argued that the musical discourse within the capoeira ring is structurally weighted or biased toward the cooperative communal values, while the physical dialogue tends more toward the competitive combative side, all things being equal. This is because in the physical interplay martial aspects are the foreground, whereas the values of solidarity are the background, underlying the action and acting as a check on its violent tendencies. Ideally, these two values are in balance, which produces a capoeira both beautiful and deadly; but as the balance shifts between the two poles, the physical interaction can (and does) vary from the most elegant choreographed dance to the most brutal brawling. These extremes encompass contests between friends who want a good workout and enemies who are ready to maim.

The songs therefore may act to counteract both extreme tendencies, taunting and cajoling the players to keep within bounds. When someone is being overly aggressive, a soloist may sing:

s:	Vai quebrar tudo hoje	Today you smash everything
c:	quebra	smash
s:	Amanhã quem te quebra?	who will smash you tomorrow?
c:	quebra	smash

The effect in this case is to remind players that their strength will not last forever, that as they sow so shall they reap. By using the song in this way, singers can attempt to influence the action, to change the context of play, in order to keep it in line with the convention against violent intent. From time to time the *povão* (great poor masses) of Bahia (and throughout Brazil) rise up in revulsion at their poverty and go on a rampage of destruction, in a process similar to ghetto riots in the United States. Such outbursts, frequently directed at metropolitan transit in recent years, are called *quebra-quebra,* a reduplication of the verb used above ('to break, shatter; to disrupt') which conveys the idea of an orgy of riot, a loss of control, a blind hitting out in all directions (see da Matta 1980). Although people usually have some sympathy for the rioters as well, because they understand their extreme situation, a similar sense of the verb is conveyed when the song is used in this way, directed in this case at men whose anger and arrogance lead them into brutality.

Nevertheless, the physical interaction can also be seen as too nice, too easy, too cooperative. In this case, the players can sing songs to goad the opponents into greater combativeness:

s:	No nêgo você não dá	You're not giving him a thing
c:	Dá, dá, dá no nêgo	Give, give, give it to him
s:	Se não der, vai apanhar	If you don't give, you're gonna get it
c:	Dá, dá, dá no nêgo	Give, give, give it to him

This verse is difficult to translate well, because it refers to the process of attack, which is *dar um golpe.* Literally 'to give a strike,' this phrase combines the sense of 'to strike a blow' with that of 'to launch an attack.' The contestants in the ring are being told that if they don't try to attack they will surely be defeated. Once again the singers are hoping to influence play by changing the discourse context, in this case to 'stir up' the action.

Many of the songs represent a conscious understanding of the need to steer between extremes, both in terms of capoeira tactics and in the world of values and norms. One version of traditional wisdom, then, might be summarized by the familiar adage 'take the middle way.' As the above examples illustrated, those who fail to avoid extremes are subject to ridicule, but so are those who are constantly swinging back and forth from one extreme to another:

s:	oia, tira dali, bota 'qui	oh, take it from there, put it here
c:	Idalina	*Idalina*
s:	oia, tira de cá, bota lá	oh, take it from here, put it there
c:	Idalina	*Idalina*

This song literally seems to be referring to a scenario in which Idalina is a servant being ordered by her mistress or master to do contradictory things, or to do and then undo. The intent is usually to lampoon those who don't know their own minds and thus make life miserable for others. In the context of the game the song can be used, for instance, to ridicule the futility of a player's tactics, if he is constantly overreacting and thus telegraphing his moves to an opponent. But it can also be used in the opposite way, in praise of a player who always foresees the moves of his comrade and thus forestalls the latter's attempts to attack or defend himself. When used in this second sense, the player who takes the middle way can be seen as one who is able to move less but accomplish more than his counterpart, who expends a tremendous amount of effort in defeating himself.

The same principle applies in the realm of cultural values, as well: if one fails to moderate one's emotions or desires, one inevitably suffers:

s:	se ando limpo sou malandro	if I'm clean I am a hoodlum
	se ando sujo sou immundo	if I'm dirty I'm a bum
	se não falo sou calado	if I don't talk I am tongue-tied
	se falo muito sou falador	if I talk a lot I'm a braggart
	se não como sou mesquinho	if I don't eat I am stingy
	se como muito sou guloso	if I eat a lot I'm a glutton
	se não ligo sou covarde	if I don't fight I'm a coward
	se mato sou assassino	if I kill I am a murderer

Here the singer seems to be bemoaning his fate as a human, always condemned by others no matter what he does to avoid censure. Upon closer examination, however, it is apparent that, whatever others think, if the singer can avoid extremes he can also avoid trouble. The counsel here might be to pay no attention to what others say, but also to avoid extremes of behavior. If one walks the middle path, in fact, there is less chance that one will be noticed, surely an advantage when most notoriety takes the form of censure. This is the advice of the wily pragmatist, as are so many of the ideas expressed in the most traditional songs. Such advice is not destined to create heroes, but calculated to enhance survival in a hostile world.

The lyrics above come from a traditional *ladainha*, the source of much of the most profound wisdom in capoeira discourse. Recall that the litany solo precedes play, since it is sung while the players are preparing to enter the ring for the first time. Therefore it only frames the action that follows and has a different relation to context formation than songs which accompany active play. One effect this has is to reduce or constrain the metacommunicative function of such songs, giving them a more fixed relation to context in the game. Briggs has captured this kind of difference by proposing a continuum between 'contextual' and 'textual' genres among Spanish-speaking New Mexicans (1988: 223). Following this framework, *ladainhas* (and *chulas*) are more textual, and *corridos* are more contextual songs, since the former occur in relatively restricted settings, with more syntagmatic and structural constraints, while the latter vary greatly in pragmatic effect, depending on the context of physical interplay which they index. This also helps explain why overt capoeira values are most clearly stated in *ladainhas*, why ambiguity is reduced, because these songs invariably frame play as a whole, as well as a specific (but always future) interchange, and thus need to encompass a totalizing perspective on the game. Since there is as yet no action to connect them to an emergent context (except past events), these songs must be relatively more context-independent.

If it is true that *ladainhas* were once sung more frequently, as play was often stopped to highlight important contests, this contextual framework also suggests why solos were often improvised in the past, since their relation to ongoing action would then have been more immediate and contingent. Given that the current tendency is to sing them primarily at the beginning of events, this correlates well with the loss of improvisation; the relative fixity of the litany texts corresponds to their more fixed relation to contexts of physical play. At present, most masters have memorized a few standard *ladainhas*, and the ones selected are those which most clearly express fundamental values of play which apply generally to many interactive situations.

The *ladainha* and the *chula* are always paired, as I have noted, so they both function in the same fashion as relatively textual subgenres, establishing frames for an entire sequence of bouts to follow. Even in these orienting texts, however, the term *malícia* is rarely invoked directly, although it is common in the spoken commentary of *capoeiristas* as they discuss the sport. In the *chula*, players often sing instead of *malandragem*, 'hooliganism,' a synonym for capoeira which evokes the image of the *malandro*. Both words are related to *malícia*, but carry with them the added connotations of social stigma: poverty combined with a lack of regard for social conventions and laws. On his record, Mestre Bimba sings a *chula* verse in praise of *falsidade* ('falseness'). Like *malícia*, this is frequently interpreted as the falseness of the dissembler who must cover up his feelings in order to survive. As with some terms in black English (for example, 'bad'), semantic inversions can take a word with negative intent in one social domain and turn it into something positive in another. Such reversals might be seen as structurally equivalent to body inversion on the physical plane.

Mestre Bimba is also reported to have said that the essence of capoeira is 'treachery' (*maldade*).[9] This is another term related to the ones above, but it is the darkest of all. Although *malícia* can mean 'evil intent,' and similar things hard to praise, it is usually used in a much lighter sense, and Brazilian people would generally not be offended if accused of having acted with *malícia*. Even if they were not *capoeiristas*, they might take it as a compliment. The same cannot be said for *maldade*, which is one of the primary words for 'evil' in the Portuguese language. My interpretation of Bimba's comment is that he was basically referring to the same complex of related meanings I have identified with *malícia*, but that his personal bitterness in the face of what he felt were life's injustices made it come out stronger and darker. It is true that evil for one group may be seen as virtue by another, and I believe this is what Bimba was referring to, not an 'absolute' evil of the kind usually envisioned in the Christian ethos.

The *ladainha/chula* complex contains many references to the comradeship between players. Every line of the *chula* refrain ends with the word *camará* ('comrade'), for instance, invoking the solidarity of the players repeatedly in the ritual frame establishing the game (see next chapter). Accordingly, the *ladainhas* frequently invoke the ideal of friendship, as in the following:

s: é verdade meu amigo	it's true my friend
nossa vida é um colosso	our life is a colossus
mais vale nossa amizade	our friendship is worth more
do que dinheiro em nosso bôlso	than money in our pockets

This poem seems even more eloquent if one remembers that it comes from a social milieu of extreme poverty in which having money can literally be a matter of life or death. The comradeship of *capoeiristas* does not need much more emphasis than this, but it should be remembered that it is always a cautious friendship. The love between master and disciple in capoeira can be as close as that kind of bond in any culture of the world. The master's praises are usually sung right after those to God in the *chula*. Nevertheless, the master can and does subject his disciple to great pain and suffering in capoeira training, and he may deliberately betray the student's trust in order to teach him the lesson of *malícia*. Friendship and rivalry between fellow players can become almost indistinguishable in the capoeira context, but in both cases they are very intense. As one young master from São Paulo put it, "Sometimes your best friend can be your worst enemy and your worst enemy can turn out to be your best friend."[10]

Conclusion

DISCOURSE WITHIN THE RING

The discussion of the individual semiotic domains or channels for expression in capoeira has already revealed a substantial amount of interdependence between them. Indeed, I argued that this must be the case from theoretical grounds, since it is true of other multiplex phenomena such as linguistic and social systems. In the first place I have demonstrated a striking parallelism between formal structures in the physical play, the instrumental music, and the singing. In all three there are essential dichotomies or dimensions of contrast, complemented by mediating structures capable of neutralizing or balancing those contrasts under certain conditions. In the physical dialogue, the fundamental distinction is attack/defense, or initiative/response, mediated by the *ginga;* in the instrumental music it is high tone/low tone, mediated by the buzz tone; in the vocal dimension, call/response is mediated by silence and by overlapping solos. Finally, in the domain of symbolic or conceptual structure, I have been arguing for a primary contrast between *malícia* and comradeship, in this case mediated by ambiguity, about which I will say more below.

Each channel can and does function independently, since they all can constitute expressive genres in their own right outside of the capoeira setting. The basic oppositions and mediations serve to maintain both dynamic tension and homeostasis within each domain of signification. In addition, the structural iconicities between domains can be thought of as redundancies in the total system of capoeira discourse, since they can function to reinforce the connections between the channels and thereby emphasize a given type of expression. Not only can the subsystems reinforce each other, they can also counterbalance or counterpoise one against the other in order to decrease a tension created when one channel verges toward an extreme, or to create more tension, or more ambiguity, when the expression becomes too routinized. This was seen to be the case, for instance, when the music, well suited for the maintenance of harmony between systems, is used to counteract an increasingly violent interaction between players in the ring. An increase in tempo, however, or the choice of a certain song, can have just the opposite effect.

The subsystems of capoeira discourse function so well together partly because of these iconicities between their structures, and another important result of the discussion has been to demonstrate how such icons within a given expressive form can propagate into, or resonate with, their isomorphs in the symbolic system of Bahian and Brazilian culture outside the ring. I showed how this could happen, for example, in the cases of 'accommodation' and 'pretend to run away,' as well as in the more conceptual realms of *malícia* and comradeship. The scenario of the 'blessing,' discussed as the first example of *malícia* in action, can also operate either outside the ring or inside. An alternative way to describe the 'blessing' interaction might be to call it 'pretend to shake hands.' This phrase highlights the social convention that is violated in the interchange and underscores the similarity between that scenario and 'pretend to run away.'

Pretense is clearly an essential aspect of *malícia,* and one could construct a long list of 'pretend' scenarios, all of which are used in capoeira but which can also function to deceive victims outside the ring as well. The list would include: pretend to lose sight of the opponent; pretend to be injured; pretend to have something in one's eye; pretend there is something amazing (or dangerous) behind the opponent and point to it; pretend to stop playing; pretend to get angry; pretend to be afraid; pretend to be drunk; and so forth. All of these scenarios revolve around social norms of behavior and take advantage of a victim who follows the rules for how one is 'supposed' to act. Establishing and breaking rules within the game and in society will be a major focus of this chapter.

Although I have been describing *malícia* as a value central to capoeira, I also noted that it is a term that can be used and understood in a similar (though less multivocal) sense by Brazilians in general. Indeed, the idea of pretense is an important and often cited property of people throughout the society, especially those in positions of power. A frequently heard phrase, in general use, which captures this propensity is *jôgo de cintura* (literally, 'game of the belt,' or 'game of the waist'), which often refers to the creation of facades or smoke screens behind which to hide shady activities. For example, this phrase applies to the frequent elaborate attempts to cover up government corruption. Viewed in this light, *malícia* in the capoeira world can be seen as a special, more intense and elaborated, version of a general social value. When practiced by victims of the political/economic system, deception can become laudable; when the dominant elites play the game to dupe the public, most people react negatively.

It is interesting to notice how iconic propagation or redundancy can generate intermediate structures between the micro and macro levels of discourse—for instance, within the performance syntagms. If call/response is the central structure in the vocal channel, a moment's consideration is enough to reveal that solo *ladainha,* followed by choral *chula* is simply an elaboration of that basic form. Even though the *chula* itself contains a call/response sequence, it is of a specialized or marked type, involving the echoing of the soloist by the chorus. That distinctive repetition by echo, combined with the mandatory linking of the two subgenres, together reinforce the structural iconicity between call/response and *ladainha/chula*. Another example is the isomorphism between each bout of two contestants and the overall structure of the *roda* or capoeira event. Essentially a *roda* is just a sequence of bouts strung together, a continual iteration of the basic syntagm, with some elaboration at the beginning and the end, depending on the style.

If these points are clear, they should provide enough conceptual apparatus to make the final synthetic step, which is to consider in detail the relations between interactions within the capoeira ring and those outside, in Brazilian society at large. In the following discussion, it should be stressed that when I rely heavily on data from the *ladainha/chula* complex and the *chamada* subroutines, I am referring primarily to the ludic style of capoeira *Angola*. Although there was a period in which it seemed that this form was doomed to extinction, it has recently made something of a resurgence, and the latest developments in what I am calling *atual* style seem to indicate that the trend toward more agonistic play, begun in the 1930s, may be reversing itself. It is too early to predict what will happen, but it is certain that events in the United States and other foreign countries will have some influence on this future. This internationalization process will be discussed as part of the concluding focus on frameworks for understanding capoeira in a multiplicity of cultural systems.

INSIDE THE RING AND OUTSIDE

Setting aside a special or 'sacred' space is regarded as an essential aspect of all games by most scholars of the subject, since it establishes a microcosm in which certain rules apply and certain interactions are to be expected (Handelman 1977: 185; Huizinga 1955: 14). The capoeira ring is such a space: a framework which aids in the definition of how events within it are to be interpreted. For Goffman and Bateson, games constitute a type of frame in which behavior is 'transposed' from a primary context to a secondary one (the game) and therefore mean something different in the new context than they would have in the old. Thus, Goffman uses a musical metaphor, comparing game behavior to a melody that is transposed into another key, and calls the game framework a 'keying' (1976: 45). Goffman shares with Bateson the idea that there is something inherently deceptive in games and play, something paradoxical even, since play events "do not denote what would be denoted by those actions" in another context (Bateson 1972: 180). Games are a specialized kind of play, and one of the basic differences between the two, in my view, is that games are institutionalized or routinized forms of play in which the rules are more or less firmly established, as is the space within which the play is to occur.[1]

In setting up a framework for play, drawing boundary lines between what is 'in play' and what is 'out,' one is therefore creating a distinction between two contexts, not just defining one. This point was made elegantly clear by Spencer-Brown, for instance, who showed that drawing any line is making a distinction (1979: 1). Therefore, the establishment of the capoeira ring does not just frame the play space, it also frames the 'non-play' space: the social world at large against which the capoeira world can and must be compared and contrasted. This distinction is not merely implicit, as it is in many games, but is made explicit both verbally and nonverbally in capoeira:

s: ó que mundo velho grande	What an old, huge world
ó que mundo enganador	What a deceitful world
Eu digo desta maneira	I speak in this way
Foi mamãe que m'ensinou	as my mother taught me

Here the singer seems to be speaking of the world at large, but the words come from a *ladainha,* the ritual introduction to the contest in *Angola* circles, and the word 'deceitful' adds a further indication that there is intentional ambiguity here. The double meaning of 'world' becomes explicit during the *chula,* as the players sing praises and prepare for the action to begin:

s: é hora é hora	it's time, it's time
c: iê, é hora é hora, camará	it's time, it's time, comrade
s: vamos embora	let's go
c: iê, vamos embora, camará	let's go, comrade
s: pelo mundo fora	out into the world
c: iê, pelo mundo fora, camará	out into the world, comrade
s: que o mundo dá	what the world provides
c: iê, que o mundo dá, camará	what the world provides, comrade
s: dá volta ao mundo	take a turn around the world
c: iê, dá volta ao mundo, camará	take a turn around the world, comrade

This illustrates the repetitive echoing structure of the *chula,* with a few of the many possible verses. Notice again the high degree of comradeship expressed: the chorus echoes the soloist, and each line of the chorus ends with an appeal to the solidarity of fellow players (*camará*). Here the contestants are about to enter the ring to begin the physical dialogue, yet the song sends them to the world (*fora*), the 'outer' world. Clearly, there is an isomorphism being declared between inner and outer worlds, in line with the teachings of many masters who say that lessons learned in the ring must be applied outside as well. It is interesting that this line could also be transcribed as *"pelo mundo afora,"* which would mean 'throughout the world.' Since these lyrics are part of an oral tradition, exact renderings in written form are debatable, and indeed verbal punning based on homophony is fairly common. One could argue that both meanings apply, since they reinforce the very point being made here.

Referring to the inside of the circle as 'the world' is a metaphor linking the two spheres, as in the phrase 'take a turn around the world,' which becomes a technical term for circling the ring. As in all metaphors, the iconicity between spheres is never exact, since it is the contrast, as well as the similarity between the two, which provides the richness of the trope. In this case, by identifying the capoeira world with the outside world, practicioners are 'saying,' as a first reading, that social life is really a combat like capoeira, a struggle between dominance and submission. That it may not appear that way is due to the 'deceit' of hypocritical conventions which mask the underlying reality.

This interpretation will be reinforced during the following discussion, but the reader should recall again that in the scenario of 'the blessing,' and the entire 'pretend series' listed above, the tricks can be used either inside or outside the ring and that they revolve around the unmasking of social conventions as well as capoeira conventions. For instance, shaking hands is a general icon of solidarity, of implicit cooperation, but it is often used as a social lubricant between people who really distrust or even hate each other. The 'blessing' kick can therefore be seen as an unmasking of the aggression and desire for dominance which underlie the social niceties. The lesson for capoeira players is clear: don't be fooled by the appearance of friendliness, don't trust anyone too far, and always be ready to defend yourself. A person who always follows these maxims is someone with *malícia*, a quality of value in both inside and outside 'worlds.'

This first set of structural relations between capoeira and society at large might therefore be diagrammed as in figure 7.1. The convention to be followed in all of the diagrams in this chapter, except where otherwise indicated, is for the outer line to represent the overt, foregrounded interaction in a domain: a commonsense,

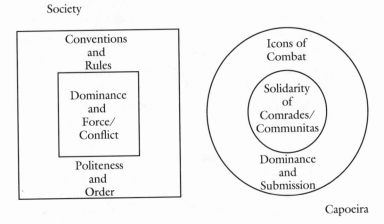

Figure 7.1   Metaphoric Inversion

consensual interpretation of that situation. The inner circle represents covert or latent (background) patterns which underlie the overt interaction and may constitute the privileged interpretations of a subgroup, such as capoeira adepts or poor Afro-Brazilians.

Capoeira is represented in figure 7.1 as an inversion of society, since relations of dominance and submission, and especially the use of force, are usually masked or latent in normal social interaction, and when they do become overt it is usually because of a failure of customary practice. Capoeira, on the other hand, takes the form of active combat, and it requires active reflection to realize that conventions of fellowship constrain the icons of force, keeping a check on the potential violence of the interplay. This apparent inversion is seen by the players as an unmasking of various truths about society, as they repeatedly emphasize the identity between inner and outer 'worlds.' This metaphoric identity has the effect of a social critique, implicity revealing that what seems overt in society is really a sham, and what underlies is the true reality. Therefore the worlds are both 'deceptive': the outside world attempts to cover its ugly face; the capoeira world uses trickery to reveal that face.

The same line in the *chula* that speaks of the 'outside' world has an alternate version, "*pela barra fora*," which refers to the conditions of battle. *Barra* means 'bar' or 'rod' and in Bahian parlance frequently is extended to mean the receipt of blows from a rod, and, by extension, all difficult conditions. Likewise, another phrase from the *chula* makes reference to the 'field of battle' ("*no campo da batalha*"). Again, the point is that capoeira is a 'field of battle' and so is the outside world, in which one is likely to receive hard knocks. By singing and speaking in this way the players are foregrounding the violence of the outer world, and by training in the game they are preparing themselves to survive in that greater battle. This view of society as a battlefield has become general folk wisdom, especially among the poorer sectors, and I frequently heard Bahians remark when going to work, "*Vou batalhar*" ('I'm going to battle'). Given recent events in Brazilian economic life, this point of view seems to be spreading to include greater and greater proportions of the population, even those who formerly saw themselves as members of the middle and upper social sectors.

When the two players crouched at the foot of the lead *berimbau* move into the center of the ring to begin physical play, it is called the *saída*. The verb *sair* means 'to leave' and is frequently used by people inside a building to indicate that they are going out. Yet when the players use this term they are not going out, they are going *in:* they are entering the ring. The term makes linguistic sense because the partners are said to be "leaving the foot of the *berimbau*." This peculiar circumlocution provides further evidence for the metaphorical identity of inner and outer worlds. When the players *enter* the ring, they are simultaneously going 'out' into 'the world.' They are literally entering the capoeira world and figuratively going out into the social world at large, since they are training for its battles.

GAMES WITHIN THE GAME REVISITED

What I have called the 'inner games' of capoeira include the 'callings' (*chamadas*), 'circling the ring' (*dá volta ao mundo*), the *saída,* and the 'money game' (see chapter 4). During all of these events, different rules apply than those in force for 'normal' capoeira, and the routines are indexed by the breaking of some lower-order rules (see table 4.3). I believe these encounters to be at the heart of traditional capoeira, since they provide a subtle forum for 'commenting' nonverbally on the rules of the game and, by extension, on the rules of society at large.

Although many authors have argued that folk expressions are frequently reflexive, that they may 'comment' on their own progress, for example (see Handelman 1981: 333), I believe it is unusual for an art form to be so explicit as to allow the players to comment on how rules can and should be applied in the process of play. Capoeira achieves this with the aid of verbal language in the songs, to be sure, but this aid is utilized primarily to set the basic frame or 'key' as represented in figure 7.1. The subroutines are literally games within the game, or 'rekeyings' in Goffman's terms (1976: 79–81), in which normal capoeira interactions can themselves be imitated; they are tropes of tropes. By moving back and forth between 'normal' interactions and these subroutines, between game and inner game, players can 'comment,' largely nonverbally, on the application of the rules themselves and thereby on the application of social norms and conventions.

To simplify the discussion, I will restrict my analysis to only one subroutine, the *chamada de bênção,* in all its variations (see table 4.3 and the related discussion).[2] All of the inner games function in approximately the same way, although the others tend to be less elaborate, and their rules aren't as clearly defined. To review what was said previously, *chamada* means 'call' and the subroutine is initiated or indexed by an apparent breaking of some lower-order rules: player A stops moving, pretends to leave himself open, and may even turn his back on B. If B is familiar with the convention of the *chamada,* he responds with a series of solo acrobatic moves (the *floreios*), followed by a careful approach to A, low to the ground. As B gets close to A, the tension heightens, since it is dangerous to be in the near kinesphere of another player, because it is harder to avoid a sudden attack. Sudden attacks may occur at any time during the *chamada* but are most common during the approach and the separation phases. A sudden attack indexes the resumption of normal play whenever it occurs and aborts the sequence of the subroutine syntagm. In

Goffman's terms, this is a frame break, since it signals a return to the primary key of the game, with the normal or default rules in effect. Such a break must occur eventually, however, at least by the separation phase, although it is still dramatic because either player may initiate it.

Tension is always present in normal capoeira play, since it is a combat and there is always danger. The initiation of a call temporarily breaks the tension, since the players have tacitly agreed to suspend hostilities in order to perform the subroutine. Phases 1 and 2 (table 4.3) are therefore relatively relaxed, and tension begins to build again as the players come together in Phase 3, waiting to see when and how the frame break will occur. The entire *chamada* can therefore be seen as a truce, a pause in the warfare, with renewed hostilities threatening to break out at any time.

Phase 4 is the climax of the *chamada* and the dramatic focus, since it represents the truce most fully, with both players hand in hand and, seemingly, fully cooperative (see fig. 4.7). The icons of combat have now given way to icons of cooperation, and the movement style is very different from normal capoeira action, which is why I have jocularly called it 'the waltz.' There is no *ginga* during this duet, which sometimes resembles simple walking, and other times a sort of mock ballroom dancing. Joining hands is always significant in the capoeira context, as noted previously, since there are times when it must be done (to begin and end the physical interaction), but it is always a somewhat dangerous activity as well (as in the scenario of the blessing). It can be a sign of communitas, but also a fertile field for deception. Hand position is the trickiest part of learning how to do the *chamadas*, since one must always be prepared to block a potential attack.

The trick of the blessing can be seen as an abbreviated version of the *chamada* interchange, since both are based on conventions of truce, symbols of comradeship, which can then be suddenly and unilaterally abrogated by attacks, symbols of *malícia*. Note that the attack is the index, the moment of secondness in Peirce's terms,[3] but it is the deceptiveness of the attack, especially when breaking a convention or expectation, which turns that index into a symbol of *malícia*. The subroutines intensify the drama of capoeira by providing a break in the tension (and the action) that then can be highlighted and reframed. What starts as a release of tension, however, turns into an 'intensification,' an increase in tension as the players come together. This union creates the eventuality, the inevitability, of a frame break that is simultaneously a release of tension and a resumption of the 'normal' tension of capoeira play. In addition, the creation of frames within frames (keying and rekeying) allows for the breaking of some rules without the destruction of the game framework itself. That is, lower-order rules, which apply to the subroutines, can be temporarily violated without damage to the structure of the higher-order rules that define the game. I demonstrated this using the interchange between Curió and Moraes in chapter 4.

In table 4.1, I organized the rules for capoeira play into two groups, following Bailey's distinction between normative and pragmatic rules in political (metaphorical) 'games.' This distinction captures an important principle of capoeira interaction but, as I noted, the boundary between the two rule types is often hard to clarify in practice. I suspect that this is true for many cultural genres of performance in which the rules are transmitted orally and informally and for which the very notion of 'rule' overlaps significantly with what might also be called the 'esthetic' of performance. By dividing the rules in this way, I was trying to indicate the extremes on what I really see as a continuum between latent and patent knowledge in capoeira practice and to highlight the importance of pragmatic principles (in Bailey's sense) for defining the esthetics of play.

Insofar as one might abstract from capoeira discourse one fundamental principle, it would be something like "Never trust anyone too far; especially those you have good reason to trust." This is one version of the law of *malícia*, of course, illustrated in the scenario of the blessing, and it follows most directly from pragmatic rule 7 (table 4.1), "Try to deceive your opponent." If one's opponent in the ring becomes (by iconic extension) one's opposite in any interaction, one's interlocutor for instance, the assumption of the intent to deceive is correspondingly extended, therefore the danger of trusting becomes universal. The normative rule which corresponds here is number 3 (table 4.1), "Always be ready to defend against an attack." This illustrates the close blending of normative and pragmatic principles, but also the dominance of the pragmatic order. The law of self-defense is the law of survival here, a hermeneutic of suspicion (in Ricoeur's phrase), which supercedes all social conventions, norms, niceties, and normative rules of the game.

In addition to the rule/esthetic and tacit/overt continua, the other important principle for organizing capoeira play is the notion of rule hierarchy. The work of Hofstadter, among others, has clarified the general understanding that in hierarchical cybernetic systems, some rules are more mutable than others. Mutable rules (lower-order) are those which can be changed relatively easily, whereas immutable (or less mutable) rules tend to be more strictly adhered to, since the system depends on them to preserve its essential structure (1985: 70–77). As I suggested above, the pragmatic principle of self-defense and the assumption of malicious intent can be seen as the highest-order, or default, principles which supercede all other rules or conventions in capoeira, inside the ring or out. Normative rules for capoeira play can always be suspended in deference to these fundamental principles, even if this means the framework of the game itself is broken. This is why the inner games are so important: they allow for a set of lower-order conventions that can be violated at will, leaving the higher-order rules, and thus the game framework, intact. As I tried to indicate in table 4.3, the very conventions that signal the onset of the inner games take the form of lower-order rule violations, which can then be 'set right' when the *chamada* frames are broken. In this way, the inner games represent a kind of meta-commentary on the mutability of rules and the tactics of rule-breaking. Instituting a 'call' is a concise, nonverbal way of 'saying' that rules are made to be broken.

This playing with rules in the transitions between normal play and the inner games is what allows for the full expression of *malícia*, the joy of deceptive rule breaking, while at the same time controlling it, keeping it within the bounds of the capoeira ring. If *malícia* is allowed to run rampant it can, and sometimes does, destroy the very fabric of the game, just as it was a threat to the social fabric during the slave era. Even today at the public festivals, police platoons will often ostentatiously stroll through the capoeira rings while play is under way, a tangible reminder of the default set of social rules that will be invoked should violence prevail.

Examples of games being destroyed due to the violation of normative rules are easy enough to document. The most common case is when mock combat turns to real combat, and the opponents begin trying to hurt each other in earnest. In this case, the circle collapses and everyone converges on the fighting players, trying to separate them. The game has dissolved and cannot be resumed until the fight is broken up. The same thing happens if onlookers decide that one player is trying to hurt the other one or is using unacceptable tactics. They can descend on the offending player and eject him from the game, which brings everything to a halt until the problem is resolved. Likewise, if a player gets injured by accident (or intentionally), the game may be discontinued until he is seen to, depending on the seriousness of the injury. The master of the *roda*, in games which have one, may stop the physical play at any time by stopping the music (yelling, "*iê!*"), which he may do for the purpose of instruction or to lecture players whose behavior he doesn't like. I have seen this happen when players don't respond in chorus to his calls, for instance. This was how rules were enforced in the traditional setting, how *malícia* was kept in bounds.

The structural relations expressed by the addition of games within the game to the models of capoeira and society above are complex and subtle. I will represent them graphically using a shaded line (inner game/frame; rekeying) inside a solid line (outer, 'normal' game/frame; primary key). The inner games are 'within' the regular game of capoeira in two senses: (1) in a conceptual sense, in that special rules apply, but these rules only have meaning within a framework of the normal, default rules of capoeira play; and (2) in a syntagmatic sense, since normal play both precedes and follows them in the sequence of events. However, the physical space used for the 'inner' game is the same as that in the primary key, the entire capoeira ring. Since each of these frames also has both covert and overt aspects, the potential for expression can be seen to multiply.

The inner games are embedded within capoeira play just as

capoeira itself is embedded in the social world, and this allows for an immediate reflexivity of expression. Comparisons between play in the subroutines and normal capoeira play can initially be seen as iconic with comparisons between capoeira play itself and social interaction. In this way, capoeira creates a structure within which it can 'comment on' its own relation to society. This structural iconicity is represented in figure 7.2.

If normal capoeira play is a mock combat, then the inner game can be seen as a mock truce, an uneasy respite always in danger of reverting to warfare. But even the default state of capoeira warfare is still only play warfare, since real fighting destroys the game. Real battles, such as slave rebellions in the past and political demonstrations at present, are fought outside the ring, in the social world. Any activity in the ring, no matter how aggressive, should still be mere play. Masters concur that, even in the past, serious fighting was properly kept out of capoeira games. Action in the ring could cause hostilities that resulted in real fights, but it was inappropriate for such fights to be staged at a *roda*. This iconicity provides further support for the complex metaphoric relation expressed in figure 7.1, since the structure embodies an implicit hierarchy of violence, with the social world

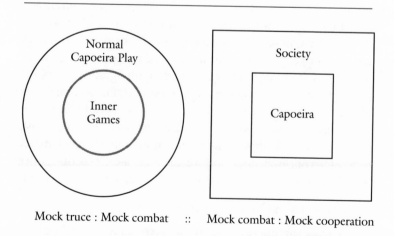

Mock truce : Mock combat   ::   Mock combat : Mock cooperation

Figure 7.2   Icon I: Metaphoric Inversion

on top. Capoeira uses icons of combat to critique the extreme violence of the social world, where one can easily be tortured and killed.

Although the inner games are embedded within capoeira play, when they are being enacted there is a sense in which normal capoeira play is also embedded within the *chamadas*. This is because the regular interplay of attack/defense is the default state, the 'subject' of the game, and the inner games simply exist to highlight normal play. In other words, the *chamadas* have no meaning in themselves, but are made to be destroyed, to be subsumed back into the flow of normal play. They represent a frame which exists in order to be broken. Accordingly, the whole tension of the inner games revolves around when and how they will revert to default capoeira, and the immanence of this reversion always 'inhabits' the play of the *chamadas*. So while the inner subroutines are in effect, the normal play of capoeira is always lurking 'within' the action, waiting to emerge as the frame breaks. This perspective on the embedding of domains produces another set of iconic relations between capoeira and society.

By seeing normal play as embedded within the inner games, the iconicity between capoeira and society increases, and the identity between the worlds is quite apparent. Mock combat, the normal state of capoeira, is latent within all the inner subroutines, and, by direct analogy, actual violence is latent within society, though often disguised by cultural conventions such as blessings and handshakes. Now the true force of the metaphor in figure 7.1 should be felt very clearly if one regards both figures 7.2 and 7.3 together. As in all metaphors, capoeira is both like and unlike its object, society. Where it is similar, it can comment by imitation and iconic representation. Where it is dissimilar, it can unmask and critique, and ultimately express an entirely different moral order. Of course, it does both of these at once, and this is the glory of its complex expression and, therefore, of its enduring life.

CAPOEIRA AND SLAVE SOCIETY

When analyzing the relations between capoeira and Brazilian society it is apparent that one must confront the problems of meaning which result from the multiplicity of potential and actual

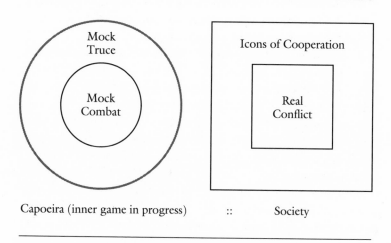

Capoeira (inner game in progress)   ::   Society

Figure 7.3   Icon II: Metaphoric Identity

social contexts. Capoeira means different things to people in Salvador than it does to those in the interior of Bahia and different
things to Bahians than to those in other parts of Brazil. In particular, the relations between the sport and the surrounding society were expressed differently during slave times when the sport
was being developed than they are today in the modern context.
I will argue that the more traditional, ludic style of capoeira, the
Angola form, has a special affinity with slave society, since it was
presumably being created during that period, whereas the more
agonistic styles arose in conjunction with the growth of industrialization in Brazil. Therefore, I will begin this section by exploring what the frameworks outlined above can reveal about master/
slave relations in the Brazilian past. I will then return to the
modern world of Bahia and the rest of Brazil, with an emphasis
on the development of the agonistic styles. Finally, I will conclude
with a few comments on the latest developments in the *atual* style
of capoeira and the influence of capoeira in the United States on
the emergence of that style.

The rules and conventions of a society are an attempt to en-
sure its smooth functioning by enforcing the cooperation of its
members. In a slave society there are an inordinate number of

elaborate rules, because separate conventions of behavior apply to slaves versus ordinary citizens (Mintz and Price 1976: 18–19). As a result, slaves in Brazil took special joy in bending, twisting, and breaking the rules, when they could, as a form of resistance against this double standard. The inversion in figure 7.1 establishes the opposition between capoeira and the social world, which could be used to express the slaves' awareness of and revulsion for the hypocrisy of the two-faced society in which they were captives. Furthermore, this distinction indicates their (partially masked) desire to turn things around: to do battle directly rather than indirectly, as they were usually forced to do. The underlying communitas between capoeira players extends in principle to all slaves, or oppressed people, and is an expression of the solidarity which exists, or should exist, between them in the face of the oppressor.

From this point of view, the inner games can be seen as icons, not so much of slave society as a whole, but of the dominant group, the Luso-Brazilian masters. The conventions of the subroutines thus become an acting out of the hypocrisy of surface politeness and even as an imitation of the white movement style. That might explain why joining hands in 'the waltz' seems almost like a burlesque of European ballroom dancing, and rather foreign to an African esthetic in which dancers (especially of the opposite sex) usually do not touch. Ironically, African movement style, such as pelvic rotation, was denounced by the Europeans as 'barbaric' or 'shameless,' while Africans often held European couple dancing to be similarly obscene! The movement from inner to outer games can be seen, from this perspective, as a transition from an imitation Euro-Brazilian world to an idealized Afro-Brazilian world.

In a slave society in which tensions and struggles are narrowly contained by a veneer of politeness and convention, the slave was a victim of the rules, so learning how to manipulate these rules was a matter of basic survival. When a member of the slaveowning class became 'friendly' with a member of the slave class, he was in effect saying, "Let's have a truce; let's dance hand in hand and suspend the combat between our groups." For the black slave, or even a freedman in a slave society, there was always the question,

"How long does this last? When do we revert to the normal (bi-ased) rules? When do you betray our friendship (or when do I)?" The poignancy of this problem was suggested in the first chapter in connection with the emotion-laden terms *ioiô* and *iaiá*, used by slaves for the sons and daughters of plantation owners. These con-flicts are perfectly expressed in the movement between the inner and outer games of capoeira, which is also why the attack that breaks the truce is often accompanied by laughter among the au-dience. Frame breaks are funny in general, especially if they ex-press deep and painful social truths, like the constant betrayals experienced by slaves or other oppressed groups. By moving from the inner to the outer games in a frame break, the players also express their desire for confrontation, for rebellion against domi-nation, without having to incur the dangers of actual rebellion.

Slaveowners and slaves had diametrically opposed views of social violence, for the most part. For slaves, outbreaks of violence which upset the social system could be positive, in that they al-lowed opportunities for liberation. The masters feared such out-breaks and set up elaborate controls to prevent them, yet at the same time they were forced to use 'orderly' violence, such as flog-ging, to keep the system working. This distinction can be used to generate a series of oppositions that represent the range of com-plexity found in the relations between capoeira domains and slave society in Brazil. This simplified scheme (see fig. 7.4) is based on a single distinction, between attitudes toward violence and social control, but even so it entails considerable subtlety and ambiguity of expression.

As a first reading, *a* might be seen to represent the slave view of society, in which controls or conventions are viewed as intol-erable constraints masking a potential violence against the system, which could mean liberation. This contrasts with *b*, the normal state of capoeira, in which violence must be controlled in order for the game to benefit the players. In *c*, the inner games, violence is again masked, this time by a truce, and if capoeira combat breaks out, it will destroy the frame in which the routines can be enacted. But it was emphasized above that the inner frame is cre-ated only to be broken, since in movement terms the interesting action is normal capoeira play, which is the point of the whole

OVERT/PATENT	COVERT/LATENT
a. controls	violence
−	+
b. violence	controls
−	+
c. controls	violence
+	−
d. −	+

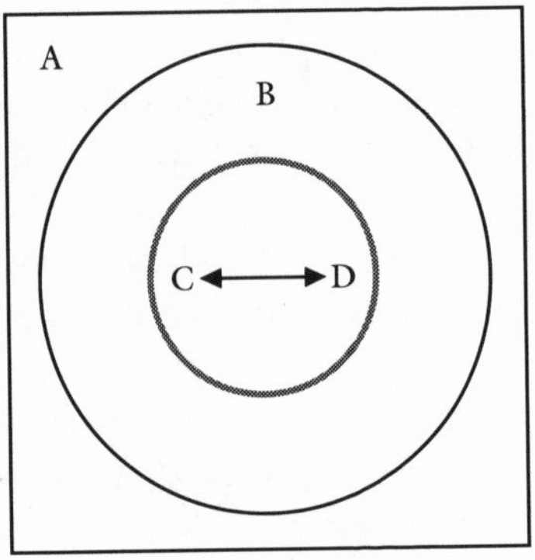

Figure 7.4   Universe of Discourse in Slave Society

performance. Since the inner game is only effective as a dramatic highlight for, and reframing of, the main action, it might just as well be the latent 'violence' (only a mock violence, of course) waiting to emerge from these routines that is positively valued. In that case, the overt truce, an imitation of boring European movement patterns, becomes a negative value. This situation is represented in *d*, whereby the essential ambiguity of the inner games is captured in the dissonance between *d* and *c*. The subroutines are important as frameworks within which to focus the conflicts of capoeira, but are of interest primarily as stages for the ingenuity of framework breaking, not for intrinsic properties of their own. They are icons of the ridiculous, but as symbols they are sublime.

The ambiguity in the inner games prompts a rereading of the relations in figure 7.4, motivated by the inversion of values between *c* and *d*. As it stands, *d* is identical to *a*, but since both *d* and *c* are possible interpretations of the same inner game, and since the inner game is an icon of society (fig. 7.3), what would it mean for *a* to be identical to *c* as well? If the positive and negative values of *a* were reversed, making *a* equivalent to *c*, the result could represent the slaveowners' view of society, where controls were seen as necessary checks on the potential violence of slave rebellion. This reinforces the iconicities, both of movement style and structural relations, between the inner games and society at large in the slave setting. It also demonstrates that capoeira is capable of expressing both fundamental aspects of slave society: the role of the dominant as well as the dominated.

Although violence is negatively valued during normal capoeira, as in *b,* mock violence is positive (as in *d* also), since it is what makes the entire performance possible. Changing the valences of *b* exhausts the possibilities of the scheme in figure 7.4 and reproduces a likeness of slave rebellion against oppressive controls, where violence is overt and positively valued. This is arguably one of the psychological keys to the popularity of the game, now and in the past. In a compelling sense, defeating one's opponent in capoeira is identified in a player's mind with liberation from oppression. This is reinforced by the persistent oral tradition that slaves used martial skills developed through practice of capoeira in order to escape from and rebel against their masters. In that case, the mock violence of the game was converted into actual violence in the outside world.

I have argued that, even in slave times, actual violence against the system was not always the desirable strategy, even though it might have been psychologically appealing, since the dangers of failure, and subsequent penalties, were so great. Instead, a majority of slaves chose to fight *indirectly* against the system, to manipulate the rules for their own benefit. The game of capoeira and the value of *malícia* are able to express both types of rebellion, indirect and direct, at the same time, as the series of relations diagrammed in figure 7.4 has made explicit. Thus, while training in martial skills which might be effective in an actual confrontation with authority, players could immediately experience the thrill of physical victory over an opponent, imagining that opponent to be the oppressor, which one day it might be. In this way they could also savor the psychological triumphs of humiliating and making fun of an opponent, thereby perhaps reducing their personal frustrations under oppression. At the same time, by practicing techniques of deception, players could learn how to manipulate the rules within the system, thus surviving situations where direct conflict was not feasible. In that case, they could

actually sing songs discreetly making fun of the slaveholder, imitate his movement patterns, and learn techniques of bending the
rules that could be immediately applied in the social arena.

The line between mock violence and real violence is easy to
cross, and defeating one's opponent in a martial contest without
violence is very difficult indeed. The ambiguity of capoeira depends on maintaining a constant balance between extremes like
attack and defense, competition and cooperation, and achieving
this balance is the measure of mastery. It is this ambiguity of
the encounters, dancing on the knife-edge between oppositions,
which makes capoeira so expressive and also so difficult to perfect.
Kochman has argued that there is a fundamental difference between Afro- and Euro-American approaches to conflict, namely
that African-Americans often rely on an attitude he calls 'strategic
ambiguity' (Kochman 1986; see also 1983). In the examples he
uses, participants make verbal challenges which are intended to be
neither hostile nor playful, but are perched squarely on the border
between the two states. If the reply is hostile, they are ready for a
fight; if playful, they are ready to banter, depending on the response of the hearer. Capoeira lends weight to the validity of his
analysis, since it is an excellent example of the maintenance of a
'strategic ambiguity' in African-derived play, both in the verbal
and in the nonverbal arenas.

CAPOEIRA IN MODERN SOCIETY

In pointing out the similarities between colonial and imperial
slave society and modern Brazilian society, I stressed the persistence of economic and social oppression based on ethnic and racial discrimination. These continuities are reflected in the fact that
the *Angola* style is still being played in the modern context and,
therefore, that many of the same relations diagrammed above still
hold in Bahia today. However, there have also been many changes
since the slave era, and some of those changes are expressed in the
development of the agonistic style of capoeira, as it emerged from
the older tradition in the 1930s. I have called *Regional* agonistic
in the first place, partly to indicate that it was more combative,
more competitive, and therefore that the underlying comradeship
between players was submerged. If it is true, as I argued in

chapters 5 and 6, that music and song intrinsically foreground communal, harmonic relations, relative to the more aggressive physical interaction, that helps explain why they frequently assumed a vestigial or perfunctory character in the *Regional* style of capoeira. This led over time to the virtual extinction of the *ladainha/chula* invocations in that style, which put a major stress on one of the most important roles for older masters in the sport. Finally, an overriding interest in the efficiency and effectiveness of the self-defense aspects of capoeira led to a deemphasis on, and eventually a virtual loss of, the various *chamada* subroutines in *Regional* style.

Along with these structural losses, however, came many gains in other areas. The most important was the creation of the academy setting and the institutionalization of capoeira as a legitimate sport in the eyes of most Brazilians. This allowed for the expansion of the sport to many parts of the country where it had never existed before (as well as its reintroduction to parts where it had) and eventually into the international community. It is probable that the institutionalization of capoeira saved it from extinction, but at the very least it breathed new life and vitality into it and created an immense pool of players from all strata of Brazilian society (and outside). As capoeira moved off the streets and into academies, there were improvements in training techniques, in martial applications, and in the general level of physical play, since competition was much tougher. The status hierarchy of students became much more complex, including rites of passage such as christenings, presentations of ranked belts, and graduations of new instructors. Tournaments were organized by state and national capoeira federations, and groups of local academies began affiliating into societies.

During the initial period of the divergence of styles, as I have shown, the *Regional* style of capoeira became the dominant form, especially outside of Bahia. The simplifications in performance syntagm and standardizations of movement repertoire made it easier to teach, but these changes also resulted in a different expressive emphasis in play. Both the *ladainha/chula* complex and the *chamadas* represented framing conventions whose loss reduced the pragmatic potential of interactions to comment on social and stylistic habits. The result was an increasingly intense focus on the physical interplay only as contest, with group participation in musical and verbal commentary becoming vestigial, rather than integral, to the action. The narrowed scope of interest, more goal-oriented, seemed to highlight individual rather than group process, and mastery became primarily a matter of physical superiority rather than esthetic or moral excellence. Emphasis on the values of competition and efficiency implies a meaning system in which there is a single set of normative social rules for all and, therefore, no need to expose hypocrisy with deceit. Without the musical and verbal reinforcements of comradeship and solidarity between players, there were fewer constraints on the aggressive forms of combat, so there was a tendency toward greater violence. When this agonistic style was taught to poorer players it became especially dangerous, because their frustrations with the system often caused a lack of interest in restraints of any kind.

Notice that the image of personal, direct competition is in line with the dominant ideology of many industrialized societies, often combined with a 'democratic' mythos that in order to win one needs only to work hard. It might be argued that such a view was fairly common to many middle- and upper-middle-class Brazilians during the initial period of the split in capoeira styles, especially the 1940s and 1950s. Since that time, it has become increasingly difficult for Brazilians of any class to maintain optimism about the virtues of hard work and 'fair' competition, because the systemic inequalities of the economic system, both locally and internationally, are so apparent. This brings the views of the middle economic sectors closer to those of the predominantly dark underclass, which have remained essentially pessimistic. It is interesting that this renewed skepticism about economic and social progress should correlate with the reunification of capoeira in the stylistic trend I have called *atual*. This ongoing process involves the reintegration of many of the semiotic and structural forms previously abandoned under the *Regional* approach, along with the resurgence of participation in the *Angola* style itself. Of course, even *Angola* tradition, though teachers avow a conservative orientation, has changed and is changing as it is performed in new settings in Brazil and internationally.

I have repeatedly emphasized the close connection in the minds of the players between what goes on in the capoeira ring and events in outside society, a link that is reinforced by the reflexivity of the inner games. Therefore, from one perspective the sport can be seen as a kind of a fight magic, an alchemical attempt to influence the outer world by deeds in the inner world. *Capoeiristas* hope to translate power in one domain to power in the other, but is this just a fantastic dream or are there concrete ways in which capoeira expertise can lead to socioeconomic advancement? D'Aquino examined this question and concluded that there was a direct correlation between power within the ring and increased social status outside (1983: 156–70). I don't agree that this is usually the case, since upper-class groups, especially in Bahia, do not consider capoeira prowess to be a legitimate form of social status. Many of the best *capoeiristas* are respected within their own peer group, and even gain recognition nationally among enthusiasts of the sport, but this does not often translate into mainstream social acceptance. In terms of economic success, there is at best a very limited advantage to capoeira mastery, in most cases, as I showed in chapter 3. A few teachers, especially in southern Brazil, have succeeded in making a fairly good living from the sport, but the majority of masters depend on other occupations to make ends meet.

The division between the *Angola* and *Regional* styles of capoeira began in the 1930s and continued to be important into the 1970s, when the first national tournaments were held. The organization and adjudication of those competitions, under the direction of the Federação Brasileiro de Pugilismo, caused many disputes between state delegations, which eventually led to a massive disillusionment with the tournament format altogether. There were always some masters, even in the southern states, who had adhered to a more traditional, ludic style of play and had resisted participation in organized competitions. Because of the unprecedented growth in the number of academies and players in Brazil, there was more and more interest in the roots of the sport, and players began to research its origins and document the life histories of older masters in Bahia and elsewhere. By the late 1970s and early 1980s, this effort was encouraged by the inquir-

ies of players from the United States and Europe who began going to Brazil to train and learn more about the sport. Many of the
U.S. players were themselves African-Americans and were interested in the African aspects of the game, since it gave them a sense
of historic continuity with the tradition. It was during this period
that what I have been calling the *atual* style began to be a force
in the development of capoeira.

Teachers who had refused all along to identify exclusively
with either *Regional* or *Angola* schools of play simply taught what
they wanted, incorporating some of the innovations of the agonistic approach and rejecting others. Two notable examples of this
tendency were Mestre Nô in Bahia and Mestre Suassuna in São
Paulo. At the same time that some masters were beginning to turn
away from the tournament format and question the trends of the
agonistic movement, there was a resurgence of interest in the *Angola* style of capoeira, influenced by such masters as Mestre Moraes, who at that time was having a great impact on the style of
play in Rio. By the early to mid 1980s, many of the older *Angola*
masters in Bahia had come out of retirement and opened academies, and fewer and fewer masters anywhere were identifying
themselves as proponents of the *Regional* form. At present, this
convergence of styles is continuing, and the vast majority of players and masters could now be placed within the category *atual*.
Although many masters in Bahia have recently joined an association of *Angola* academies, the styles of their students reflect the
individual training of a particular master more than any coherent
genre. In short, the time may be rapidly approaching when the
capoeira motto quoted previously will be realized: "There is only
one capoeira."

These most recent events pose an interesting case for social
scientists, since they problematize the relation between performance arts like capoeira and social movements in the world at
large. The institutionalization and modernization of capoeira begun in the 1930s coincided with what was then (and perhaps still
is in political circles) a standard model of economic development
for 'third world' countries generally, but was less frequently
applied to the arts of ethnic minorities within them. Recently,
however, with the reincorporation of more and more traditional

elements into capoeira, the trend in that sport might just as well be called 'antimodernization,' as the new styles are looking increasingly ludic. Huizinga argued that the play element in culture tended only to diminish over time, under the influence of increased social organization and routinization (1955: 75). He did not envision the process as a pendulum swing that might reverse itself at the extremes. The most recent studies of ethnicity have begun to note similar, conservative trends in many societies, as minority peoples who once embraced 'progress,' at least to some extent, begin to question that choice (for example, Clifford 1988: chap. 12). Native peoples everywhere seem to be returning to or recreating 'traditional' lifeways and languages as part of an increasing struggle against the ravages of industrialization and ecological destruction. Ironically, this kind of postmodern discourse between the historic and the mythic is nowhere stronger than in the most 'developed' countries, like the United States and the Soviet Union.

FRAMES WITHIN FRAMES

I indicated in the introduction that I conceived of the main framework for capoeira as a kind of play, and toward the beginning of this chapter I discussed some of the paradoxical properties of a related frame, that of game. Some students of these and related frameworks for cultural context have taken pains to clear up generic muddles in the classification of expressive phenomena, and I want to conclude this study with an examination of how capoeira might aid in this attempt. I refer especially to the work of MacAloon (1984) and his enlightening discussion of embedded frameworks within the spectacle of the modern Olympic games. It seems to me that contextual frameworks are aids in the interpretation of meaning and that, therefore, they are types of 'interpretant' in the Peircean perspective.[4] This implies that although there must be a certain social consensus for such frames to function, it is also possible, indeed expected, that different individuals and groups should frame the 'same' event differently. In other words, an interpretive framework is not a static object, open for all to read, but is constantly being restructured and reconstituted by participants in a social situation.

To demonstrate how this works, consider the relation between two possible frames for the performance of capoeira. In the first place, capoeira can easily be viewed as a kind of 'spectacle,' especially by a naive audience. The frame of spectacle has been distinguished by MacAloon as being visually and emotionally compelling but morally suspect (1984: 246–50). Capoeira is spectacular because of its acrobatic movements, principally, and because there is always a potential for violence. Brazilians unfamiliar with capoeira and foreign tourists, for example, might well view the game solely as a series of impressive contortions, perhaps with an added *frisson* of potential danger, much as they might watch a troupe of itinerant acrobats. For participants or aficionados, however, the spectacle frame is relatively unimportant, even nonexistent, as the acrobatics and/or violence are noticed as interesting sidelights on, or even diversions from, the important events. In this way, the 'same' performance can be framed as spectacle by one group of observers and as game by another.

There is a relatively new context in which the spectacle frame takes on overriding importance, and that is the domain of show capoeira: principally the folklore shows for tourists in Salvador and other Brazilian cities. In these shows, some of which also go on world tours, all the expressive genres (such as candomblé, samba, etc.) tend to lose significance, and in capoeira even the game framework is usually lost, since the players are frequently going through a choreographed routine in which competitiveness is a sham. Such a performance is usually not even play for the participants, since it quickly becomes reduced to the routine of a job.

One of the first folkore shows I ever saw was as the guest of Mestre Moraes, who took me to see one of his old teachers, Mestre João Grande, then starring in the show. During the capoeira segment, Moraes went onto the stage where he improvised a stirring *ladainha* to commemorate the occasion and proceeded to play an exquisite game with his master. Chills went up my spine during this classic interaction, but as I looked around, I realized that no one else in the audience realized anything unusual was happening. For them it was still just an interesting spectacle; as far as they knew the same thing happened every night.

Although the first folklore shows in Bahia seem to have originated after World War II, it seems clear that the spectacle frame for capoeira is considerably older. When I was visiting the Recôncavo region of Bahia, I spent time with two brothers in Muritiba who had gathered a capoeira group around them. These were the same two I described in the act of verbal dueling in chapter 6.[5] This group performs capoeira occasionally at local festivals and their style of play is more theatrical than I had hitherto experienced. That is, the players were obviously (to me) putting on a show: they had a tacit agreement not to compete seriously, but were cooperating to make the performance entertaining to spectators in the hope of getting spare change and free drinks. Their capoeira bouts included mock knife fights, mock arguments, and several other prearranged scenarios quite different from anything I had previously seen on the streets. This kind of reduction in the game framework in order to play for the audience, thus encouraging an interpretation of events as theatre or spectacle, is clearly an option available to players in many settings and may have been as common in the past as it is in modern show business. There are moments, such as gestural 'asides,' which represent frame breaks into the theatrical mode, present in much of current capoeira play, and the group from Muritiba seem to have exploited and elaborated this possibility to develop a distinctive style.

During a local festival, the above group had started a *roda* in the middle of a crowd of spectators when a stranger jumped into the ring, asking to play.[6] He was a young, light-skinned fellow who obviously was an adept of the sport, since he had a *berimbau* tatoo on his upper arm. We subsequently learned that he was from the south, from São Paulo, and was visiting Bahia on vacation. As he began to play, it was evident that he didn't understand the tacit solidarity of the spectacle frame encouraged by the brothers, since he had been schooled in the agonistic martial traditions common in the south. At one point he grabbed one of the local players, lifted him up, and dumped him forcefully outside the ring. This level of aggression was confusing to the other players, who could not understand why he would want to humiliate a fellow that he didn't even know (and therefore could have no grudge against). The locals were all friends out for a good time, hoping to make a little money and add to the festival atmosphere. Their orientation toward the audience strengthened the ties between players, since all money collected was to be shared, and any conflict between them was understood to be only an act, to fool the spectators into giving more. The fact that the player who had been dumped did not react by getting angry, but only by shaking his head in wonder, underlined the fact that what I had seen was a conflict of styles, of interpretive frameworks. The outsider had different assumptions about the tacit rules of the game than the local group did, and his competitive behavior was simply incongruous in that theatrical frame, as it would also have been in the context of a professional folklore show.

This clash of expectations might also be used to illustrate further the difference between games and freer types of play. Play in general is often said to involve an alteration of the means/ends relation relative to normal social interaction, such that means are not determined by their ends, but attain a relative autonomy.[7] Games, as specialized forms of play, tend to be less free in this respect, since the object of the game frequently influences, to a greater or lesser extent, enjoyment of play for its own sake. In this view, ludic capoeira, especially of the extremely cooperative kind played by the group above, is closer to pure play: moves and music enjoyed for their own sake and presented as spectacle for the crowds. The agonistic style of the outsider, in contrast, was goal-oriented: he conceived of the game as a competition in which his tactics were determined by their martial effectiveness. The directness of the game framework is characteristic of institutionalized capoeira, as opposed to more 'folkloric' varieties, the indirectness of which approaches the ideal of freedom in play.

In the traditional setting, I pointed out that capoeira was often played at festivals, especially during the pre-Carnaval cycle in Salvador. This was never the exclusive context for capoeira, though it was arguably the most important one in the past. Even today, the tradition continues in a somewhat attenuated form, since many of these street *rodas* no longer attract the best players. In such cases, the game frame is embedded within the larger framework of festival, capoeira play being only one of a variety of activities during such celebrations. Since festivals are only one setting for capoeira play, now as in the past, the festival frame is clearly an optional, not a necessary, condition for performance. Because capoeira can be performed either in free play mode or as a more structured game, and therefore can optionally be embedded in the framework of festival, it follows that its overarching framework is rather mutable or 'weak.' This is evidence in support of Handelman's analysis of play phenomena in general, as opposed to other genres, such as ritual, which have more 'resilient' or immutable frames (1977: 190).

The festival cycle in Bahia that frames some capoeira is itself embedded in church ritual, which is the sacred 'excuse' for the secular celebrations. In the article cited above, Handelman's main point is to distinguish play and ritual as metacommunicative types, which he sees as quite close in some ways, but ultimately as opposed or complementary social domains. Following his analysis, I want to conclude by showing how the interplay of these two frameworks, play and ritual, accounts for much of the ambiguity in capoeira. One important difference between the two frame types, Handelman argues, is that ritual serves to define a moral community whereas play is fundamentally amoral. While both frames are capable of constituting social critique, ritual criticizes from the point of view of ultimate truth, whereas play pokes fun at social foibles for the sake of humor, without offering an alternative model of behavior (1977: 189).

In the ludic style of capoeira, the *Angola* form, the introductory *ladainha/chula* complex clearly establishes a ritual framework for the play to follow. Fundamental values and philosophies are alluded to in those songs, and God is directly invoked: overtly in Christian terms and, perhaps, covertly in a more African form as well. Since these invocations have been omitted in many of the agonistic events, the obvious conclusion would be that such styles have lost the ritual framework, being therefore reduced to mere play or game. I believe this would be a hasty conclusion, however, the actual situation being, as usual, more complex than that.

To begin with the original, ludic style, the *Angola* tradition would seem to be made up of equal parts of ritual and play, and one could argue that either framework was embedded within the other.[8] This involves a series of paradoxes, as I have indicated, which in Handelman's terms include such oppositions as: morality/amorality, harmony/disharmony, faith/pretense, and so forth. Does the normative communitas between capoeira players, for instance, form the basis for a moral community? The answer would seem to be ambiguous, yes and no. In the slave era, when the ritual frame was probably stronger, the social critique was also based more solidly on a shared sense of injustice reinforced by ethnic solidarity. In that context, capoeira and Afro-Brazilian arts in general did, in effect, form an alternative moral community. In the modern world, however, although capoeira still implies something of a social critique, the basis for that criticism is much less clearly defined and usually falls more into the realm of amoral ridicule. This is not only related to the weakening of the ritual frame, or virtual extinction in some settings, but also reflects the ethnic and class diversity of the players and is further manifested in the anarchic battles between various schools and masters. Nonetheless, even in the most agonistic of contests, the game usually takes on an air of moral seriousness, related to the uncompromising truth of lessons learned in the ring: truths which can help the player to adjust to life in the outside world. In the ludic styles, these basic truths were the 'true deceptions,' namely learning how to unmask pretense and hypocrisy in society at large. In the agonistic styles, the truths became the virtues of hard work and efficient combat, to prepare oneself for the competitive battles outside.

The evidence of the latest turn back to ritual in the convergence of styles to a more unified *atual* form of capoeira perhaps indicates a new moral and social community developing, the bases of which remain to be delineated clearly in the future. In his examination of frameworks for understanding the Olympic games, MacAloon plays with a host of similar embedded and contrasting contexts which cause problems in classification. Instead of frames that clearly define the activities within them, such as "this is game," he asks if it might not be more appropriate to use the interrogative mode, "Is this game?" in order to capture the ambiguities of interpretation (1984: 258–62). Such transformations seem very appropriate in the case of capoeira as well and could generate a host of similar ambiguous questions which summarize the arguments of the book. One could begin with normal capoeira play and ask, "Is this a real fight, or are we really cooperating now in order to fight better outside?" Turning to the inner games, one could similarly ask, "Is this a truce, or are we actually intensifying the combat potential by pretending to cooperate?"

These and many similar questions turn on the ambiguities generated by alternative framework possibilities and by the maintenance of a balanced tension between oppositions within those frameworks. The creation of strategic ambiguities in capoeira allows it, like many art forms, to reveal on the one hand while concealing on the other, playing at the border between overt and covert images. What is communicated in performance may be a style or a complex of feelings, things not easily compacted into language alone, or even at all.

The journey into the ring of capoeira, barely begun in this work, reveals rings within rings, games within games, and at the heart a profound ambiguity which remains unresolved. In this ambiguity is potential, a possibility space that is open to the future, since it can be continuously defined and redefined in conformity with new cultural needs. The sense of infinite potential within the game is, I believe, the key to its continuing success and expansion into the international scene. It is what challenges the players to ever greater creative effort and what gives them the transcendent sense of liberation in the act of play. This sense of freedom is fresh, but it is rooted in the piercing vision of slaves who glimpsed long ago a spark of brightness in the midst of the dark night of domination.

APPENDIX A

Laban Notation of Capoeira Ginga

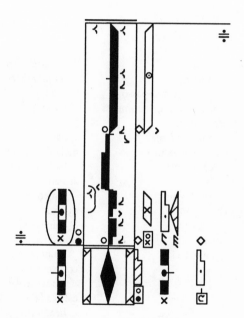

Notation courtesy of Ilene Fox, with the resources and personnel of the Dance Notation Bureau, New York City.

Movement Repertoire (Partial List)

Golpes ('Strikes')	*Ataques* ('Attacks')	*Base* ('Base' ginga)
		Contragolpes ('Counterattacks')
Mortais 'mortal'	*Traumatizantes* 'Traumatizers'	*Desequilibrantes* 'Takedowns'
meia-lua de compasso	bênção	rasteiras
half moon in a compass	blessing	sweeps
rabo de arraia	martelo	vingativa
stingray's tail	hammer	vengeful
chapeu de couro	meia-lua de frente	bandas
leather hat	half moon in front	trips
chibata	armada	bôca de calça
small whip	armed strike	pants 'mouth' [cuff
cruz	queixada	arrastão
cross	chin strike	pull down
coice	ponteira	tesouras
mule kick	point strike	scissors
	cotovelhada	
	elbow strike	
	cabeçada	
	head butt	
	palma	
	palm strike	
	chapa	
	metal plate	
	joelhada	
	knee strike	

Defesas
('Defenses')

Esquivas	*Fugas*	*Floreios*
'Escapes'	'flights'	'Flourishes'
negativa	aú	parafuso
negation	cartwheel	screw
resistência	macaco	relógio
resistance	monkey	clock
esquiva	mortais	pião
escape	mortal jumps	spinning top
cocorinha	's' dobrado	canivete
defecation	double 's'	can opener
rolé		sacarolha
roll		corkscrew
queda de quatro		queda de rins
fall on all fours		fall on the kidneys

Names of Masters Cited

Mestre	Given Name
Acordeon	Ubirajara ("Bira") Almeida
Besouro	Manoel Henrique
Bimba	Manoel dos Reis Machado
Caiçara	Antônio da Conceição Morais
Camisa	Rafael Tadeu Carneiro Cardoso
Canjiquinha	Washington Bruno da Silva
Cobrinha Verde	Rafael Alves França
Curió	(unidentified)
Ezequiel	Ezequiel Martins Marinho
Gato	José Gabriel Goes
Itapoan	Raimundo Cesar Alves de Almeida
João Grande	João Oliveira dos Santos
João Pequeno	João Pereira dos Santos
Moraes	Pedro Moraes Trinidade
Nô	Norival Moreira de Oliveira
Pastinha	Vincente Ferreira Pastinha
Suassuna	Reinaldo Ramos Suassuna
Vavá	Valfrido Viera de Jesus
Virgílio	Virgílio Ferreira
Waldemar	Waldemar da Paixão

Notes

1. In older accounts, one also encounters the term '*brinquedo*,' from the same source, meaning 'toy' or 'plaything.' This sense of 'toy' for a game or sportive movement is reminiscent of early uses of the word in English, common by the eighteenth century, originating perhaps in Elizabethan times.

2. This distinction was first pointed out to me by Bira Almeida, Mestre Acordeon.

3. Although Geertz notes the importance of their work in developing the 'game' metaphor for current interpretations of culture (1983: 24–26), he does not make the connection to his own use of the metaphor in "Deep Play," nor does he elaborate on the theoretical implications of the contextualizing process.

4. For example, Guttmann (1978: chap. 1); most modern analysts follow Huizinga (1955: 7–8). Caillois notes that the ancient Greeks distinguished between uncontrolled freedom, *paidia*, and rule-governed play, *ludus* (1969: 55).

5. One prominent elaboration of these ideas has been the work on 'flow,' by Csikszentmihalyi (1971; 1974); see also Gadamer (1975: 94).

6. For a good discussion of the history of the play/work distinction in anthropology, see Schwartzman (1978: 4–6); also Norbeck (1974). Blanchard and Cheska base their entire theory of play on this sort of distinction (1985: 38–52).

7. For general works on Brazilian Carnaval, see Brissonnet (1988), da Matta (1984; 1980) and Crowley (1984).

8. Although Huizinga is most often given credit for these ideas, Sebeok points out that he borrowed his fundamental insights from Schiller, and the latter's concept of the centrality of *spieltrieb* (Sebeok 1981; Schiller 1967).

9. This phrase comes from Habermas (1971), who uses it not only in relation to slavery, but for all forms of institutionalized domination.

10. This distinction is taken from Parmentier (1985b: 134).

11. For Peirce's phenomenology, see his *Collected Papers* (1931–58); following the tradition of Peirce scholarship, I will cite selections from this work as follows: *CP* 1.222 (volume 1, paragraph 222). A useful selection of excerpts from Peirce's work can be found in Buhler

(1955); one of many good summaries of Peirce's semiotics is Zeman (1977). There are now many examples of the use of Peircean semiotics in anthropology; some of the best are: Briggs (1988), Parmentier (1985a; 1985b), Daniel (1984), Singer (1978), and Silverstein (1976). Much of my understanding of the importance of Peirce to anthropological thought I owe to E. Valentine Daniel, although any errors in presentation are mine alone.

12. As a first approximation, an iconic relation is any quality seen as shared between a sign (or representamen) and its object, such as shape (isomorphism), color, or smell; an indexical relation is seen as one of contiguity, co-occurrence, causality, but also salience; a symbolic relation is taken to be one of arbitrary convention, rule, law, habit, but also continuity.

13. A useful review of the literature on this approach can be found in Briggs (1988: 11–16).

14. This metaphor comes from Daniel (1984).

15. This is my view, of course, which is not necessarily echoed by other students of play and sport: cf. Caillois (1969) for one contrasting approach.

16. Although I arrived at this formulation independently, Turner makes a similar point in (1988: 76–77).

17. For recent work on Bahian *candomblé*, see Wafer (1991) and Omari (1984); a discussion on the relation of these systems to Brazilian religion in general is found in Brown (1986).

18. This is the third pole in the fundamental semiotic triad: representamen (sign vehicle), object, interpretant. The implication is that signs do not 'have' meanings, intrinsically, but they are *taken* to have certain meanings by interpreters: signs determine meanings *to* someone or something (*CP* 2.228). Therefore one expects that the 'same' sign vehicle will actually be *different* for different interpreters, since it will constitute different interpretants; this is also true for a given interpreter at different times.

19. Bourdieu (1979) has been especially influential in demonstrating the importance of this emergent quality of cultural practices. Notice that the concept of 'habitus' occupies a place in his system comparable to the notion of 'habit' as employed by Peirce.

20. For instance, the work of Paul (1982) on Sherpa and Tibetan symbolic thought. The discussion of *mestre/discípulo* relations in chapter 2 employs a strategy reminiscent of Paul's work, though I arrived at it independently.

21. For Laban in English see, for example (1956); a working summary of the essentials is found in Dell (1977). The competing system most well known to anthropologists is Kurath (1974).

CHAPTER TWO

1. As Daniel states, his argument draws liberally on the insights of Olshewsky (1982).

2. This was revealed in talks between Bira Almeida and his students before the publication of his book; Marin Co., California, 1980.

3. In my experience, this view was found primarily among the intelligentsia, especially in Bahia—namely, those blacks who, although lower-class in origin, had managed to acquire a university education or were well-read on their own. See discussions by J. Turner (1985) and Fontaine (1985).

4. For *l'agya* or *ladjia*, see Michelon (1987) and Dunn [Dunham] (1939); for *maní*, see Ortiz (1985: 394–429).

5. For *kalinda*, see Hill (1972); on *maculêlê*, see Mutti (1978) and chapter 3.

6. In addition to the passing reference in Gwaltney (1981: 94), I have interviewed several people from Alabama and Louisiana who claim to have seen something like this in their early childhoods.

7. I only recently became aware of the Michelon study of *ladjia* (1987) and have not yet had a chance to consult it.

8. Only those indigenes purportedly captured in 'just wars' against unpacified tribes could be legally enslaved, the rest were supposed to be hired at a wage (which rarely happened). They died in large numbers from lack of antibodies to such diseases as measles and small pox. It was relatively easy for them to escape to the interior and find refuge with unpacified tribes. They were not seen as good workers, slave or free, which may have been partly a result of the 'anomie' resulting from forced acculturation, including their unfamiliarity with hierarchical social structures, and in some cases unfamiliarity with agriculture itself. By the late sixteenth century, they were increasingly being replaced by slaves from Africa, though Indians continued to be used as well (cf. Schwartz 1985: 51–72).

9. See Curtin (1969: 276); Rawley confirms these figures (1981: 283–306).

10. This is described and pictured in Fresu and de Oliveira (1982: 28–32), but apparently taken from an earlier work from the 1950s. I heard several descriptions of the money game in capoeira which, in times past, reportedly involved picking up coins, though currently only paper money is used. See also poorly documented photos from Mozambique in the Brazilian magazine *Iris* (no. 331, Oct., 1980) which portray moves similar to the *relógio* of capoeira.

11. Hegel was probably the first to make this point, but it has frequently been reiterated and reformulated since: for example, Mattoso (1986: 190); Patterson (1982: 97–98, 310); Mintz and Price (1976: 14). Similar relations also apply in peasant forms of domination, as Scott argues (1985).

12. See, for example, the recent Brazilian film "Quilombo" by Carlos Diegues (1984).

13. The book is called *Memórias da Rua do Ouvidor*. I have never seen the original, but it is cited by Lyra Filho (1974: 328). Almeida also cites the Lyra Filho reference, but for some reason gives an incorrect date of 1700 in both editions of his book (1981; 1986).

14. Some local ordinances were passed earlier; for instance, capoeira was specifically banned in Recife in 1831 (Freyre 1963: 261).

15. He reports that arrests on this basis are recorded as early as

1810 (1989: 647). Holloway is also careful to point out, however, that it is not clear what this charge actually meant in practice, in comparison with the sport as we know it today. There is some circumstantial evidence that it was associated with music or musicians, even then (1989: 667).

16. In this historical section, I temporarily return to the old usage of 'capoeiras' as practitioners. Elsewhere I will continue to use *capoeirista;* see Preface.

17. The related police term was *malfeitor* (Holloway 1989: 675).

18. Especially famous are the novels of Jorge Amado, like *Tenda dos Milagres* (1948) and *Os Pastores da Noite* (1964), both of which deal with capoeira.

19. A short film was made in 1952, perhaps one of the first films about capoeira, called "*Vadiação*," by Robatto.

20. In Rio de Janeiro, for example, there were two famous rival gangs (*maltas*) of capoeira fighters called *Guaiamums* and *Nagoas* (d'Abreu n.d.). Holloway makes the point that there is frequent confusion in the literature over the distinction between gang members who simply fought and those with some knowledge of the sport of capoeira (1989: 649).

21. This connection was first pointed out to me by James B. Watson.

CHAPTER THREE

1. See discussion in chapter 2, under holiday festivals.

2. This account is taken from Mutti (1978) and from interviews with Mestre Vavá and others in Santo Amaro.

3. This was the "old market" (*velho mercado*), which burned down in the 1930s. After that, the Mercado Modelo was constructed nearby, also next to the water but not quite on the same site. Right after the fieldwork period, the Mercado Modelo itself burned, but was immediately restored in the same place.

4. I am indebted to Catherine Howard for reminding me that *contramestre* is also a named status in the famous *escolas de samba* of Rio de Janeiro. In general parlance, the term often refers to an 'overseer' or 'subforeman.' This is another example of the links between capoeira discourse and other specialized, as well as ordinary, domains of Brazilian social life.

5. I found that the monthly fees were usually about the same as entrance fees, not substantially less as d'Aquino reports (1983: 64).

6. Even this is slightly controversial. Some masters recite the names of famous women capoeira players of the past, but others insist that these were simply 'tough women' who could fight but did not necessarily play the sport. It's interesting that this same comment was sometimes made about former male players as well. One Santo Amaro resident even told me that Besouro himself, although a great fighter, was not a *capoeirista*.

7. Personal communication from members. *Paulista* is the term for residents of São Paulo.

8. The LMA term 'kinesphere' refers to the space around the body defined by the reach of the limbs without changing position. It is some-

times subdivided into 'near reach' and 'far reach' in a manner reminiscent of Hall's categories of 'intimate' and 'personal' space (1969: 116–20).

9. Another possible problem, of course, is whether it is appropriate to abstract the quality of 'inversion' from a set of named moves and give it the status of a category to be interpreted. This is justified, I think, only if the players themselves make such a distinction, or if it can be shown indirectly that such a (covert) category has significant effects within the system. In this case, some players do make the distinction overtly, while for most it remains an operant, though covert, category. Indications of how this happens will be discussed in the following chapters.

10. This follows from Peirce's phenomenology, since icons are firsts, thus associated with mere possibility, with "positive qualitative potential" (*CP* 1.123).

CHAPTER FOUR

1. Adapted from a diagram in d'Aquino (1983: 38).
2. Simon Ottenberg, personal communication, 1984.
3. It is possible to view this sort of interaction in light of the Freudian theory of group formation and male bonding. In that framework, many all-male sports, as well as political groups, are said to function by marshaling sublimated homosexual libido, which sometimes can become overt (cf. Paul 1982: 60). It is not clear to me what such a theory would add to an understanding of capoeira, as opposed to the many other similar sports (as well as governments and businesses) which foreground aggression and dominance.
4. This term is taken from Peirce's pragmatic theory, which locates the meaning of signs in their interpretants—that is, in their effects on potential and actual interpreters (*CP* 5.457).
5. For a discussion of prototype theory in semantics, see Rosch (1973; 1977).
6. The LMA system uses the word 'flow' as a technical term, along an axis of 'free' versus 'bound.' Free flow is when muscles act in concert to reinforce a movement, and in bound flow they oppose each other to impede or constrain a movement (Dell 1977: 13–19). Capoeira play exhibits both kinds of flow 'effort' at different moments. During testing or combative encounters, bound flow predominates, and when the players are cooperating and relaxed, they are often in free flow. There is a slight preference for the second state among many players, since flow should never get so bound that it becomes difficult for movements to string together into sequences. When sequencing is interrupted by extreme bound flow, the players are usually fighting and this is generally seen as ugly or even 'non-' capoeira. I am indebted to Pam Shick for noting the importance of sequencing in capoeira interactions.
7. This kind of tactical pattern-breaking is common to many martial arts, of course, at the level of the microstructure. In fact, any feint or 'fake,' common to nonmartial sports as well, is effective for similar reasons. What is perhaps unique to capoeira is the creation of an explicit value, *malícia*, that expresses this tactic as a general principle with social implications.

8. Note that this sense of 'syntagm' as opposed to 'paradigm,' well established in linguistics, is quite different from the usage, especially of 'paradigm,' common in general scholarly discourse (as in Kuhn 1962, for example). Although first established in the work of Saussure (1966) and Hjelmslev (1963), the distinction was crucially linked to the poetic functions of metaphor (selection/paradigmatic) and metonymy (combination/syntagmatic) by Jakobson (for example, 1956: 55–82). I believe further that syntagmatic relations are essentially indexical, in Peirce's terms, and paradigmatic relations are fundamentally iconic.

9. The word *ié* primarily serves what Malinowski originally called the 'phatic' function of language; the term was elaborated into a systematic approach in Jakobson (1960: 355–59). Words used in this way signal that the communicative channel is open or closed. Thus *ié* is used to stop the action while play is in session, or to begin the action with an introductory solo.

10. Sometimes the *chula* is also called *entrada* ('entrance' or 'beginning').

11. This refers to the African-based medicine man or sorcerer complex, mentioned above and in chapter 2. I don't attempt to translate *mandingueiro* as 'sorcerer' here, because it is not clear to me that this meaning is consciously intended by most players. Rather the term seems to involve a diffuse Africanity, with mysterious overtones, associated with capoeira practice, especially in times past.

12. Associating this intensely 'malicious' interchange with the *mandingueiro* complex examined above. D'Aquino (1983: 58–60) refers to these *chamadas* as '*oferecendo golpe*' or '*balão fingido*' ('offering a blow' or 'false rumor'). I never heard these phrases used in this way, but their meanings are in character with the nature of the routines as described.

13. D'Aquino noticed this aspect as well, comparing it with Mukarovsky's notion of 'foregrounding' oneself (1983: 141).

14. Break dancing in the United States employs a similar move. Perhaps this is evidence of some influence from capoeira. Since it is such an unlikely and difficult move, it seems improbable that it could be an independent invention, but not impossible.

15. Some indications of increasing anger and aggressivity can be expressed well with LMA terminology. For instance, movements tend to go from 'sustained' to 'quick'; there are frequent 'recovery' periods between strikes; and blows are thrown with more 'strength' and 'directness' (cf. Dell 1977). In Peircean terms, the transition is from icons to indexes of combat.

16. Kochman suggests that African-Americans in general may deliberately push the limits between play and fight in a number of contexts, a propensity he calls "Strategic Ambiguity" (1986); also, see chapter 7 in this volume.

17. Mintz and Price have reference to this 'deeper level' of cultural patterning, which they refer to as "cognitive orientation," and they argue that it is more basic than culture, underlying it (1976: 6). I would argue instead for a continuum between cognitive, covert 'habits' and overt conceptual patterns, mediated through signs.

CHAPTER FIVE

1. This is still controversial for some generative grammarians advocating revised versions of a Chomskyan model of linguistics. An early argument against the autonomy thesis as it relates to syntax can be found in Newmeyer (1978).

2. Rego notes that in Bahia the *reco-reco* is also called *ganzá*, a name usually given to another instrument elsewhere in Brazil: a metal rattle often played in Carnaval groups (1968: 85).

3. As usual, there are differences as to the names. Some call the medium-sized one *gunga* and the largest one *beira boi* or *contra-gunga*. All agree that two of the three sizes are *viola* and *gunga*.

4. *Atabaques* are called *lé* (smallest), *rumpí* (medium), and *rum* (largest). Cuban *bata* drums are *ikónkulu* (smallest, 'child'), *itótele* (mid-size, 'father'), and *iyá* (largest, 'mother'). This information comes from various sources, including musicians in the traditions, and names vary somewhat from source to source.

5. For a comprehensive treatment of Umbanda, see Brown (1986).

6. This scheme was related in a personal communication from Gary Harding, an *ogan* (ritual specialist) of an Umbanda *terreiro* ('house') in São Paulo, who now resides in Seattle.

7. Similar to Almeida's description of a "buzzing" effect (1981: 70).

8. From a Peircean perspective, the buzz note is a clear example of a 'first' in its indiscriminate potentiality. It is from this inchoate source that distinction and opposition (secondness) arise. Since it also mediates between extremes, allowing a smooth flow between tones and providing the rhythmic continuity, it must also be seen as a 'third,' and thus embodies the idea of the 'thirdness of firstness' (cf. Apel 1981: 95).

9. Although an argument might be made that the rhythms could be heard in cycles of four or even eight, I have conformed to what has become the standard convention of notating them in 2/4 time (see Onori 1988; Shaffer 1977). My notations are similar to the ones in these sources, except that I identify certain motifs as the signature 'themes' in order to highlight comparisons between the *toques*. Since I argue that many of the variations are interchangeable between *toques*, I don't bother to notate them, although no *toque* can be played without both theme and variations. Another difference with these other sources is where the accents come in the measure, since I believe the accented tones are frequently off the beat (especially the 'one' beat), as I have indicated. I am aware of the many controversies surrounding the use of Western musical notation in the analysis of non-Western musical genres. In adhering to a modified version of standard notation, I am making no claims about the appropriateness of such an enterprise, but am simply employing the system I am somewhat familiar with. Accordingly, I would welcome other approaches to the notation and analysis of capoeira music, if they could capture aspects of its structure more clearly. I take it for granted that any analytical system inevitably shapes, to some extent, its objects of inquiry.

10. Ottenberg (personal communication, 1984) noted that male/

female oppositions are also common in African call and response singing. In this case the one/many relation is also neutralized.

CHAPTER SIX

1. The term glossed as 'guy' (*nego*) is a shortened form of *negro* ('negro' or 'black'), which in Bahia is an affectionate term, among many speakers, for any friend or acquaintance, regardless of racial characteristics.

2. Cf. Abrahams, pp. 215–40, in Kochman (1972) for some United States examples.

3. See section on holiday festivals.

4. There is a burgeoning literature on women's roles and perceptions of gender typing in Brazil, but less is available, of an analytical nature, on *machismo* or gender typing from the male perspective. For examples of the former, see Hahner (1978; 1984). For a fascinating analysis of how women are represented in the legal system, see Corrêa (1983).

5. One exception is Mestre Jelon Vieira, now living in New York, who does believe possession to have been part of the tradition.

6. He should not be confused with Saint Benedict 'the moor,' a sixteenth-century black saint. In Portuguese, the latter is São Benedito.

7. See Rego (1968: 198); he says it actually means 'like the ocean.'

8. See chapter 3, section on "Play Space, Social Space."

9. Almeida (1986: 1); I learned in a personal communication that the actual word used by Bimba was '*maldade*.'

10. Personal communication from Marcelo Pereira, Mestre Caveirinha, 1986.

CHAPTER SEVEN

1. Guttmann (1978: 4–14); but, as I noted previously, other scholars of play disagree with this view (for example, Blanchard and Cheska 1985: 53–54).

2. I refer to *chamadas* in the plural because there are several variations on the basic pattern, mostly having to do with the hand and body positions of the players (see chapter 4). All of these variations can be referred to by the same phrases, usually either *chamada de bênção* or *chamada de mandinga*, which are synonymous.

3. In Peirce's phenomenology, secondness is (to simplify) the experience of the world as resistant to our ideas about it and is correlated with indexicality in one semiotic dimension (*CP* 1.23–6; 1.325; 1.418–28).

4. See chapter 1, note 18.

5. Olavo Paixão dos Santos and his brother Airto.

6. This interchange occurred during the *micareta* (a kind of festival) in São Felix, May 9, 1982.

7. Miller (1973), cited and elaborated in Handelman (1977).

8. Since all 'serious' play begins with *ladainha/chula* in *Angola* style, play can be seen as framed by ritual. However, since everyone comes to play, already expecting a game, the ritual could equally well be seen as

conceptually 'preceded' or framed by play. In that case, the invocations might be taken as perfunctory nods to a ritual frame, without seriously affecting the action to follow. A similar argument could be made for some types of liminoid phenomena, like the singing of the national anthem before a baseball game.

Glossary

academia: capoeira school
agogô: two-tone clapperless bell or gong
aluno: student of capoeira master; same as *discípulo*
Angola: a traditional or conservative style of capoeira; also a 'nation' of
    candomblé
Angoleiro: a practitioner of the *Angola* style
arame: metal string on a *berimbau*
arrastão: capoeira takedown, pulling both legs from under an opponent
ataque: attacking move or movement initiative
atual: an emerging style of capoeira (my term), combining aspects of
    both *Angola* and *Regional* styles
aú: cartwheel
aviso: a *berimbau* beat, formerly used to warn players of a police raid
balanço: part of the basic capoeira movement (*ginga*); torso rocks for-
    ward and back as the weight shifts
bamba: someone adept at verbal and physical dueling; synonym for ca-
    poeira expert
banda: movement to trip or flank an opponent
barravento: a *berimbau* beat; name refers to a prepossession trance state
base: base, the *ginga*, the fundamental movement
batizado: the capoeira initiation ceremony; christening
batuque: a music and dance event in the Afro-Brazilian style
Batuque: a genre of martial arts in Bahia, probably extinct, involving
    verbal and physical competition
batuqueiro: participant in a *batuque*
bênção: blessing; a front kick
berimbau: lead instrument in capoeira, a musical bow
bôca de siri: 'crab's mouth' movement
brincar: to play like a child
cabaça: gourd used as the resonator of the *berimbau*
cabeçada: head butt
camará: comrade; capoeira colleague
candomblé: a major variety of Afro-Brazilian religion

capoeirista: a capoeira player; an adept of the game

cavalaria: 'cavalry,' a *berimbau* beat used to warn players of a police raid

caxixí: woven rattle played with the *berimbau*

chamada: 'call,' a named subroutine of capoeira play, the basic kind of inner game; short form of *chamada de bênção* or *chamada de Mandinga*

chula: special introductory song, always follows *ladainha*

cocorinha: squatting movement; refers to the defecation position

comprar o jôgo: to buy the game, entering the ring by cutting in on another player

contragolpe: counterattack; response to an initiative

contramestre: an instructor working under a master's guidance in an academy

cordão: colored sash or belt awarded to mark grades of advancement in some academies; same as *cordel*

corridos: call and response songs accompanying action in the ring

danado: cursed, damned; wily, clever

dá volta ao mundo: take a turn around the world, a named subroutine of play that involves circling the ring

defesa: defensive move or movement response

desequilibrante: movement that unbalances the opponent

discípulo: disciple, student of capoeira master; same as *aluno*

dobrão: coin used to play the *berimbau;* same as *moeda*

esquiva: escape movement

fechar o corpo: to close the body, physical and/or spiritual defense

floreios: 'flourishes,' acrobatic moves

folguedo: pastime; entertainment

formatura: graduation ceremony for a new capoeira master

fuga: flight, a category of defensive or escape moves

ginga: the fundamental capoeira movement; in various forms, it also refers to rowing, swaying, or fancy footwork

golpe: strike or blow; attacking movement

iaiá, ioiô: terms used by slaves for daughters and sons of the master

jogador: player

jogar: to play games

jôgo: game

ladainha: litany, an introductory solo, usually sung by a master

ligeiro: swift, quick; nimble, agile; slippery, dishonest

maculêlê: another martial dance to music, involving rhythmic stick play

malandragem: hooliganism, shady activities; synonym for capoeira play

malandro: street tough, hoodlum, scoundrel, con man, bad guy

malícia: deception, trickery, cunning, double-dealing, dissimulation, indirection

mandigueiro: sorceror; healer; synonym for capoeira player

mangangá: medicine man; praise name for Besouro

martelo: 'hammer' kick; a rhymed song form

meia-lua de compasso: 'half moon in a compass,' a spinning kick

mestre: master, senior capoeira teacher

mocambo: fugitive slave community; same as *quilombo*

moeda: coin used to play the berimbau; same as *dobrão*

moleque: street urchin

nome da guerra: 'war name' given to a player in the course of his training, sometimes as part of a *batizado* initiation

orixá: a class of spirit beings in *candomblé*, also known as 'saints'

pandeiro: tambourine

paraná: body of water; river of the same name

passada: footwork, especially in the *ginga*

patuá: protective amulet

pé: 'foot'; position in front of the *berimbau*

pião: 'spinning top,' headspin (no hands)

queda: fall, basic way to lose advantage in the game

quilombo: fugitive slave community; same as *mocambo*

rabo de arraia: 'stingray's tail' kick

rasteira: sweep, trip-'em-up; the basic takedown

reco-reco: ribbed bamboo scraper in capoeira musical ensemble

recuo: retreat move, usually with one hand on the ground

Regional: innovative, modernized style of capoeira, associated with
Mestre Bimba

roda: ring, space for playing capoeira; used to refer to a performance
event involving a complete series of bouts on a given occasion

saída: exit, most formal way to enter the ring; one 'exits' from the foot
of the *berimbau*

samba duro: hard *samba*, involves tripping people while dancing

seqüência: sequence of required moves learned by players in *Regional*
style

tocar: to play music

vadiação: loafing, hanging around; synonym for capoeira

vaqueta: stick used to strike the string of the *berimbau*

vara: wooden pole that is the body of the *berimbau*; same as *vêrga*

vêrga: wooden pole that is the body of the *berimbau*; same as *vara*

Bibliography

Abrahams, Roger D.
1983   *The Man-of-Words in the West Indies: Performance and the Emergence of Creole Culture.* Baltimore: The Johns Hopkins University Press.

Alén, Olavo
1986   *La Musica de las Sociedades de Tumba Francesa en Cuba.* La Habana: Casa de Las Americas.

Almeida, Bira
1981   *Capoeira, A Brazilian Art Form.* Palo Alto: Sun Wave.
1986   *Capoeira, A Brazilian Art Form: History, Philosophy, and Practice.* Berkeley: North Atlantic Books.

Almeida, Renato
1942   "O Brinquedo da Capoeira." *Revista do Archivo Municipal do São Paulo,* 7.84: 155–62.

Apel, Karl-Otto
1981   *Charles S. Peirce: From Pragmatism to Pragmaticism,* translated by J. M. Krois. Amherst: University of Massachusetts Press.

Bailey, F. G.
1969   *Stratagems and Spoils: A Social Anthropology of Politics.* New York: Schocken Books.

Bastide, Roger
1978   *The African Religions of Brazil: Toward a Sociology of the Interpenetration of Cultures,* translated by H. Sebba. Baltimore: Johns Hopkins University Press.

Bateson, Gregory
1972   *Steps to an Ecology of Mind.* New York: Ballantine.

Birmingham, David
1966   *Trade and Conflict in Angola: The Mbundu and Their Neighbors under the Influence of the Portuguese 1483–1790.* Oxford: Clarendon Press.

Blanchard, Kendall, and Anna Cheska
1985   *The Anthropology of Sport: An Introduction.* South Hadley, MA: Bergin & Garvey.

239

Bourdieu, Pierre
1979   *Outline of a Theory of Practice*, translated by R. Nice. Cambridge: Cambridge University Press.

Briggs, Charles L.
1988   *Competence in Performance: The Creativity of Tradition in Mexicano Verbal Art*. Philadelphia: University of Pennsylvania Press.

Brissonnet, Lydie C.
1988   "The Structuration of Communitas in the Carnaval of Salvador, Bahia (Northeastern Brazil)." Ph.D. diss., Dept. of Anthropology, Indiana University.

Brown, Diana D.
1979   "Umbanda and Class Relations in Brazil." In *Brazil, Anthropological Perspectives: Essays in Honor of Charles Wagley*, edited by M. Margolis and W. Carter. New York: Columbia University Press.
1986   *Umbanda: Religion and Politics in Urban Brazil*. Ann Arbor: UMI Research Press.

Buhler, Justus
1955   *Philosophical Writings of Peirce*. New York: Dover.

Burns, E. Bradford
1970   *A History of Brazil*. New York: Columbia University Press.

Cacciatore, Olga G.
1977   *Dicionário de Cultos Afro-Brasileiros*. Rio de Janeiro: Forense Universitária.

Caillois, Roger
1969   "The Structure and Classification of Games." In *Sport, Culture, and Society*, edited by J. Loy and G. Kenyon, pp. 44–55. New York: Macmillan.

Cardoso, Fernando Henrique
1962   *Capitalismo e escravidão no Brasil meridional*. São Paulo: Difusão Europeia do Livro.

Carneiro, Edison
1958   *O Quilombo dos Palmares 1630–1695*. São Paulo: Editôra Brasiliense.

Cascudo, Luís da Câmara
1979   *Dicionário do Folclore Brasileiro*. São Paulo: Edições Melhoramentos.

Chernoff, John Miller
1979   *African Rhythm and African Sensibility: Aesthetics and Social Action in African Musical Idioms*. Chicago: University of Chicago Press.

Clifford, James
1988   *The Predicament of Culture: Twentieth-Century Ethnography,*

Literature, and Art. Cambridge, MA: Harvard University Press.

Clifford, James, and George Marcus, eds.

1986   *Writing Culture.* Berkeley: University of California Press.

Comrie, Bernard

1989   *Language Universals and Linguistic Typology: Syntax and Morphology.* Chicago: University of Chicago Press.

Cook-Gumperz, Jenny, and John J. Gumperz

1976   "Papers on Language and Context." Working paper no. 46, Language Behavior Research Laboratory. Berkeley: University of California.

Corrêa, Mariza

1983   *Morte em Família: Representações Jurídicas de Papéis Sexuais.* Rio de Janeiro: Graal.

Crowley, Daniel J.

1984   *African Myth and Black Reality in Bahian Carnaval.* Los Angeles: Museum of Cultural History, UCLA.

Csikszentmihalyi, M.

1974   *Flow: Studies of Enjoyment.* P.N.S. report. Chicago: University of Chicago.

Csikszentmihalyi, M., and Bennett, S.

1971   "An Exploratory Model of Play." *American Anthropologist* 73: 45–58.

Curtin, Philip D.

1969   *The Atlantic Slave Trade, A Census.* Madison: University of Wisconsin Press.

da Matta, Roberto

1980   *Carnavais, Malandros e Heróis: Para uma Sociologia do Dilemma Brasileiro.* Rio de Janeiro: Zahar Editores.

1984   "Carnaval in Multiple Planes." In *Rite, Drama, Festival, Spectacle: Rehearsals Toward a Theory of Cultural Performance,* edited by J. MacAloon, pp. 208–40. Philadelphia: ISHI.

1987   *A Casa e A Rua: Cidadania, Mulher, e Morte no Brazil.* Rio de Janeiro: Editôra Guanabara.

Daniel, E. Valentine

1984   *Fluid Signs: Being a Person in the Tamil Way.* Berkeley: University of California Press.

1990   "Afterword: Scared Places, Violent Spaces." In *Sri Lanka: History and the Roots of Conflict,* edited by Jonathan Spencer, pp. 227–46. New York and London: Routledge.

d'Aquino, Iria

1983   "Capoeira: Strategies for Status, Power, and Identity." Ph.D. diss., University of Illinois at Urbana-Champaign.

de Abreu, Placido
n.d.   *Os Capoeiras*. Rio de Janeiro: José Alves.
de Almeida, Raimundo Cesar Alves
1982   *Bimba, Perfil do Mestre*. Salvador: Universidade Federal da
               Bahia.
Dell, Cecily
1977   *A Primer for Movement Description*. New York: Dance Nota-
               tion Bureau Press.
de Oliveira, Albano M.
1958   *Berimbau: O Arco Musical da Capoeira*. Salvador: Commis-
               são Bahiana de Folclore.
de Oliveira, Valdemar
1971   *Frevo, Capoeira e "Passo."* Recife: Companhia Editôra de
               Pernambuco.
Dimock, Anne
1976   "Capoeira Angola." In *Black People and Their Culture:
               Selected Writings from the African Diaspora,* edited by
               L. Shapiro, pp. 123–26. Washington, D.C.: Smithsonian
               Institution.
Dossar, Kenneth
1988   "Capoeira Angola: An Ancestral Connection?" *American Vi-
               sions* 3(4): 38–42.
Dunn, Kaye [Katharine Dunham]
1939   "L'Ag'ya of Martinique." *Esquire* 12(5): 84–85.
Evleshin, Catherine
1986   "Capoeira at the Crossroads." *UCLA Journal of Dance Eth-
               nology* 10: 1–13.
Faria, Vilmar E.
1980   "Divisão inter-regional do trabalho e pobreza urbana: o caso
               de Salvador." In *Bahia de Todos os Pobres,* edited by G. de
               Souza and V. Faria, pp. 23–40. Petrópolis: Editôra Vozes.
Fontaine, Pierre-Michel
1985   "Blacks and the Search for Power in Brazil." In *Race, Class,
               and Power in Brazil,* edited by P. Fontaine, pp. 56–72. Los
               Angeles: Center for Afro-American Studies.
Foucault, Michel
1980   *History of Sexuality*. Volume I: *An Introduction,* translated by
               R. Hurley. New York: Random House.
Freitas, Décio
1982   *Palmares, A Guerra dos Escravos*. Rio de Janeiro: Edicões
               Graal.
Fresu, Anna, and Mendes de Oliveira
1982   *Pesquisas para um teatro popular am Mocambique*. Maputo:
               Cadernos Tempo.

Freyre, Gilberto
1956 [1933] *The Masters and the Slaves: A Study in the Development of Brazilian Civilization*, translated by S. Putnam. New York: Alfred A. Knopf.
1963 [1936] *The Mansions and the Shanties: The Making of Modern Brazil*, translated by H. de Onís. New York: Alfred A. Knopf.

Frigerio, Alejandro
1989   "Capoeira: de arte negra a esporte branco." *Revista Brasileira de Ciências Sociais* 4, no. 10: 85–98.

Gadamer, Hans G.
1975   *Truth and Method*, translated by G. Burden and J. Cumming. New York: Seabury Press.

Geertz, Clifford
1983   *Local Knowledge: Further Essays in Interpretive Anthropology*. New York: Basic Books.

Goffman, Erving
1976   *Frame Analysis: An Essay on the Organization of Experience*. Cambridge: Harvard University Press.

Grathoff, Richard H.
1970   *The Structure of Social Inconsistencies: A Contribution to a Unified Theory of Play, Game and Social Action*. The Hague: Martinus Nijhoff.

Gumperz, John J.
1982   *Discourse Strategies*. Cambridge: Cambridge University Press.

Guttman, Allen
1978   *From Ritual to Record: The Nature of Modern Sports*. New York: Columbia University Press.

Gwaltney, John
1981   *Drylongso. A Self-Portrait of Black Americans*. New York: Random House.

Habermas, Jurgen
1971   *Knowledge and Human Interests*, translated by J. Shapiro. Boston: Beacon Press.

Hahner, June
1984   *Women in Brazil: Problems and Perspectives*. Albuquerque: Latin American Institute, University of New Mexico.

Hahner, June, ed.
1978   *A Mulher no Brasil*. Rio: Editôra Civilização Brasileira.

Hall, Edward
1959   *The Silent Language*. Garden City, NY: Doubleday.
1969   *The Hidden Dimension*. Garden City, NY: Doubleday.

Handelman, Don
1977   "Play and Ritual: Complementary Frames of Meta-Communication." In *It's a Funny Thing, Humour*, edited by

A. Chapman and H. Foot, pp. 185–92. Oxford: Pergamon.

1981 "The Ritual-Clown: Attributes and Affinities." *Anthropos* 76: 321–70.

Hasenbalg, Carlos A.
1985 "Race and Socioeconomic Inequalities in Brazil." In *Race, Class, and Power in Brazil,* edited by P. Fontaine, pp. 25–41. Los Angeles: Center for Afro-American Studies.

Henfrey, Colin
1981 "The Hungry Imagination: Social Formation, Popular Culture and Ideology in Bahia." In *The Logic of Poverty: The Case of the Brazilian Northeast,* edited by S. Mitchell, pp. 58–108. London: Routledge & Kegan Paul.

Herskovits, Melville J.
1958 [1941] *The Myth of the Negro Past.* Boston: Beacon Hill.

Hill, Errol
1972 *The Trinidad Carnival: Mandate for a National Theatre.* Austin: University of Texas Press.

Hjelmslev, L.
1963 *Prolegomena to a Theory of Language.* Madison: University of Wisconsin Press.

Hofstadter, Douglas R.
1985 *Metamagical Themas: Questing for the Essence of Mind and Pattern.* New York: Basic Books.

Holloway, Thomas H.
1989 "'A Healthy Terror': Police Repression of *Capoeiras* in Nineteenth-Century Rio de Janeiro." *The Hispanic American Historical Review* 69: 637–76.

Holston, James
1989 *The Modernist City: An Anthropological Critique of Brasília.* Chicago: University of Chicago Press.

Huizinga, Johan
1955 *Homo ludens: A Study of the Play Element in Culture.* Boston: Beacon Press.

Izikowitz, Karl G.
1935 *Musical and Other Sound Instruments of the South American Indians: A Comparative Ethnographical Study.* Goteborg: Elanders Boktryckeri Aktiebolag.

Jahn, Janheinz
1961 *Muntu: An Outline of the New African Culture,* translated by M. Grene. New York: Grove Press.

Jakobson, Roman
1960 "Closing Statement: Linguistics and Poetics." In *Style in Language,* edited by T. Sebeok, pp. 350–77. New York: MIT Technology Press and John Wiley & Sons.

Jakobson, Roman, and Morris Halle
1956   *Fundamentals of Language.* The Hague: Mouton.
Kauffman, Robert
1980   "African Rhythm: A Reassessment." *Ethnomusicology* 24 (3):
            393–415.
Keil, Charles M.
1987   "Participatory Discrepancies and the Power of Music." *Cul-
            tural Anthropology* 2 (3): 275–83.
Kent, R. K.
1965   "Palmares: An African State in Brazil." In *Maroon Societies:
            Rebel Slave Communities in the Americas,* edited by R. Price,
            pp. 170–201. Baltimore: Johns Hopkins University Press.
Kochman, Thomas
1981   *Black and White Styles in Conflict.* Chicago: University of
            Chicago Press.
1983   "The Boundary Between Play and Nonplay in Black Verbal
            Dueling." *Language in Society* 12 (3): 329–37.
1986   "Strategic Ambiguity in Black Speech Genres: Cross-cul-
            tural Interference in Participant-Observation Research." In
            a "Special Issue on Cross-cultural Communication," edited
            by Deborah Tannen, *Text* 6 (2): 153–70.
Kochman, Thomas, ed.
1972   *Rappin' and Stylin' Out: Communication in Urban Black
            America.* Urbana: University of Illinois Press.
Koster, Henry
1966 [1805] *Travels in Brazil.* Edited by C. Gardiner. Carbondale:
            Southern Illinois Press.
Kubik, Gerhard
1979   *Angolan Traits in Black Music, Games, and Dances of Brazil:
            A Study of African Cultural Extensions Overseas.* Lisboa: Cen-
            tro de Estudos de Antropologia Cultural.
Kuhn, Thomas
1962   *The Structure of Scientific Revolutions.* Chicago: University of
            Chicago Press.
Kurath, Gertrude P.
1974   "Research Methods and Background of Gertrude Kurath."
            In *New Dimensions in Dance Research: Anthropology and
            Dance (The American Indian),* edited by T. Comstock. New
            York: Committee on Research in Dance.
Laban, Rudolf
1956   *Principles of Dance and Movement Notation.* New York: Dance
            Horizons.
Landes, Ruth
1947   *The City of Women.* New York: Macmillan.

Lewis, J. Lowell
1986   "Semiotic and Social Discourse in Brazilian Capoeira." Ph.D. diss., University of Washington, Seattle, WA.

Loeb, Edwin M.
1948   "Transition Rites of the Kuanyama Ambo (A Preliminary Study)." Reprint from *African Studies* 7 (1, 2–3) March, June–September.

Lomax, A., I. Bartenieff, and F. Paulay
1968   *Folk Song Style and Culture*. Washington, D.C.: American Association for the Advancement of Science.

Lyra Filho, João
1974   *Introdução à Sociologia dos Desportos*. Rio de Janeiro: Editôra Bloch.

MacAloon, John J.
1984   "Olympic Games and the Theory of Spectacle in Modern Societies." In *Rite, Drama, Festival, Spectacle: Rehearsals Toward a Theory of Cultural Performance*, edited by J. MacAloon, pp. 241–80. Philadelphia: ISHI.

MacGaffey, Wyatt
1986   *Religion and Society in Central Africa*. Chicago: University of Chicago Press.

Maraire, Dumisani A.
1982   "The Position of Chipendani (Bow Instrument) in Shona Music Culture and Tradition." M.A. thesis, University of Washington, Seattle, WA.

Marinho, Inezil Penna
1945   *Subsídios para o Estudo de Metodologia do Treinamento da Capoeiragem*. Rio de Janeiro: Imprensa Nacional.

Mattoso, Katia M. de Queirós
1986   *To Be a Slave in Brazil, 1550–1888*, translated by A. Goldhammer. New Brunswick, NJ: Rutgers University Press.

Megenney, William W.
1978   *A Bahian Heritage: An Ethnolinguistic Study of African Influences on Bahian Portuguese*. Chapel Hill: University of North Carolina Press.

Mendonça, Renato
1973   *A Influência Africana no Português do Brasil*. Rio de Janeiro: Editôra Civilização Brasileira

Michelon, Josy
1987   *Le ladjia: origine et pratiques*. Paris: Editions Caribéennes.

Mintz, Sidney W., and Richard Price
1976   *An Anthropological Approach to the Afro-American Past: A Caribbean Perspective*. Philadelphia: ISHI.

Moura, Clóvis
1981   *Rebeliões da Senzala: Quilombos Insurreições Guerrilhas.* São Paulo: Ciências Humanas.
Moura, Jair
1979   *Capoeira—A Luta Regional Baiana.* Salvador: Prefeitura Municipal.
1980   *Capoeira—Arte e Malandragem.* Salvador: Prefeitura Municipal.
1983   "Capoeira: De prática de desordeiros à ginástica, uma longa história." *Jornal do Comércio* (Revista Nacional), Rio de Janeiro, June 5: 12–13.
Mutti, Maria
1978   *Maculêlê.* Salvador: Prefeitura da Cidade do Salvador.
Newmeyer, Frederick J.
1978   "The Self-Defeating Autonomy Thesis." In *Papers from the 14th Regional Meeting of the Chicago Linguistic Society,* pp. 316–25. Chicago: C.L.S.
Nketia, J. H. Kwabena
1971   "Surrogate Languages of Africa." In *Current Trends in Linguistics,* vol. 7: Linguistics in Sub-Saharan Africa, edited by T. Sebeok, pp. 699–732. The Hague: Mouton.
Norbeck, Edward, ed.
1974   *The Anthropological Study of Human Play.* Houston: Rice University Studies 60.3.
Olshewsky, Thomas
1982   "Between Science and Religion." *The Journal of Religion* 62: 242–60.
Omari, Mikelle Smith
1984   *From the Inside to the Outside: The Art and Ritual of Bahian Candomblé.* Los Angeles: Museum of Cultural History.
Onori, Piero
1988   *Sprechende Körper: Capoeira—ein afrobrasilianischer Kampftanz.* Köln: Edition diá, St. Gallen.
Ortiz, Fernando
1985 [1951] *Los Bailes y el Teátro de los Negros en el Folklore de Cuba.* La Habana: Editorial Letras Cubanas.
Ott, Carlos B.
1955   *Formação e Evolução Étnica da Cidade do Salvador.* 2 vols. Salvador: Tipografia Manú.
Parmentier, Richard J.
1985a   "Signs' Place in Medias Res: Peirce's Concept of Semiotic Mediation." In *Semiotic Mediation: Sociocultural and Psychological Perspectives,* edited by E. Mertz and R. Parmentier, pp. 23–48. Orlando, FL: Academic Press.

1985b   "Times of the Signs: Modalities of History and Levels of Social Structure in Belau." In *Semiotic Mediation: Sociocultural and Psychological Perspectives,* edited by E. Mertz and R. Parmentier, pp. 131–54. Orlando: Academic Press.

Patterson, Orlando
1982   *Slavery and Social Death: A Comparative Study.* Cambridge: Harvard University Press.

Paul, Robert A.
1982   *The Tibetan Symbolic World: Psychoanalytic Explorations.* Chicago: University of Chicago Press.

Peirce, Charles S.
1931–58   *The Collected Papers of Charles Sanders Peirce.* 8 vols. Cambridge: Harvard University Press.

Pescatello, Ann, ed.
1973   *Female and Male in Latin America.* Pittsburgh: University of Pittsburgh Press.

Pierson, Donald
1967   *Negroes in Brazil: A Study of Race Contact at Bahia.* Carbondale: Southern Illinois Press.

Plaut, Kimson F.
1980   "Samba: The Voice of the Morro, A Historical and Musical Analysis of a Brazilian Popular Form." M.A. thesis, University of Washington, Seattle, WA.

Rawley, James A.
1981   *The Transatlantic Slave Trade: A History.* New York: W. W. Norton.

Rego, Waldeloir
1968   *Capoeira Angola, Ensaio Sócio-Etnográfico.* Salvador: Editôra Itapuã.

Rodrigues, Nina
1977 [1906] *Os Africanos no Brasil.* São Paulo: Companhia Editora Nacional.

Rosch, E.
1973   "Natural Categories." *Cognitive Psychology* 4: 328–50.
1977   "Classification of Real-World Objects: Origins and Representations in Cognition." In *Thinking: Readings in Cognitive Science,* edited by P. Johnson-Laird and P. Wason, pp. 212–22. New York: Academic Press.

Rugendas, Johann Moritz
1976   *Viagem Pitoresca através do Brasil,* translated by S. Milliet. 2 vols. Brasília: São Paulo, Martins.

Saussure, Ferdinand de
1966   *Course in General Linguistics,* translated by W. Baskin. New York: McGraw-Hill.

Schiller, Friedrich

1967   *On the Aesthetic Education of Man in a Series of Letters*, translated and edited by Elizabeth Wilkinson and L. Willoughby. Oxford: Clarendon Press.

Schwartz, Stuart B.

1970   "The Mocambo: Slave Resistance in Colonial Bahia." In *Maroon Societies: Rebel Slave Communities in the Americas*, edited by R. Price, pp. 202–26. Baltimore: Johns Hopkins University Press.

1985   *Sugar Plantations in the Formation of Brazilian Society, Bahia 1550–1835*. Cambridge: Cambridge University Press.

Schwartzman, Helen B.

1978   *Transformations: The Anthropology of Children's Play*. New York: Plenum Press.

Scott, James C.

1985   *Weapons of the Weak: Everyday Forms of Peasant Resistance*. New Haven, CT: Yale University Press.

Sebeok, Thomas A.

1981   *The Play of Musement*. Bloomington: Indiana University Press.

Shaffer, Kay

1977   *O Berimbau-da-barriga e seus Toques*. Rio de Janeiro: Fundação Nacional de Arte.

Silverstein, Michael

1976   "Shifters, Linguistic Categories, and Cultural Description." In *Meaning in Anthropology*, edited by K. Basso and H. Selby, pp. 11–55. Albuquerque: University of New Mexico Press.

Singer, Milton

1978   "For a Semiotic Anthropology." In *Sight, Sound, and Sense*, edited by T. Sebeok, pp. 202–31. Bloomington: Indiana University Press.

1980   "Signs of the Self." *American Anthropologist* 82: 489–507.

Spencer-Brown, G.

1979   *Laws of Form*. New York: E. P. Dutton.

Stern, Theodore

1957   "Drum and Whistle 'Languages': An Analysis of Speech Surrogates." *American Anthropologist* 59: 487–506.

Taylor, James L.

1980   *A Portuguese-English Dictionary*. Stanford: Stanford University Press.

Thompson, Robert F.

1966   "An Aesthetic of the Cool: West African Dance." *African Forum* 2, no. 2 (Fall).

1979   *African Art in Motion: Icon and Act*. Los Angeles: University
            of California Press.
1983   *Flash of the Spirit: African and Afro-American Art and Phi-
            losophy*. New York: Random House.
1986   "Hip-Hop 101." *Rolling Stone* 470: 95–100.
1988   "Tough Guys Do Dance." *Rolling Stone* 522: 135–40.
Thompson, Robert F., and Frère J. Cornet
1981   *Four Moments of the Sun: Kongo Art in Two Worlds*. Washing-
            ton, D.C.: National Gallery of Art.

Turner, J. Mitchell
1985   "Brown into Black: Changing Racial Attitudes of Afro-
            Brazilian University Students." In *Race and Class in Brazil*,
            edited by P. Fontaine, pp. 73–94. Los Angeles: Center for
            Afro American Studies.

Turner, Victor
1977   *The Ritual Process: Structure and Anti-Structure*. Ithaca: Cor-
            nell University Press.
1978   *Dramas, Fields, and Metaphors: Symbolic Action in Human So-
            ciety*. Ithaca: Cornell University Press.
1982   *From Ritual to Theatre: The Human Seriousness of Play*. New
            York: PAJ Publications.
1988   *The Anthropology of Performance*. New York: PAJ Pub-
            lications.

Vansina, Jan
1966   *Kingdoms of the Savanna*. Madison: University of Wisconsin
            Press.

Verger, Pierre
1964   *Bahia and the West African Trade 1549–1851*. Ibadan: Iba-
            dan University Press.

Wa Mukuna, Kazadi
1982   *Contribuição Bantu na Música Popular Brasileira*. São Paulo:
            Global Editôra.

Waddey, Ralph C.
1980   "Samba de Viola and Viola de Samba in the Recôncavo of
            Bahia (Brazil)." *Latin American Music Review* 1 (2): 196–
            212.
1981   "Viola de Samba and Samba de Viola in the Recôncavo of
            Bahia (Brazil). Part II: Samba de Viola." *Latin American
            Music Review* 2 (2): 252–79.

Wafer, James W.
1991   *The Taste of Blood: Spirit Possession in Brazilian Candomblé*.
            Philadelphia: University of Pennsylvania Press.

Wagner, Roy
1981   *The Invention of Culture*. Chicago: University of Chicago
            Press.

Zeman, J. Jay
1977   "Peirce's Theory of Signs." In *A Perfusion of Signs,* edited by
            T. Sebeok, pp. 22–39. Bloomington: Indiana University
            Press.

Discography

Note that some of the Brazilian records have no dates, so I have arranged them as they are generally known within the capoeira community, by the master(s) who was/were in charge of the session. This list is not intended to be comprehensive, but it covers many of the most important recordings, excluding those made outside Brazil, in roughly chronological order.

Mestre Bimba
Curso De Capoeira Regional. JS Discos, Salvador.
Mestre Traira
Capoeira. Documentos Folcloricos Brasileiros, Editôra Xauá, Rio de Janeiro.
Mestre Limão and Natanael
Capoeira Mestre Limão. Editôra Musical Arlequim, São Paulo.
Mestre Pastinha
Capoeira Angola. Polygram Discos, Rio de Janeiro, 1979 [1969].
Mestre Caiçara
Academia de Capoeira Angola São Jorge dos Irmãos Unidos do Mestre Caiçara. Discos Copacabana, São Paulo, 1973.
Mestre Suassuna and Dirceu
Capoeira Cordão de Ouro. Discos Continental, São Paulo, 1975.
Capoeira Cordão de Ouro, vol. 2. Discos Continental, São Paulo, 1978.
Capoeira Cordão de Ouro, vol. 3. Discos Continental, São Paulo, 1983.
Mestre Joel
Capoeira. Discos Continental, São Paulo, 1979.
Mestre Carioca
Capoeira de Angola. Tapecar Gravações, Rio de Janeiro.
Camafeu de Oxossi
Berimbau. Gravações Elétricas, São Paulo, 1981.
Nestor Capoeira
Galo já Cantou. Arte Hoje Editôra, Rio de Janeiro, 1985.
Mestre Waldemar and Mestre Canjiquinha
Capoeira. Gravações Elétricas, São Paulo, [1987].

Films and Videos

There are several commercial films with sequences of capoeira in them, but I will include only documentaries whose main focus is capoeira. In addition, there is a wealth of unproduced, amateur film and video footage collected by afficionados, most of which is of quite poor quality and unavailable through normal means. This list is even less comprehensive than the discography, and some of the references are incomplete, but at least it provides a starting point for the interested scholar or martial artist.

"Vadiação" by Robatto, 16mm. Salvador, 1952.
"O Berimbau" by Tony Talbot, 16mm. New Yorker Films, 1971.
"A Dança de Guerra" by Jair Moura, 70mm. Salvador.
"Capoeira of Brazil" by Warrington Hudlin, 16mm. Black Film-maker's Foundation, New York, 1980.
"Capoeira at the Crossroads" by Catharine Evleshin, VHS. Instructional Television Services, Portland State University, 1986.
"Dança de Cultura: Capoeira de Salvador da Bahia" by Glenn Micallef, VHS. Filmsound, Portland, Oregon, 1986.

Index

255

INDEX

887 - 577